AMERICA
NOW

AMERICA NOW

Edited by

JOHN G. KIRK

with a Foreword by John W. Kluge

ATHENEUM   *NEW YORK*

1968

FOREWORD

by John W. Kluge

PRESIDENT AND CHAIRMAN OF THE BOARD, METROMEDIA, INC.

A MERICA NOW is the first of a series of books that will be produced at random intervals by Metromedia, Inc. Intended as a public service, the series represents an inquiry into topics of pressing concern to modern Americans.

Metromedia's role is that of catalyst and sponsor: determining subject areas of maximum concern, finding the best qualified authors, ensuring that each contributor has unrestricted freedom in the expression of his point of view and his conclusions. The result, I hope, will be what Professor McLuhan might call a "probe"— an exercise intended not so much to persuade as to generate insight, to find new ways of dealing with some of the diverse and confusing elements of modern life that, for good or ill, will shape our future.

America Now embodies this approach. Its subject was chosen precisely because it is both familiar and difficult. For most Americans there seems to be no coherent way of looking at contemporary America. Everyone is uneasily aware that old certainties have become unhinged and that traditional codes and patterns of behavior are shifting; but whether this is truly progress, few can tell. Half understood and something less than half evaluated, an avalanche of new facts, events and ideas pours in on us in ever-increasing volume. The first twenty pages of any day's edition of, say, The New York Times represents a mass of information which appears to be important, yet little of which can easily be assigned a firm place within our traditional conception of our society and its role in the world.

Under the circumstances, it is not surprising that sharp public debates have arisen about foreign policy, civil rights, education, welfare and many other topics. Debate on public issues is hardly new in itself, but there seems to be something new in the *quality* of our present discord: an intolerance, a violence, an impatience with normal democratic processes—all operating against the background of a deepening concern over how we are to find a common ground for judging our actions and determining priorities. None of us really wants this situation. No one who believes in democracy, for example, really *likes* to feel there is no choice but civil disobedience. We should all surely prefer to work out our problems within the framework of a far broader agreement as to ends and means.

To try to find new bases for agreement from which we may derive common action is a matter of urgent concern for all Americans—not only for individuals, political and social groups and government, but for business as well. We at Metromedia are acutely conscious of the unfulfilled responsibilities that American business might assume in the public interest. The days of the "invisible corporation" are passing. The private sector represents a vast potential instrument for the common good, and it is up to businessmen to make certain it is fully and responsibly used.

The publication of *America Now* is an example of how Metromedia is actively seeking to fulfill what we sense to be a basic obligation of the corporation of the future. The past commitments to the public interest by our various operating divisions are no longer adequate to today's needs. There must be a much larger acknowledgment of the need, by us and by all Americans. The commitment must be put to work—constructively and actively—if the common good is to be served properly.

America Now both illustrates an approach to the problem and suggests its dimensions. By their differing points of view, the contributing authors have shed much light and raised many disturbing new thoughts. That is what we asked of them; the fact that they have succeeded is not a small thing. Therefore, to all the distinguished contributors to this project, I can do no more than express again my heartfelt thanks.

New York, N.Y.
July 1968

INTRODUCTION

T HE NOTION that ours is peculiarly an age of anxiety, of complex, ambiguous challenges and of dissolving certainties, has now become a commonplace to most Americans.

In the early part of the twentieth century such dismaying perceptions were largely confined to a few intellectual circles and radical political minorities, and even then, much more to Europeans than to Americans. As early as 1897, for example, the French sociologist Emile Durkheim had written of the "collective sadness" that was overtaking Western society, of the "hate and disgust for what is, and a common need to destroy the real or to escape from it." But then, and for a long time after, a majority of Americans would have found Durkheim's description irrelevant to the American context.

It is not that informed Americans were unaware of the growing modern literature of alienation. We knew, for example, of Nietzsche's anguished jeremiads; we had heard the gloomy prophecies of Spengler and Ortega y Gasset; we had read Mann, Kafka, Huxley and the rest; we understood the Marxist-Leninist critique of capitalism. But until recently most of us did not truly *feel* that these dark visions applied to the American reality.

We had, after all, endured a shattering economic depression and two world wars to find ourselves, at mid-century, the richest, most powerful, most technically advanced, most politically stable and most economically competent nation on earth. We were prepared to admit that we had been lucky—magnificently endowed and smiled upon by history—but we also believed that we had been right. The correctness of our assumptions about the proper organization of human life had, we believed, been triumphantly vindicated by our success.

In their most explicit form, these assumptions were only slightly modified versions of the classic principles of eighteenth- and early nineteenth-century liberalism. They consisted of a body of fairly straightforward propositions about the nature and goals of government, foreign policy and social and economic organization; and they were firmly rooted in a concept of the individual as the primary unit of concern.

Less explicitly, these assumptions were expressed in terms of a characteristic "national style": faith in progress, optimism, pragmatism, a nearly limitless sense of the possible, respect for achievement, a belief that rising wealth and expanding technology would ultimately dissipate most individual and social problems, a tendency to personalize (that is, moralize about) issues and so on. Taken together—and in their most extreme expression—these spoken and unspoken assumptions amounted to a kind of ideology of Americanism that went beyond simple patriotism and became, as Seymour Lipset has said, a dynamic political creed rivaling socialism, communism or fascism.

There was very little debate about these assumptions. Republicans and Democrats regularly clashed over how principles should be applied but seldom questioned the principles themselves. Americans might argue about whether a given political procedure was really democratic; but they never doubted that it *should* be democratic. They might disagree about the extent to which the government ought to interfere in the life of society or the functioning of the economy; but they agreed that, in theory, such interference should be confined to a "necessary minimum." They might debate the relative merits of a new teaching method or a new plastic; but they did not question that progress was an historical reality which was served by universal education and advancing technology.

Yet within approximately the last decade, our attitude toward our old assumptions has undergone a serious change. We have not yet abandoned our assumptions, but we have begun to re-examine them. More to the point, we have begun to question their adequacy, to wonder whether they are wholly relevant to the new situations in which we find ourselves.

Now such agonizing over first principles is no longer the special province of intellectuals and political radicals of the Right and Left; it has become an almost universal American phenomenon. Here, for example, is a description of the prevailing mood in Washington in October 1967—a description that comes not from *Ramparts* or the *National Review*, but from James Reston writing in *The New York Times:* "That there is no common faith or body of principle to guide the people through this convulsion of change is clear. It is not even possible to get much agreement here in the capital on the guiding principle and purpose of the war, let alone find any common ground on what is primary and what is secondary in this staggering catalogue of problems."

It is obvious that any very widespread concern over assumptions and values must inevitably have important psychological, philosophical and political consequences. There is, after all, nothing harder than to try to reason about an assumption or evaluate a value. Assumptions should be the starting point of discursive reasoning, not its product; values should be the constants by which *other* things are evaluated.

This problem and its personal consequences were succinctly described by the eminent Dutch sociologist and psychoanalyst Henry Ruitenbeek in his book *The Individual and the Crowd.* "In large measure," said Dr. Ruitenbeek, "the authority of values depends on their being taken for granted. It is extremely difficult to replace one set of values with another. When a man loses his faith, that is, the values on which he has relied, he feels insecure, unrelated and *unidentified.* He may be able to establish a new identification, but that often requires fairly rigorous intellectual activity."

When such individual difficulties are projected onto a national scale, one is liable to come to something like the dismaying conclusions recently expressed by the National Committee for an Effective Congress: "America has experienced two great internal crises in her history: the Civil War and the economic depression of the 1930's. The country may be on the brink of a third trauma, a depression of the national spirit. At all levels of American life people share similar fears, insecurities and gnawing doubts to such a degree that we may be suffering from a kind of national nervous breakdown."

The events that caused so many Americans to review their old assumptions are complicated, and the significance of these events is not yet clearly understood. That, of course, is part of the trouble.

The Cold War and the advent of nuclear weaponry must certainly bear a large part of the responsibility. The Cold War dashed our optimistic post-World War II hopes for the dawn of an "American Century." And worse than the sense that we had been defrauded of a deserved victory was the dawning realization that we could not fairly be said to be winning the Cold War. Eastern Europe and China had joined the adversary camp; the Korean War was, at best, a dreary humiliation; Soviet military power had quickly come to rival—and in some areas, overmatch—our own; and both our allies and the uncommitted nations received our cherished assumptions with varying degrees of apathy and found in them little or no basis for an ideology. Inevitably, our national pride, our optimism, our sense of the possible and our faith in the universal relevance of our liberal principles suffered.

Had the Cold War been divorced from technological considerations, its effects might have been less corrosive. But the threat of an instant nuclear Armageddon injected a haunted urgency into our political life. The stakes of the game had become almost intolerably high. It was not enough that a decision should apparently be consistent with principle; it had to be right—or else. As never before, national security became a touchstone of politics. McCarthyism was one aspect of this preoccupation, but more basic was a growth of the power of the executive branch of government. The military burgeoned; vast secret agencies not even fully accountable to Congress, let alone the people, sprang up; *ad hoc* decision-making bodies never envisaged in the Constitution—the National Security Council and smaller, less formal groups without names—daily considered matters of potential life and death for millions of people throughout the world. At the center was the office of the American President, with its terrible, anomalous responsibilities. It is worth remembering that every American President since the end of World War II has been obliged at one time or another to make some major commitment to action in the interest of national security without a clear prior mandate from the Congress or the people—Korea, Lebanon, the Bay of Pigs, Vietnam, to cite only the most obvious. The urgencies of national security thus distorted the doctrine of separation of powers, widened the gap between decision making and the popular will, set further limits on our sense of being able to accomplish whatever we wanted and made it virtually impossible for us to be as moral in the conduct of foreign affairs as we felt we should be.

A fulminating technology, meanwhile, was creating other ambiguities within the nation. The blessings of nuclear explosives and ballistic missiles could be interpreted as progressive only in a special sense, but questions began to be raised about other innovations as well. People began to sense that there were obscure prices to be paid for having television sets, fastback sports cars, DNA synthesis and computers. The old assumptions are not terribly helpful about what these prices might be; they merely suggest that because advancing technology is generally synonymous with progress, the prices will probably be right. But to many Americans they have begun to seem high.

For example, the advance of technology seems inextricably linked with increasing organization and mechanization. The interests of the individual have become less and less "the primary unit of concern." Participation in the corporate activities of big government, big business, big labor and whatnot have become less humanly attractive. Neurotic dissatisfactions have noticeably increased among the already participating, and recruitment of new participants (especially among recent college graduates) has become a serious problem. The hugeness, complexity and mechanization of our institutions, with their concomitant impersonality and inertia, are among the main causes of the radical New Left's animus against the present social order. The ultimate concerns of SDS (Students for a Democratic Society) rioters at Columbia University in the spring of 1968 went far beyond any local contest about gymnasiums. In effect the SDS challenged the legitimacy of the existing university authority and, by extension, the legitimacy of every other institution of society. The implied question as to what constitutes or confers "legitimacy" was valid. To many, however, the SDS's answer seemed merely to be "power."

Meanwhile, advancing technology and rising affluence have patently *not* provided automatic solutions to the nation's oldest and thorniest social problem: that of relative disprivilege, on racial, economic, educational or other theoretically unacceptable grounds. The contemporary poor, however they compare materially to the poor of the past, feel their poverty as acutely as ever—if not more acutely. Negroes, maddened by the accumulation of two hundred years of injustice, are beginning to resort to mass violence and the rhetoric of revolution. The guilt-ridden confusion with which, for example, the white community reacted to the civil disorders following Martin Luther King's murder vividly expressed the general sense that the problem was understood but that the remedy was not.

Thus, while it is possible to see many of our contemporary problems as primary or secondary effects of an exploding technology, it seems unlikely that technology will necessarily provide the answers we need. Science and technology are, after all, mainly methodologies. They are highly logical systems animated by very simple root assumptions: that human knowledge should be extended as far as possible and that this knowledge should be applied, at least experimentally, as much as possible. Judgments as to whether a given discovery or application is humanly useful or good must usually be made on the basis of assumptions and values that are not intrinsic either to science or technology. That, no doubt, is why scientists are so nearly unanimous in insisting that neither they nor science should be held accountable for the ways in which their discoveries are used.

Ninety percent of all the scientists who have ever lived are alive today and are busily engaged in showering us with more ideas, techniques and things than we can readily comprehend. Yet not only must we comprehend, we must evaluate and make appropriate responses. To do this we are obliged to apply a logic based on a set of assumptions far more complicated than those used by science—assumptions about how human life should best be organized and conducted—about human nature, society, culture, economics and politics.

We must have such assumptions in order to act coherently— perhaps, in order to act at all. If our former assumptions now fail to produce effective actions, we must be prepared to discard or modify or reinterpret or add to them. There seems to be no avoiding that "fairly rigorous intellectual activity" that Dr. Ruitenbeek spoke of. Perhaps we cannot expect that all our assumptions will be correct, but we cannot ask less of ourselves than constantly to try to make them so.

America Now is a collection of essays by a group of American writers, each of whom was invited to discuss some portion of the body of ideas, maxims and attitudes that constitute the core of our assumptions about our country and its place in the world.

In order that every contributor should have a common point of departure, it was necessary at the outset to articulate as precisely as possible the assumptions to be considered. This proved easy enough with respect to assumptions which were derived from eighteenth-century liberal principles and which were plainly embodied in the language of the Declaration of Independence, the Constitution and the basic writings of the Founding Fathers; but far more difficult were the less explicit—in some cases, not even very clearly rationalized—attitudes that condition our thought and behavior as Americans. How should these attitudes be described? How could their universality be authenticated?

The answer to the first question was that, as much as possible, only the most familiar and explicit assumptions would be used initially and that the task of identifying and describing attitudes and characteristic behavior patterns would be left to the contributors themselves. To the extent that they perceived disparities between what Americans profess and the ways they habitually act and feel about things, the authors would thus be laying a basis for analyzing the validity of professed assumptions.

Vouching for the universality of the assumptions was something else again. Few people could be expected to agree with *all* the assumptions, as stated; and some people would not agree with any of them. But more to the point was whether most people would assume that most *other* people agreed with the assumptions. After a fair amount of informal testing (involving, among other things, polling reactions among college students), phraseologies that seemed to meet this criterion were adopted for five general categories: government, foreign policy, economy, culture, and society and the individual. Technology—which might arguably have been a sixth category—was, after some debate, omitted. The rationale for this omission has already been touched on; in any event, the theme of technology's impact on modern America runs like a leitmotiv through most of the essays in the book.

Each author was presented with a draft of the stated assumptions and assigned a general subject area. At least one author in each category was asked to comment generally on the subject, although, in practice, many others chose to do so as well. The remainder discussed various major subtopics within the categories. All authors were encouraged to use the essay form, since opinion, perception and the free play of ideas were felt to be more desirable in this case than the tighter, more circumscribed approach of formal disquisition. Authors were selected largely on the basis of the wide variety of views they represented and in the confident hope that they would fruitfully contradict one another.

The purpose implicit in this exercise was, of course, to compare concept and reality in order to discover whether they stood in appropriate relation to one another. In their most elementary form, the questions to be asked about the assumptions were: Are they adequate? Were they ever adequate? What is needed to make them adequate (that is, change the assumption or change the reality)?

It is notoriously easier to identify problems than to propose their solutions, and certainly it was not the purpose of this project to do irresponsible damage to still-viable "myths." But the operative premise was and is that the viability of many of our national myths is already in question precisely because the assumptions on which they are grounded are no longer taken for granted. And in any case, a national myth that is not viable, that is no longer consistent with reality, can be a remarkably dangerous thing.

Each reader will judge the results of the *America Now* project according to his preferences. The contributions are diverse in their content and approach and often disturbing in their conclusions. Some authors have proven to be in irreconcilable disagreement; others have agreed where no agreement was expected. Some assumptions—those relating to the ideal forms of government, for example—seem to have remained relatively immune to criticism; others, such as those concerning American foreign policy, have been roughly handled. There has been much probing—and occasionally devastating—criticism; but there is no lack, either, of positive proposals. In general, the consensus about the present relationship between our assumptions and reality is forbidding, but very far from desperate.

Inevitably, certain issues transcended the limits of any specific category. There was, as we have said, very little disagreement about what the American system of government should be, but there was evident concern about how well it is working. This is not entirely a distinction between theory and practice, for it has long been a widespread assumption that democracy should work increasingly well as certain social, economic and educational requirements are fulfilled. Thus John Stuart Mill, in admiring tribute to his father, wrote: "So complete was his reliance on the influence of reason over the minds of mankind, that he felt as if all would be gained, if the population were able to read. . . ." But today, when affluence and education have reached an unexampled universality, the quality of American democracy seems to have improved relatively little. Professor MacIver introduces this theme in the "American Government" section when he discusses continuing failures by the electorate to participate responsibly in the democratic process. And the same concern is expressed by authors writing in every other section of the book. Bigness, mechanization, the disenchantment of minorities who are unable to prevail at the polls and many other reasons are suggested to explain this; and some authors have gone as far as to speculate that freedom itself—the very object of democracy—may be partly to blame. Thus Professor Jay Martin writes (under "American Culture"): "Intrinsic to our ideals are democratic values; but it is clear that in the present state of our culture, the individual may be losing his self and finding his democracy becoming sinister." And Richard Rovere ("American Society and the Individual") writes: "Like the rich man with his money, the free individual learns that freedom cannot buy happiness."

The parallel theme of individual alienation from society likewise runs through the book; well over half the essays touch on one or another aspect of this phenomenon—its effects on government, politics, the economy, relations between the generations, education, the practice of civil disobedience, popular taste and much more. Writers such as Floyd McKissick of the Congress of Racial Equality and Eric Mann of Students for a Democratic Society see such alienation as a prerequisite to social reconstruction; most of the rest, while prepared to sympathize with the rationales for alienation, reject it as being an attitude which carries more peril than promise.

Nevertheless, the very issues that similarly concern authors writing under different headings ("American Culture," "American Foreign Policy," "American Economy" or whatever) are the ones most suggestive of inadequacies in the stated assumptions. For example, faith that majority rule is the best method for making decisions which affect a large number of people is not a matter that relates solely to the ideal form of government. Its philosophic implications permeate nearly every aspect of American life, raising problems at every turn, demanding justification of every action or intellectual position that claims immunity from the dominant opinion. What is the authority that defines "inalienable" civil rights; how can one justify calling a work of art "superior" if it is unpopular; in what sense can American foreign policy, whenever it is clearly mandated by the electorate, be called "immoral"? From varying points of view and on different levels of abstraction, the authors have wrestled with these and a host of similar questions. And in the fundamental similarity of their concerns lies, perhaps, the greatest hope either that some new assumptions may be synthesized or that the applicability of old assumptions may be better understood.

Equally pervasive among the essays is the (no doubt very American) impulse to find specific solutions to immediate problems. Thus George Gallup proposes reforms in the way we elect our congressional representatives; Robert MacIver outlines ways in which the teaching of secondary-school civics courses should be improved; Richard Rovere, T George Harris and Howard Zinn discuss action which might be taken in the war on poverty; Bernard Rosenberg suggests a program for raising the level of popular aesthetic taste; Floyd McKissick exhorts Negroes to unite in the civil-rights struggle; Russell Kirk calls for an end of American

xix

interference in the affairs of emerging African states; and so on. Even among specific proposals, ideas tend to cross the lines of category and, sometimes unexpectedly, converge. Thus, for example, Russell Kirk ("American Foreign Policy") and Edmund Stillman ("American Government")—writing from politically different points of view—find themselves in agreement that the American Constitution cannot successfully be exported to most underdeveloped nations.

The fact that so many authors have proposed concrete measures of reform may no doubt be taken as prima facie evidence that they are not yet ready to abandon faith in the idea of social and political progress. But most of the contributors do seem to feel that such evolution is vastly slower, more uncertain and more painful than most Americans had once supposed. Not only does our competence set limits on our ability to do all the things we wish, but our vision is far from being so clear that we can be certain everything we wish to do is wise or good.

This growing sense of limitation is perhaps simply a sensation appropriate to nations—as to men—approaching middle age; but the sense of uncertainty is surely inherent in the democratic system itself. "It is the essence of democracy," Professor MacIver reminds us, "that it is not tied to any transcendent creed, to any particular doctrine of man's role or his destiny." To put it bluntly, democracy is a system of government based on a confession of ignorance, an admission that most ultimate truths remain unknown. If they *were* known, majority rule would presumably be as irrelevant as dissent.

Most of the great eighteenth-century theorists of democracy—Rousseau, Locke, Montesquieu and the rest—were conscious of this fundamental uncertainty. They believed in the reality of natural law and they believed that its discovery and application to the ordering of civil society was the true end of government. Democracy, they felt, offered the best hope of making and applying this discovery; and they permitted themselves to be optimistic about democracy's prospects for doing so. We Americans, the heirs of the liberal philosophy, have traditionally shared and elaborated upon this optimism.

Perhaps, the contributors to this volume now seem to be suggesting, we have overelaborated, and are paying the price of disillusion for an excess of optimism. Yet sanguine hopes were never crucial to the justifications for democracy. Perhaps we need to remind ourselves again of democracy's essentially experimental nature, of the fact that its genius is to treat hopes and principles alike not as eternal dogmas, but as hypotheses. Most fundamentally, we believe in democracy because we find it superior to all other systems that claim to know more of the Truth.

If, then, all but the most elementary core of our assumptions are to be treated as problematical, we should expect to find ourselves, in some degree, perpetually in that "unidentified" state that Dr. Ruitenbeek wrote of—perpetually challenged to "fairly rigorous intellectual activity" in the testing, discarding and reformulating of our working hypotheses. Even granting that at least a qualified faith in social progress is implicit in this formula, it sounds nerve-racking. No doubt it is. But democracy was never so much a gift as a challenge.

John G. Kirk

New York, N.Y.
July 1968

CONTENTS

I AMERICAN GOVERNMENT

The Genius of Democracy: The American Experiment
ROBERT M. MAC IVER   3
American Government: The Limits of Reason
EDMUND STILLMAN   24
Violence in American Politics
ROGER D. MASTERS   36
The Failure of Leadership
GEORGE GALLUP   49

II AMERICAN FOREIGN POLICY

Myths and Realities in American Foreign Policy
HENRY STEELE COMMAGER   59
The Objectives of American Foreign Policy
FRANK N. TRAGER   87
The Problem of Motives
WILLIAM PFAFF   107
The African Example: American Ritualistic Liberalism in Action
RUSSELL KIRK   114
Today and Tomorrow
SENATOR GEORGE MC GOVERN   125

III AMERICAN ECONOMY

America's Economy: The Qualified Uproarious Success
KENNETH E. BOULDING   143

Contents

The Political Economy of Partnership
    ELSPETH DAVIES ROSTOW   162
The Politics of the American Economy
    HOWARD ZINN   170

IV AMERICAN CULTURE

American Culture: The Intersection of Past and Future
    JAY MARTIN   185
The Public Taste
    BERNARD ROSENBERG   217
The Arts Versus Most of the People All of the Time
    OTIS L. GUERNSEY, JR.   230
Students and Their Universities
    ERIC M. MANN   245
America Revisited: Radicalism and Alienation
    WILLIAM JOVANOVICH   257

V AMERICAN SOCIETY AND THE INDIVIDUAL

Alienation and the Future of Democracy
    RICHARD H. ROVERE   279
Generations and American Society
    JAMES W. CAREY   293
Society, U.S.A.
    FLOYD B. MC KISSICK   306
From Rugged-Individualism To Helpless-Individualism
    T GEORGE HARRIS   315
America the Unimagining
    BENJAMIN DE MOTT   325

Notes on Contributors   339

Index   345

I

American

Government

ASSUMPTIONS

Democracy is the most desirable form of government.

The United States is modern history's most nearly perfect example of democracy.

The bases of American democracy are:

1. *A wisely conceived Constitution that makes possible regular and peaceful political change according to the will of the majority, safeguards individual rights and, through a system of checks and balances, prevents undue concentrations of power.*
2. *A vast popular consensus that supports the basic system; an increasingly enlightened electorate that makes all ultimate decisions.*

ROBERT M. MACIVER

The Genius of Democracy:
The American Experiment

"Democracy . . . always unfinished
business."

*Americans are almost unanimous in believing that their demo-
cratic system of government is inherently excellent. What to the
Founding Fathers were revolutionary, unproven and perhaps
unprovable theses are to us articles of faith so taken for granted
that we seldom think about them at all. When foreign or domestic critics challenge our system, we often begin by being surprised and end by being shocked or angry. No doubt our system
is as defensible now as it was in the eighteenth century, but it can
hardly be well defended—or operated—by people who no longer
bother to think about it realistically. More democracies have
failed in history than have succeeded, and our own is not proof
against catastrophe. Few Americans can have thought longer or
more deeply about the problems of American democracy than
has Robert MacIver. It is appropriate that* America Now *should
open with his words.*

ALL MEN are created equal. So proclaimed the Declaration of Independence, as did the preamble to the Universal Declaration of Human Rights of the United Nations. All
men have certain inalienable rights, to life, liberty and the pursuit of happiness. Resounding words. They ring out over the land
every Fourth of July. Once they were the trumpet call of revolution. Now, undefined, elusive, transcendent, they no longer sing
in the hearts of men.

3

What then is the political creed to which our citizens respond, whether they act in accordance with it or not? Its two major tenets are democracy and capitalism, normally regarded as close associates. Together they are thought to be the essential conditions of "progress." We like to suppose that we are practical, not ideological, in our creeds.

Various other assumptions stem from these major tenets. For example, we commonly view our American democracy as the greatest and the most perfect embodiment of the democratic principle, a model for the rest of the world. It has the most stable and well-conceived of constitutions, safeguarding us from the revolutions that have beset other democracies. This assumption, to be sure, is at present challenged by the massive discontent exhibited by our disprivileged Negroes and Puerto Ricans and the incipient revolution they have organized in nearly all our larger cities. We normally meet their challenge by the answer that the fault lies not in our democratic system but in our persistent violation of its demands. No doubt, but there is more to it than that.

All human behavior is conducted in the misty light of what we think we know, but do not or cannot verify. We think we know enough about many tangled situations when we have only a nodding acquaintance with them. We believe so much and we inquire so little. Our beliefs are grounded in our indoctrination, our upbringing, our lot in life and the influence of associates and leaders. They are colored and skewed by our special interests and our native urges.

Our beliefs—including our beliefs about democracy—fall into patterns and form complexes that develop and become modified with the years. They express our personality and determine the essentials of our behavior. We pursue, often fitfully, the ends or purposes they inspire.

In one of my books, *The Web of Government*, I call the two forms of human creativity respectively *myths* and *techniques*. In this classification our myths are our belief-complexes, value-

4

impregnated conceptions of actualities. "Every civilization, every period, every nation, has its characteristic myth-complex. In it lies the secret of social unities and social continuities, and its changes compose the inner history of every society. Wherever he goes, whatever he encounters, man spins about him his web of myth, as the caterpillar spins its cocoon. Every individual spins his own variant within the greater web of the whole group. The myth mediates between man and nature. From the shelter of his myths he perceives and experiences the world. Inside his myth he is at home in his world."

Our belief-systems determine the background of our mode of life and influence the trends of social change, but much of our everyday behavior escapes the injunctions of our professed beliefs. Frequently we disguise their sway by pretending and even believing that our private interests serve public interests. What is good for General Motors is good for the country. We are serving the cause when we serve ourselves. We entertain assumptions that reconcile our wishes, our inertia and our own gratification with the common good.

The term *techniques*, on the other hand, includes all the procedures, plans, devices, controls, managerial activities and other contrivings through which we pursue or advance our objectives. Every step on the road from primitiveness has been made possible by the development of techniques. Men learned to sow seed instead of merely gathering fruits or roots and so came the first stage of agriculture. So it has been all the way up to the computer and the nuclear reactor. Every new technique puts a new power into the hands of men. Everything, even our myths, our ideologies, can be turned into techniques to serve some ulterior end. But still the "word" comes first—the conception, the idea, the suggestion, the hypothesis, the myth itself in one or another of its forms.

Every group—religious, ethnic, professional, occupational, academic, family, artistic or whatever—has its own belief-system. It develops a tradition, a way of life, a set of mores. There are

5

endless variants. In a modern society a man belongs to several disparate groups, and the demands they respectively make will sometimes be in conflict. Every individual who thinks at all acquires an overall belief-complex that accepts some parts of the codes of the groups to which he belongs, fusing them into a particular pattern. The reformer and the genius cherish distinctive belief-systems that reject whole areas of public opinion.

Nothing is so effective for unifying and giving coherence to a group—any group from the family to the great nation—as common traditions, shared belief-systems. And one serious drawback to the practical realization of democracy in present-day America is its failure to develop any pervasive common tradition. When the Republic was founded it was united not only by the dominating urge for self-government but also by the prevalence of traditions that stemmed from the British elitist form of limited democracy developed in the seventeenth and eighteenth centuries. This tradition found its typical expression in the doctrine of John Locke, began to lose hold under the Jacksonian regime and was grossly shaken by the cleavage of the Civil War and Reconstruction. But it was the successive waves of immigration in the later nineteenth century that turned this country into a loosely pluralist society, united by some common usages, dominated by the pursuit of social advancement and wealth, but owning a common tradition no more.

Our belief-systems or myth-complexes combine conceptions both of how things are and of how they could be and should be. This holds true alike for religious creeds, political doctrines, economic policies and social attitudes. These valuations are the dynamic of action. Our decisions, our conclusions, our enterprises of every kind rest on assumptions generated by our beliefs. These assumptions are often unprobed, untested, resistant even in the face of opposing evidence. Often enough they mislead us, deceive our assessments of the prospects of success, prevent us from reaching worthwhile goals. It is therefore important that in the conduct of all matters of consequence we should scrutinize the available evidence and be willing in its light to correct our untutored notions.

Let us now consider some popular notions about the character, role and function of our American democracy and see how they compare with the operation of the specific system of government established under our Constitution.

The American democratic form is in certain respects unique. Its Supreme Court is the guardian of the Constitution. The Court can nullify and revoke such acts of the legislature as in the Court's free interpretation and reinterpretation of the Constitution are contrary to its provisions. The American President has a remarkable amount of potential authority, combining the attributes that in various other democracies are divided between the president and the premier. Our party system is extraordinarily simple and, in its curious way, effective. Over a vast federal area, with great regional diversity in tradition, culture, ethnic composition, occupational concentration, degree of urbanization and economic resources, a simple bi-party affiliation continues, almost irrationally, to reign supreme. It makes strange bedfellows, with some left-wingers in the more rightist party and right-wingers in the more leftist, as well as a whole cohort of Southern Democrats who have been the most antidemocratic group in the legislature. But it works, in spite of—and possibly because of— some of its contradictions. Moreover, we are fortunate in that, unlike the democracies of the Old World, ours is not troubled by a big Communist Party bloc. It is perhaps all the more curious that we are so mightily concerned by the presence of a handful of Communists in our midst, as is evidenced by the blatant warnings of the FBI, the heavy-fisted activities of the Committee on Un-American Activities, and the still considerable number who cherish McCarthyist tendencies.

The very peculiarities of American democracy make suspect the common assumption that ours is a model of what a democracy should be. The quality of a democracy can never be assessed on the basis of its form alone. The structural features of a democracy are a mere façade unless made operative and meaningful by the democratic spirit of the people. The realization and maintenance of democracy is a matter of the attitudes and practices of the people and their leadership.

Every democracy is imperfect; no democracy lives up fully to the principles it proclaims. There is never complete equality before the law. Wealth, power, prestige, influence and prejudice have some weight in the courts. Only in a quite limited sense do the people choose who shall govern them, and how. The government is never in all respects—and most notably in the making of foreign policy—held responsible to the people. It was an ancient Greek saying that the fine is the difficult, and that the best way of governing, the democratic, is the most difficult. Democracy requires, to be at all viable, a long initiation, a well-established tradition, a reasonably well-educated public interested in political affairs, the possession of an economic competence by a majority of the people and a number of competing focuses of economic power. It is not a commodity that can be exported to countries lacking these prerequisites, and what has happened in so many new African states offers a painful illustration of this fact. If we now proceed to expose some flaws in our own system and some serious discrepancies between our assumptions and the actualities, this should be viewed in the perspective of the insufficiency of all democracies to live up to the principles they proclaim.

Two main types of shortcomings can be specified in our attitudes toward our American democracy. One is the breach between our professed principles and our behavior. The other is the incongruity between our assumptions about the way certain of our democratic forms work and the way they actually do.

The most grievous exhibit of the difference between our professions and our behavior is the treatment we have meted out to the ethnic and racial minorities in our midst. For over a century they have been held in various degrees of subjection. Negroes, Orientals, peoples of East Europe, Puerto Ricans and other in-

8

comers have been exploited and denied the opportunities and rights of free citizens. The most flagrant expressions of this treatment are the segregationist policies of the Southern states and the ghettolike confinement of Negroes and Puerto Ricans in the helpless squalor of our city slums. It is manifest in the exclusion of these groups from the better residential areas and in the denial to them of equal opportunities for education, employment and upgrading, and of equal protection by the police and, not infrequently, the courts.

Some realization of the cost and the waste resulting from these gross violations of our democratic principles has at length led to a significant movement for reform. Segregationist laws have been abolished; some positions of relative importance have been opened up to disprivileged minorities; and laws against discrimination on grounds of color, creed, ethnic origin or religion have been enacted by the federal government and by a considerable number of states. But the net improvement is partial and halting. Public opinion lags far behind the demands of the new laws. The "inalienable rights" of men and of citizens are still flagrantly denied. The unfulfilled promise has led to an explosive situation in the slums of our cities, with outbreaks of destructive violence and bloodshed. But this ominous object lesson is still misread by many of our people, who think the answer has to do with more police rather than with rigorous adherence to our most basic political beliefs. Certainly criminal acts cannot be allowed to go unpunished, but repression is an expedient, not a solution, and many outbreaks have been sparked precisely by rash or brutal behavior by the police, notably in Watts, Harlem, Philadelphia, Detroit and Newark. That the police often fail to be the guardians of law and order they are presumed to be, is a remark that is relevant to other democracies as well as to our own. Many reforms are needed before we get in sight of the goal of equal justice for all citizens. The legacy of a century's disregard and exploitation cannot be cancelled at a stroke. It requires major changes in attitudes and in behavior, and it calls for the massive

9

and initially costly undertaking of the conversion of our slums into decent habitations. But our welfare depends on our willingness to pay the price.

Conflicts between our professed beliefs and our behavior are usually easier to identify than misconceptions about how our democracy really works. One such misconception centers around the doctrine that in a democracy the people rule, in the sense that they determine who shall govern, and for how long, and to secure what ends. The clash here is directly between assumptions and actualities. In the first place a large percentage of citizens do not care enough to record their votes, and many of those who do are motivated by concerns other than the issues that divide one party from another. Many vote as the bosses or the local leaders bid them to. Many know little about the persons they vote for and even less about the policies they represent; opinion polls regularly expose the astounding ignorance that prevails about the political situation. Many vote for a candidate because he is a local man or the friend of a friend or because he wangled the funds for a new post office in their town. And at best the average voter has little to do with the choice of candidates. That function is taken over by the party machines, the inside group of manipulators whose choice is determined by the prospect of gaining or retaining influence, control and spoils.

Moreover, there are some powerful influences that, by purveying biased or at least one-sided information, may mislead the voter. The press is mostly in the hands of wealthy groups, predominantly supporting one party, and too many newspapers not only present the news in a manner favorable to that party but leave unrecorded some items unfavorable to it. Other interests—those of advertisers or of stockholders—may be similarly privileged. Since newspapers with large circulations require much capital to carry on, and since with greater circulation goes greater advertising, the number of daily newspapers has been much reduced through mergers and the swallowing up of the less successful by the more successful. Thus daily newspapers have become quasi-monopolies. There are comparatively few that maintain high standards and present with reasonable fairness information on both sides of controversial questions. Thus *The Wall Street Journal*, a daily that is notable for the accuracy of its reporting, presented in its issue of July 25, 1967, a remarkable indictment of the manner in which certain newspapers distort and falsify the news they print, giving chapter and verse for leading newspapers in Chicago, Boston, San Francisco and other cities.

But the news media are not solely at fault. We cannot absolve the federal government. Quite frequently the news emanating from Washington regarding the situation in Vietnam has been shown by later revelations to have been falsified. The Government has also made a series of promises respecting the degree of involvement of the United States that it failed to keep. Thus has arisen the "credibility gap" that has led to widespread distrust in the minds of intelligent citizens regarding anything the civil or the military authorities say about this unhappy undeclared war. Nevertheless it remains a remarkable fact that somehow or other, in the shorter or in the longer run, a majority of the people in a democracy like ours do resist the influences and pressures exerted by entrenched power and wealth.

In passing we should observe that while we cannot hold our citizens entirely responsible for being misled by misinformation, we can at least condemn a lack of alertness in their tendency to accept it. If people really cared, they could more easily recognize the one-sidedness of what biased informants tell them, and they would no longer, when it suits their interests or their prejudices, invite misinformation.

Some responsibility for this failure must be imputed to our educational system. Public-school education in civics, in the character, problems and demands of democratic living, has long been deficient. The textbooks in the field have ranged from humdrum accounts of our form of democracy (the stages, for example, that a bill goes through in the process of enactment) to laudatory accounts of the freedoms and the benefits we enjoy, with purple passages from the speeches of Washington, Webster and Lincoln. Citizens whose parents had come from other lands rarely receive any realistic training in the responsibilities, as well as the rights, of democracy. I can testify on this subject from some personal knowledge. In 1952 I was approached by Alvin Johnson, former president of the New School for Social Research; Margaret Lewisohn, the distinguished lady who was then head of the Public Education Association; and others who were disgruntled with the teaching of civics in the New York Public Schools. Securing the permission of the Board of Education, they invited me to give an experimental course in civics to some junior-high-school students. I obtained a number of the textbooks then used in schools, thoroughly agreed about their inadequacy, and undertook the task. A junior high school (No. 7) in the Bronx was selected and after testing the various grades, I chose youngsters of twelve and thirteen. Some teachers shook their heads on learning that I talked of the differences between Republicans and Democrats, organized debates on issues of the times, sent the children out at election time to report on the speeches of candidates and ended by giving them a neighborhood litter-clearing job.

My experience provided conclusive evidence that these quite young students were ready and indeed eager to take a course in realistic civics, in place of the generalities, laudations of democratic liberties and administrative formalities that characterized the school texts at the time. What they needed to learn was that democracy is a boon every generation has to win anew for itself. They had to recognize its problems, its conditions and its responsibilities, if as future citizens they were to maintain its privileges and rights. Students learn these things when we bring them face to face with current political issues, providing them with relevant data, but leaving them to take their own sides. They learn them better by practicing democracy in their own ways, by running their own elections and debating controversial questions.

Behind false assumptions about the nature of democratic rule lies a particularly dangerous attitude towards democracy itself. Democracy is not a legacy bestowed on a people, simply to use and to enjoy. Democracy is a responsibility people must fulfill if they are to benefit by it—if they are even to maintain it.

In our dealings with poor and industrially undeveloped countries we have failed to understand that they cannot be democracies except after lengthy preparation and experience. Such countries cannot unify their tribally and geographically diversified regions except under some form of oligarchical control. They cannot develop their economic resources except under some kind of socialistic system. They cannot operate a party system that doesn't soon transform itself into a one-party system, probably after a coup by some military junta. A democracy is viable only after a long process of maturation and education.

One other prerequisite of a democracy, to which we have already alluded, is of signal importance: a number of focuses of specialized but relatively independent powers, free to express their opposition to such policies of the government as they may dislike. This is why a fully socialized state can never be a democracy. It lacks the four relatively autonomous agencies that are most effective in bringing pressure to bear on government—those of business, finance, free trade-unionism and nonestablished religious organizations. In a fully socialized state it is hazardous for the average citizen to protest against any policy of the government, since he is its employee. In a democracy the protests of any important group of citizens, though they may represent only a minority, can carry weight and lead to the modification of administrative policy. At the time of writing, this consideration is exemplified by the groups that protest against the war in Vietnam. The growing unpopularity of this war was a serious concern of government, even when a majority still supported it. Criticism was met on the one hand by pledges of peace-probing endeavors, and on the other, by renewed insistence that the war was necessary to safeguard the "free world" and stay the advance of Communist aggression. But events have discounted this justification to such an extent that it is now by no means certain that the official position still enjoys majority support.

This may be an appropriate place to point out that war itself, or the serious threat of war or large-scale preparation for war, has nearly always been the enemy of democracy. Occasionally, a revolutionary war has replaced a dynasty or imperial rule by establishing a democracy in its stead, and our own republic is an example. But the case remains exceptional. Massive preparations for war augment the role of the military forces and the power of their supporting industries. In consequence, the demands of the armed forces tend to be supported by both the industrial and governmental sectors. The demands of war are paramount, and democratic processes fall into abeyance. It is an old saying that during wars the laws are silent. The militaristic executive is in the saddle, and its supremacy tends to endure after the fighting ends. Democracy itself is wounded in war, and the wound may be slow to heal. The harsh truth is that the unparalleled wars of the past half century have in fact brought to an end the march of democracy that was so hopefully prognosticated in the later nineteenth century.

Assumptions about the extent of popular control over democratic government are not the only ones which need reappraisal. There are others inherited from the time when the Constitution was born. The most important of them applies to the system of checks and balances. The Founding Fathers were anxious to safeguard the new state against two dangers. In the first place they feared that the stability of a well-ordered government might be weakened by hasty acts of the popular legislature; they preferred to think of the new order as a republic rather than as a pure democracy. In the second place they were concerned lest one of the trinity of governmental powers—the legislative, executive and judiciary—might encroach on the sphere of another and make itself supreme. This apprehension particularly concerned the undue arrogation of power by the executive or the legislature. The founders had been much impressed by the argu-

14

ment of Montesquieu's *The Spirit of the Laws,* and they approved of his prescription, which they understood as implying the clean-cut separation of the powers. The legislature would independently enact the laws, the executive would independently apply them. The United States Supreme Court would keep the legislature in its place by curbing its tendency to override the Constitution. The Constitution itself would be protected from hasty amendment by the size of the majority necessary to effect any change in it and by the complicated process prescribed for amending it.

This latter fear was not without justification. The executive has in a number of former democracies usurped ruling power, especially in times of crisis. One device sometimes resorted to, notably in France, has been to issue "decree-laws," a form of quasi-dictatorial government. Moreover, the military forces are an executive arm, and coups and insurrections organized by them have been, in Latin America and elsewhere, a frequent occurrence.

Nevertheless, the assumptions underlying the nearly total separation of powers are, I think, erroneous. Montesquieu was principally concerned with the peril to all human liberties when the powers are invested in a single person or organ of state, as in an absolute monarchy. If the lawmaker were also the judge who freely decided when the law was violated, and if the executive were the lawmaker and judge as well, the way would be open to the grossest abuses of power. Every power holder is certain to use his position in an arbitrary and oppressive way when he is not limited by other powers. But insofar as Montesquieu's principle implied that the various powers should not only be separately embodied but also kept separate and independent in the fulfilling of their respective functions, he was wholly mistaken. Yet that was the way the Founding Fathers tended to interpret his meaning.

A system of checks and balances is proper enough if it is designed to prevent one power from arrogating authority that be-

15

longs to another or from exercising its own authority in ways that violate the Constitution, as would happen, for example, if the Congress passed an act that favored a particular religious group. The Supreme Court is in this respect a guardian of the Constitution. The Constitution in turn is guarded by the complexity of the conditions requisite for any amendment. But checks and balances also take forms that militate against the integration and the smooth operation of our system of government, and that unfortunate consequence follows from the narrower interpretation given to Montesquieu's principle.

The separation of powers offers us no assurance against abuses by any one of them. On the contrary, separation makes it easier, since each power pursues its own policy and makes its own decisions without direct restraint by the others. Occasions arise in practically every state when the executive is tempted to usurp entire control, and it can do so the more easily when there is no coordination in the making of policy. Its opportunity comes when there is serious unrest or dissension among the people or when there is much laxity and corruption in the conduct of government.

Legislative and executive action are, after all, different parts of a single process, the process of lawmaking. It is the task of the executive to put into effect the decisions of the legislature. They must function together for efficiency of action. The experience of the United States confirms this, as did the experience of England before it developed its special form of coordination, the cabinet system. Under the American system we can have the difficult situation in which a President belonging to one political party must deal with a Congress having a majority of the other. And even when this is not the case, the President has only a minimal and indirect association with the Congress. A more curious form of stultification occurs when a Democratic President has a nominal congressional majority but only with the inclusion of the Southern Democrats who on many issues cast their votes with the Republicans. Frequently they support amendments to Democratic bills that emasculate or defeat Democratic legislation. Still another anomaly is the power of "a third plus one" of the Senate to reject or nullify treaties with foreign powers. Thus under the leadership of Senator Henry Cabot Lodge a Senate minority defeated President Wilson's ardent desire that the United States should join the League of Nations. We may argue that the Treaty of Versailles, to which the inclusion of the League was attached, was a vicious and vengeful spoliation of defeated peoples and that, in any case, the United States was basically isolationist at that time. But these considerations do not alter the fact that a smallish Senate minority can defeat the foreign policy of the administration. It is significant that Woodrow Wilson himself, in his treatise on the state, had in earlier days pointed out the vexatious consequences of the lack of coordination created by our system of checks and balances.

Foreign policy is the area of government that by its very nature is screened from public knowledge. Decisions in this area are made *in camera,* and only such "information" is vouchsafed as suits the interest or the convenience of the government. Its memorandums and records are "classified," "secret," "top secret," and only after the lapse of many years are they made available to historians. These are no doubt proper precautions, but that is all the more reason why Congress and the administration should be in knowledgeable accord on all significant decisions.

The situation at the time of this writing illustrates the defectiveness of our system. To the Congress belongs the authority to declare war. But we are waging war on a very considerable scale against North Vietnam and the Vietcong without any such declaration. The Congress, it is true, was on the side of the President, and in the Gulf of Tonkin Resolution of August 1964, gave him carte blanche to use any means at his disposal to repel armed attack against any member of the Southeast Asia Treaty Organization.

The contrast between the power wielded by President Johnson in the making of a war and the earlier impotence of President Wilson in his ardent efforts on behalf of a plan for international peace illustrates how greatly the control of the President varies from time to time. Wilson was wholly frustrated in the making of foreign policy. Johnson was given a practically free hand. Some Presidents, like Eisenhower, delegate important responsibilities to the Secretary of State and other ministers; others, like Johnson, assume direct control over all significant aspects of policy making. Such differences are not diminished but may instead be enhanced by the separation of powers.

The continuous escalation alike of the number of American troops engaged in the Vietnam war and of the range over which the conflict is waged, including the bombing of Hanoi itself, is an indication of a type of weakness in our American democracy that we have already mentioned. This war, though supported by a majority of the people until recently, has never been popular, but only reluctantly approved because of the representations of the Government that it was being fought in defense of democracy and to stop a Communist policy of aggression that otherwise would swallow up all of Southeast Asia. A large proportion of American scholars and leading educators rejected from the first these representations as specious and wholly misleading, but they received little credence. Nevertheless, there were, from the beginning, some fairly obvious facts that, though minimized or ignored by Government spokesmen, were easily accessible to anyone who cared to inquire—facts that, if widely known, might have raised doubts about the morality and wisdom of our policy. But the public—at least until recently—was not sufficiently concerned to ask such questions. And in the end, it was not those ignored considerations that led to increasing public disgruntlement. It was the continuous escalation, the expansion of our forces in Vietnam finally to more than half a million men, the casualty lists running often to over a thousand dead and wounded per week and the lack of any cogent evidence that our side was winning the war, all of which belied the pledges and the time-refuted reports of progress, until at length the polls showed approximately half of the samples expressing disapprobation of the conduct of the war. By then the confused public was entrapped.

So far, we have been discussing matters that are specific to the American form of democracy. But as I have said earlier, American democracy is in many ways—and not always necessarily for the best—unique. Since the problems of popular rule and of the separation and balancing of power under a constitution inevitably lead to thoughts about the nature of democracy in general, it might now be appropriate to turn briefly to some of these fundamentals. They bear repeating precisely because we so habitually take them for granted that we often think we are living by them when, in fact, we are ignoring them. Yet they are terribly important, for they give us an external conceptual standard against which to measure our own practice.

We have concentrated on the problems of popular rule, since the "sovereignty" of the people is the core of democracy. Yet it is by no means the simple proposition it is often taken to be. There are both popular and more sophisticated misconceptions about it. An example of the former is latent in the common remark, "It's wrong, there ought to be a law against it." A moral code should not be identified with a legal code. People have different standards of morality. If any one of these standards were established as law, the consensus on which the very existence of democracy rests would be disrupted. The same error underlies the doctrine, held by a small minority of political theorists, that perfect democracy means the absolute, unlimited right of the people to decide *all* issues by a majority vote. Austin Ranney and Wilmore Kendall, in a book entitled *Democracy and the American Party System* (1956), state that "any attempt to place *formal* institutional limitations upon the absolute power of popular majorities logically results in the establishment of minority rule," which violates the first principle of democracy. This position may claim some abstract logic on its side, but it is wholly inconsistent with the real meaning of democracy. If, for example,

19

a majority decided that their religion should alone be permitted within the state, or denied the members of other religions the rights of citizenship, as was so often done in the past, there would be a cleavage ruinous to the existence of democracy. The consensus on which democracy rests must include an agreement that certain matters are not the concern of government and should not be controlled by government.

I do not mean by this to deprecate the role of government; but the *community* is different from and greater than the *state*. In the community—in society as a whole—are the rich differences and spontaneous life that create the future. This is why the cultural values of men and of groups must remain essentially free from the uniformizing activities of government. What a man believes should not be the badge of his citizenship. It is the high virtue of democracy that it upholds this distinction.

The form of democracy puts the common interest, not merely that of some majority, above the divisive interests of all groups. Certain rights, obligations and liberties are held to be essential to the very existence of democracy and to override the special interests of either majorities or minorities. They are embodied in a constitution; but true democracy is wary of defining more than a necessary minimum of such values.

Democracy asserts the value of personality as a universal good and implies that there is a welfare of the whole to be attained through the cultivation of that value in all men. This, in turn, implies the desirability of individual liberty. But there is no sacred totality called "the liberty of the individual." The particular rights assured by democracy represent merely the central core of human liberty. If a man is not denied the right to communicate his thoughts, if he can associate freely with his fellows, if he is a citizen whose opinion counts equally with that of everyone else, then his personality is protected against the worst repressions. What he needs beyond is rather more opportunities—social, educational and economic—than more liberties.

Individual liberty is plainly incompatible with the unrestricted

20

rule of the majority, and "majority rule" is *not* the definition of democracy. The rule of opinion differs from all other kinds of rule in that it requires the continuous coexistence of opposing opinion. In a very real sense, democracy has no more precious asset than its dissenting minorities. It is the first duty of any true democracy to give its minorities the full measure of protection and respect they deserve. The faith of a small minority is as inviolable as the faith of a multitude.

Thus democracy, in recognizing the right of minority dissent, asserts it as a value. In this respect, democracy affirms the community by recognizing the existence of faction within it. Yet democracy is, nonetheless, a system of government, and as such must keep order and make effective decisions. Its method, of course, is to strike a balance between majority rule and institutionalized dissent, and in so doing, to infringe upon the perfect freedom of both.

I have already alluded to the limits that democracy must place on majority rule, but it may be worthwhile to say a few words about the limits it must also place on dissent. The first point to note is that there are certain types of faction within the community that cannot automatically be solved by the institutionalized right of dissent. The democratic form provides no ready solution to the impasse created by the discrimination of group against group within the community. Legal equality may not constitute sufficient protection for a minority that is the victim of discrimination by the majority, yet, short of revolution, there seems to be no answer save a gradual adjustment of group relations in the direction of equality of opportunity through an arduous process of social education.

What about undemocratic forms of dissent—either in the milder form of civil disobedience or in the ultimate form of revolution? A democratic system does not, in principle, deny the right of its dissenting citizens to advocate the abandonment of democracy altogether. Here the only condition consistent with democracy is that the exponents of these opinions accept, as the media for their translation into policy, the same democratic processes that give them the right of expression. If men are not content to win their ends by making enough converts to turn their cause into the cause of the majority, they are rejecting the only ground on which, in a democracy, they are entitled to ask for the liberty of their opinions. It is a primary duty of every government to maintain order and prevent not only violence, but incitements to violence. But if an antidemocratic minority, by its persuasive appeal, should succeed in winning a majority, then democracy can do no more than mourn its failure.

The final, and perhaps the most important thing we should bear in mind about democracy is its essentially pragmatic and experimental nature. We do not define democracy by its spirit. It is not a creed, but a form of government. It is the essence of democracy that it is *not* tied to any transcendent ideology or to any particular doctrine of man's role or his destiny. It puts into office a government pledged to drastic reform, then ousts it in favor of a government dedicated to stability. So it went from Wilson to Harding and from Hoover to Roosevelt. The power of the people alone sustains democracy; nearly all other powers, consciously or unconsciously, fight against it. The peoples' freedom is their responsibility.

I have felt free to state some positions and offer some evaluations that others would dispute, but there can be no dispute over the major conclusion to which this whole exposition leads. The misunderstandings, mistaken assumptions and misleading associations that clog the operation of our American democracy stem from a major weakness, the lack of any pervasive tradition of democracy and the failure of the establishment to help our citizens to acquire it by realistic civic training in the dangers, promises and responsibilities of democracy. Our people almost universally proclaim a love for democracy and their happiness at living in a country where they enjoy the freedom it bestows. Rarely is any voice raised in public in support of an oligarchical or other antidemocratic system. But we fail to recognize how often we violate its principles and how little we do positively to ensure its reality.

Nevertheless, amid all the confusion and misunderstanding that beset our American democracy there is one most encouraging sign of advancement. At length, in the last three decades, there has developed a concerted effort to remove the worst obstacle to any democratic progress, our treatment of ethnic and racial minorities. The Supreme Court decision of 1954 betokened a profound change. Public opinion moves, if laggardly, in the same direction, in the wake of a spate of antidiscriminative laws. Nothing in this new legislation holds more significance for the future than the laws forbidding discrimination in the provision of education. A better-educated public, embracing the more disprivileged groups, should mean that the voters will be more concerned about the kind of candidates they support and more likely to influence the policies of their government. Over this whole area the gap between assumptions and realities is lessening.

Our democracy was not born in 1789. It had its roots in an older land. It is still on the move, returning again to its always unfinished business.

EDMUND STILLMAN

American Government: The Limits of Reason

> "The prospect is . . . rather murkier than most middle-class Americans dare suspect."

The inherent rationality of a system of government is one thing; the rationality of the people responsible for making that system work is something else. Whenever people permit their principles to become confused with dogmas, they become vulnerable to challenge. Edmund Stillman does not disagree with Professor MacIver on this point; indeed, he places much more emphasis on it. His forecast of a "time of troubles" that lies ahead for American democracy makes sobering reading.

> Here are no aristocratical families, no courts, no kings, no bishops, no ecclesiastical dominion, no invisible power giving to a few a very visible one. . . . The rich and the poor are not so far removed from each other as they are in Europe. . . . We have no princes for whom we toil, starve, and bleed; we are the most perfect society now existing in the world. Here man is free as he ought to be; nor is this pleasing equality so transitory as many others are.
>
> JEAN DE CRÈVECOEUR,
> *Letters from an American Farmer*

> Howl!
>
> ALLEN GINSBERG

I T IS an apparent paradox of political character that, on the one hand, the American typically sees his nation as unique in history, as a society and a polity different in kind from any other in the world, and that on the other, he persists in projecting his nation as a prototype for all mankind.

The resolution of the paradox, of course, is merely the powerful current of political—indeed it may be quasi-theological—messianism that pervades American life. America was founded in the deliberate effort to create a New Jerusalem in the wilderness. We were God's American Israel, as Reinhold Niebuhr has observed; and the sense of America as witness, the chosen vehicle for the social and moral redemption of mankind, has informed our political life ever since.

This messianic sense has lent a peculiar quality of self-conscious display to the governmental process in America. To Thomas Jefferson, as a founder of the new state, "A just and solid republican government maintained here will be a standing monument. . . . The inquiry which has been excited among the mass of mankind by our revolution and its consequences will ameliorate the condition of man over a great portion of the globe."

To Lincoln, at the time of the nation's great Constitutional crisis, ". . . The Declaration of Independence . . . [gave] liberty, not alone to the people of this country, but hope to the world. . . ." And well over a century after the founding of the Republic, Woodrow Wilson, who may well be the archetypal American acting in the world arena, infused with a special moral fervor wedded to an intolerant ignorance of complexity abroad, proclaimed the New Freedom, asking: ". . . Are we preserving freedom in this land of ours, the hope of all the earth?"

Such passionate, indeed anguished, theatrics might seem easy to parody in our own more cynical age; yet criticisms of the naïve messianism that is the dominant political tradition in America commonly function in the past tense only. So self-consciously a professional diplomatist as the present Secretary of State, Dean

Rusk, defines America's foreign policy goal as a "victory for all mankind . . . a worldwide victory for freedom." His detractors, who decry the military intervention in Vietnam as their grand-fathers denounced the American imperialist adventure in the Philippines, do so precisely out of a guilty sense that America has fallen from its high estate.

In foreign affairs, this sense of American singularity has tended to produce the old moralizing isolationism, a movement now discredited but never far beneath the surface of American political discourse. It is an isolationism that would transform the world by example—keeping clean hands because, in Péguy's phrase, "it has no hands." Conversely it has produced isolationism's merely apparent opposite, the philosophy of what might be termed "the new globalism." This is a doctrine which, in its most extravagant form, holds that it is America's special mission to preside over the modernization (for which read Americanization) of the world, taming disorder and transforming history.

On the purely domestic scene, this sense of singularity, coupled to the penchant for moralizing politics, accounts in good measure for one of the peculiar rhythms of American politics: eras of "normalcy," somnolence even, characterized by the stagnation of public life and the growth of private corruption, punctuated at random intervals by passionate programs of economic and social reform.

After the commitment and tragedy of the Civil War, there ensued an unparalleled era of venality and political apathy in America, to be succeeded in its turn by a Populist movement in the 1890's declaiming against the specter of a nation "brought to the verge of moral, political, and material ruin. Corruption dominates the ballot-box, the legislatures, the Congress, and touches even the ermine of the bench. The people are demoralized."

For Theodore Roosevelt, for Woodrow Wilson, for Franklin Roosevelt, social reform was moral crusade. Even in our own time, at the close of the somnolent Eisenhower years, John Fitzgerald Kennedy, accepting the Democratic nomination for the

Presidency at Los Angeles in 1960, lapsed into the language of Biblical exhortation.

To note the missionary and ultimately theological (though now secularized) component in the American's sense of national identity is not to challenge the fundamental accuracy of the popular perception of separateness. For that perception there is abundant evidence—in the testimony of foreigners and in the material situation of the country as well. Not the least striking feature of America's role in history is the fact that, by and large, the world has chosen to accept America at its own evaluation. *Amerika,* Goethe put it in his apostrophe, *du hast es besser;* and as early as the opening years of the American Revolution, Turgot had observed: "All right-thinking men must pray that this people may arrive at all the prosperity of which they are capable. They are the hope of the human race. . . . They must prove to the world, as a fact, that men can be both free and peaceful. . . ." Tocqueville, that dispassionate observer of the early America, did not doubt that he was witness to a drama of universal relevance; and almost a century later Lenin could hardly do better than couch his near-magical ambitions for the socialist order—his vision of a new economic and social dispensation—in terms of comparison with the United States. Nor can his successors in the Soviet Union do better to this day.

America is a datum, a bench mark for the world—not only as it is, but as it would itself be. The American claim to being a chosen people has won the acceptance—sometimes the uneasy acceptance—of the world. Hostile visitors to the America of the last century, like Dickens and Mrs. Trollope, betrayed by their stridency their grudging half-acceptance of the myth. Even the *intellectuels méchants* of St. Germain, like Sartre and Simone de Beauvoir, so savage in their criticism, have often seemed in the hysterical quality of their anti-Americanism more like disappointed lovers than congenital skeptics.

If the common consent of mankind, then, be taken as some indicator of truth, America *is* unique. But the sadder truth is that it is unique in other ways than being merely the focus of the hopes of mankind. For underlying the American—and world-wide—perception of singularity is a more somber perception: while America functions (though less and less) as the symbolic incarnation of a nearly universal hope, that hope is at bottom unreasonable. America is unique precisely because the conditions that have made America are hardly duplicable elsewhere in the world, and certainly not on the American scale.

America had, in its formative first century and a half, a security afforded by geographical isolation; it had a vast endowment of national wealth; and it had the happy situation that its minorities were either overmatched aboriginals and detribalized slaves (or quasi-slaves) or immigrants who voluntarily sought to assimilate to the majority standard rather than contest it. Americans may in fact be a chosen people, but they are all the less likely for that to be the prototype of an emerging social order elsewhere in the world.

Thus the old sense of separateness evidences a fundamental intuition of America's essential isolation from mankind—an isolation which, on another level, is insistently denied. It is one of the contradictory elements in the national myth that while America is held to be unique, a peculiar treasure (and so, by extension, individual Americans, too), nevertheless popular doctrine has it that all men are essentially the same: all men would be like Americans if they could, and only a vincible ignorance or objective evil circumstance keeps them from becoming so.

The American credo is relentlessly pre-Freudian. What is needed, the American credo would seem to say, is a government of wise laws and a sufficient material portion (itself the product of rational, purposive and "virtuous" endeavor) to smother the demons in man. This is a faith independent of party affiliation or class. The political debate in America, in nearly two centuries, had usually been at the level of tactics, of means, and hardly ever at the level of goals. Only, as we shall see, in the recent past has a new questioning come to be heard—and then, as formulated by the New Left and the self-consciously alienated, formulated in

28

slack and sentimental terms. The dominant American political movements of both Right and Left still meet in their essential faith: the manipulability of human affairs and the sovereign curative power of material wealth. One might caricature this shared faith as holding that in this world there are no bad men, only poor men.

In holding to this dual theory of government and society, Americans quite obviously are faithful to their special past. The American Constitution is the great practical achievement of eighteenth-century politics—the triumph of the rationalist state-craft of the Enlightenment philosophers who held that man was essentially good, or at least corrigible, if subject to wise laws and a just ordering of society. The Constitution is the political expression of a self-consistent eighteenth-century world view that demanded, in Basil Wiley's words, to recognize the natural order "as 'controlled, sustained, and agitated' by laws in some way akin to those of human reason. To be no longer at the mercy of nature, no longer to be encompassed by arbitrary mystery—these benefits were to be accompanied by the great new gifts of power, power to control the natural forces and turn them, in Bacon's phrase, to the 'occasions and uses of life,' and the 'relief of man's estate.'" The nineteenth-century contribution to this faith was merely the more vulgar element of the materialist obsession.

This is the faith of the United States today. While two world wars, together with the plenary horrors of the Stalinist purges, Buchenwald, Dresden and Hiroshima have all supervened, chastening the rest of the world, and inducing a congenital pessimism, the majority of America has remained true to its naked childhood faith.

This isolation of America from the deepest experience of tragedy—certainly over the past hundred years—accounts in good measure for the unsatisfactory nature of the American dialogue with the world ever since the nation broke out of isolation in 1941 and took up a global role.[1]

[1] The great American experience with tragedy was, of course, the Civil War,

The effect of the American political intervention in world affairs, enormous in scope, has been to stagger the world with this nation's raw strength and vitality, but to bewilder it as well. Superficial American traits—the love of gadgetry, the informality, the intoxication with speed and mechanical power—are imitated everywhere. But too often the inner content of the American style is consistently missed. The American politics-by-consensus has certainly not exported well to our Afro-Asian stipendiaries; and in this the Americans, though now assiduous at area studies and the learning of exotic languages, do not help much. Few Americans thereby comprehend the endemic violence, the repetitive tragedy, even of such closely kindred (and, to some of the population, ancestral) societies as those of Central Europe or Sicily, let alone such alien value systems as those of the Arab Middle East—and Vietnam.

America's proffered remedies—the counsels of "reason," as we define reason, thrust on fanatics too inflamed by political and national passions to be able even to agree on a definition of the conflict at hand—have proved to have startlingly little relevance outside of the limited arena of Western Europe. There, in conditions closely related to our own, American economic aid and the doctrine of consensus politics have achieved some success—though whether Europe has, in fact, cast out its old demons of ideological politics and fratricidal war and achieved a long-lasting peace is far from certain.

---

in which 364,000 Union soldiers died from all causes. Confederate losses are difficult to assess, but this was a war which left a permanent scar on the defeated South and caused that region to stand somewhat aside from the facile optimism shared by the rest of the country.

Appalling as such losses are, they are hardly unique in history, or even, as one or one and a half percent of population, especially severe. It is reliably estimated, for example, that in the Thirty Years' War (1618–1648) the population of Bohemia, the pivot of the fighting and ravaging, fell from 2,000,000 to 700,000. In Germany and Austria the population fell from 21,000,000 to 15,000,000. Three hundred years later (three centuries not themselves especially peaceful) Germany lost well over 6,000,000 dead and wounded in the course of World War I. France lost one in every twenty-eight of population. In World War II, Russian losses (from all causes) may be estimated as something like 20,000,000 dead, or 10 percent of the whole, while Germany (excluding Austria) lost 3,250,000 battle dead and a further 3,350,000 dead from "other" causes, including Allied air raids and forced population transfers, between 1939 and 1945.

Elsewhere the American political intervention has normally proved the reverse of helpful. American theories of society and politics are resisted nearly everywhere our aid missions go. Our efforts to foster the novelty of "constitutional" government, as in Greece and Vietnam, have proved embarrassing failures. While the American Constitution is an organic growth in this country, stemming from native Protestant and rationalist traditions, and has reflected a powerful underlying consensus, the Greek and Vietnamese constitutions are not and do not. Thus the disappointments for democracy in Greece and Vietnam.

It might, for example, be argued that the ruling junta in Vietnam was *more* legitimate before the electoral process of 1967 than after. For one thing, in any society, there is a kind of authority and respect that derive merely from the successful exercise of power over a protracted period of time. This much "legitimacy" the military junta in Saigon had partly achieved by crushing most of its foes. In Vietnamese society, where political theory is traditionally derived from the Chinese, the electoral process has no real precedent except at the level of the local community. Legitimacy of the central ruler is traditionally accorded to that person or group which governs successfully: *de facto* power is *de jure*. By agreeing, under American pressure, to a contested election, the Thieu-Ky junta may be said to have conceded its prior illegitimacy and found itself unable to gain new legitimacy through an electoral process hardly warranted by Vietnamese custom and, in any case, too flawed in its operation to have proved convincing to the population at large.

That American political and social precedents are of limited relevancy to the world has, of course, begun to dawn on some critics at home. More widespread is the understanding that American optimism and idealism, when formulated into an official doctrine, too often reflect an unpleasant and underlying pharisaism—the "arrogance of power."

But intellectual questioning by Americans of the *premises* of American society and government is not yet widespread. This is so despite the fact that in the mid-1960's America, at home and abroad, has been brought into violent contact with a kind of total dissent from its dogmas. By a kind of historical accident that has about it some of the sense of Greek tragedy—*hubris* meeting its check—the American dogmas about man, purpose, fate and time are now meeting desperate challenge both on the internal and external fronts.

At home, the assumptions of the official society are challenged not so much by the classical Marxist Left, which is itself, in its own way, made obsolete by events. The new dissenters are, in part, the angry and dispirited children of the triumphant (and traditionally normative) American middle classes. These are the beat and hip movements, the new drug and motorcycle cultists, the New Left. In part—and I believe far more complete in their challenge—they are the new Negro militants.

Abroad, the optimistic American theories of human action are challenged by many in Vietnam (hardly, on a purely material income and land-ownership scale, the poorest or worst-exploited of the traditional Asian societies) whose reaction to the American presence in their country, and to the American efforts (and they are extensive) to reform and redeem it, is to reject all that the Americans try to do and all that they stand for. Rank-and-file insurgents find it all the easier to accept Communist direction because the intrusive, alien and detested Americans are anti-Communist. The insurgents therefore behave, to Americans, in a wholly "unreasonable" way, preferring autocracy to constitution, and war to foreign aid.

Among the domestic challengers, the white alienation movements clearly evidence a growing societal malaise; but their chief significance lies in their rejection of middle-class affluence. They express an anguish—a kind of intolerable psychic itch—hardly accessible to the calming effects of material wealth. Yet these white movements are not yet, curiously enough, quite total dissents. While they dissent from official *values*, they do not, even on the New Left, dissent very much from general American perceptions of the world.

They are, at bottom, movements which, along with the beliefs of their elders, express a fundamental American confidence in the benignity of the universe. For the "flower people," universal love is a tenable belief precisely because, together with their middle-aged and middle-class parents, these young have banished tragedy from their vision. Hatred, greed and ruinous lust are not part of their cosmos; these qualities are un-American, so to say.

For the New Left, with its revolutionary heroes, the mood is anger; but so is a facile optimism and meliorism which the traditional American also manifests. Fundamental skepticism about life seems as alien to the Students for Democratic Society as to the Young Republicans. The young revolutionaries hold, in effect, that millennium can be won by attitudinizing—without, in short, subjecting oneself to a harsh discipline like the dialectic or without subjecting oneself to the onerous but life-or-death organizational discipline of the revolutionary conspirator.

And if the motorcycle gangs are violent, nevertheless together with the beats, the hip and the society at large they share (even if they evidence their belief by a total indifference) a fundamental belief in the ultimate reliability of an economy and society which they ostensibly contest but which tolerate and support them.

In this sense, the white dissenting movements are less a challenge than evidence of the limited application of the American myth even in the society that generated it. More significant may be the growth of Negro militancy, which, should it fall into the hands of its extremist leaders, would constitute a basic challenge. Precisely because these vanguardists no longer wish to be incorporated *into* the American society—the consensus—precisely because they are by now indifferent to the issues of political and economic melioration as such, but react to the racial degradation of the Negro over two centuries, precisely because they wish to bring the society down, they are the first serious challenge to the consensus since the Constitutional challenge of the Civil War. Somber too is the fact that the Negro militants—and I for one believe they represent the wave of the future—are thus the truly alienated, coming, according to the pattern of most revolutionaries, at that moment in history when the lot of the submerged class is improving and the dominant class has lost its self-confidence. Modern America, then, may be confronted with an unassimilable nodule within the body politic—a group that is profoundly anti-reformist and that truly challenges the consensus —in something like the terms that Sudeten Germans challenged the Czechoslovak liberal-parliamentarian consensus before 1939, or as Buddhist activists in Hue or Da Nang today challenge the would-be consensus imposed by the Saigon central authority. Such a group, as I have said, wishes to bring the established order down.

None of this is to argue the inevitability of an American breakdown. It is to argue the likelihood of a "time of troubles" in contrast to the facile assumption that American politics and society constitute an infallible system within which dissent and disorder can always be contained.

Certainly the foreign challenge to America, as exemplified by the endemic disorders of the Third World—those political paroxysms of the *déracinés* and the detribalized—is unlikely to achieve sufficient cohesion and power to threaten the United States directly. As for Vietnam, viewed in perspective, it is not likely to function as a central challenge to the American consensus, but rather as a bitter learning experience in which America confronts some of the stuff of tragedy and learns that, for all the insistent optimism of our myth and for all our immense material power, life too often remains intractable still. The lesson is that any nation, however great, is fallible; that any nation, however strong, can construct a task too great for its powers. Vietnam, then, may be merely an instance in a long future series of heartbreaking events by which Americans will at last lose their innocence abroad.

But failure at home is another thing.

The alienated movements of our day and their likely successors of tomorrow are all a flight from the notion of a rationalist politics, even as they condemn the official system as inherently unreasonable and deadening. These movements are all, as yet, dissent without coherent content; but their emptiness of belief is not a condition likely to persist for long. Into the moral and emotional vacuum these movements prepare, a new ideology must eventually flood. If it too is anti-rational—and it is hard to see how it can be anything else—then an activist nihilism will have been let loose in American life, a doctrine profoundly incompatible with the inherited Enlightenment ideals, however debased, that rule America today.

The view is now gaining ground that the traditional society is corrupt. In this respect, if its treatment of the hip phenomenon is any guide, even *Time* magazine has a guilty conscience. But this view cannot be expected to deflect a Negro militancy which for the first time begins to *reject* rather than *demand* integration.

The contemporary tragedy of America may be that at a time when the Negro might begin to follow the classic assimilation pattern of past American minorities by adopting the mores and character structure of the dominant society, many of the best or most promising children of that society are engaged in a process of self-proletarianization. And to call it self-proletarianization may miss the point, for many of the new social movements may well be, at two or three removes, a white imitation of traditional Negro life. This too may be a vengeance of the conquered.

The prospect, then, is murky—rather murkier than most middle-class Americans dare suspect.

Nearly a century ago, in 1877, the American anthropologist Lewis Morgan sounded the note of hope for his age—the political philosophy of his nation and the credo of social evolution: "Democracy in government, brotherhood in society, equality in rights and privileges, and universal education, foreshadow the next higher plane of society to which experience, intelligence, and knowledge are steadily tending."

Writing today, one suspects he would be less sure.

ROGER D. MASTERS

Violence in American Politics

"Are American democratic institutions
more closely related to bloodshed . . .
than we have dared to admit?"

*Central to the democratic system is the ordered process by which
a minority transforms itself into a majority. Americans usually
characterize this process as "peaceful political change" and assume that the phrase describes the reality. Professor Roger Masters doubts that this has always been true in the past and, like
Mr. Stillman, Mr. McKissick and several other contributors to*
America Now, *suspects that it may be even less true in the future.*

"A GOVERNMENT of laws, not of men" ranks high
among the cherished principles of American democracy; most Americans assume that we have come close to achieving a society in which political conflict is channeled through
peaceful, legal means. At least until recently, we have believed
that the greatness of our nation was intimately connected with
our ability to resolve issues at the ballot box rather than the bar-
ricades. Indeed, it is precisely the depth of this conviction that
makes assassination or violence in the Negro ghettos so shocking;
the call for "law and order in the streets" seems to be a fulfillment of the genius of our institutions, not a way to repress a disadvantaged and rebellious racial minority.

The waves of looting, arson and death symbolized by Watts,

Detroit or Newark demand a reassessment. Has the American ideal of a government of laws actually meant the substitution of peaceful political and social competition for the use of force and coercion? Does our society rest on a consensus that makes extralegal and especially violent action a marginal exception? Or are American democratic institutions more closely related to bloodshed—and the threat of bloodshed—than we have dared to admit?

As every schoolboy knows, America's rise to political maturity was twice marked by the recourse to armed conflict. The American Revolution and the Civil War represent moments in history when the fundamental principles and orientation of our society could not be established by peaceful means. But these two wars can be viewed as exceptions that prove the rule: in each case, a fundamental principle of the American consensus was at stake. The colonists took up arms only when they felt their rights under the British constitution could be secured in no other way; the Civil War was rendered inevitable by the unbridgeable gap between the principles of equality enshrined in the Declaration of Independence and the reality of slavery in the South.

Since "a house divided against itself cannot stand," conflict on such basic issues was inevitable as a means of establishing a government of laws. Hence, it is usually argued, large-scale violence occurred in the American context only at the two points when the principles underlying our institutions were at stake; apart from these crises, political competition has been essentially peaceful and legal.

This judgment is revealing, for it suggests that—as Jefferson put it—the "tree of liberty must be refreshed from time to time with the blood of patriots. . . ." But most Americans rest comfortable in the assumption that such means are no longer necessary, at least within our society. Our regime, once independently established by the Revolution and firmly cemented by the forcible denial of a right to secede, seems to have rested on a popu-

37

American Government

lar acceptance of the Constitution and a willingness to work only within it.

This general belief has not been shaken by the striking fact that in the last century four Presidents (Lincoln, Garfield, Mc-Kinley, and Kennedy) have been assassinated in office, and others (Theodore Roosevelt, F.D.R., Truman), unsuccessfully attacked. For example, one recent historian, Marshall Smelser, in *American History at a Glance* (New York, Barnes and Noble, 1965, p. 251), describes the tragic end of John F. Kennedy's career as follows:

> All of this promise came to a bitter, senseless end when President Kennedy was shot to death by rifle fire on November 22, 1963, while riding through the streets of Dallas, Texas. . . . President Lyndon B. Johnson gravely and with assurance assumed the awful burden of the office. . . . The ancient Western notion of limited government which operates through known and just laws again showed its ageless vigor.

Without denying that the peaceful transition of power reflected the effectiveness of legal procedures, it might be argued that the assassination of four heads of state in less than a hundred years represents another tradition in American politics.

Although the political murders of Martin Luther King and Robert Kennedy have focused attention on violence, its role in our past has been curiously underestimated by both historians and public opinion. True, the attempted and successful Presidential assassinations were the acts of individuals—or at most of small groups (like the Puerto Rican nationalists who tried to kill President Truman in 1950). But they reflect a tradition of violence that has been more prevalent in our political life than has been popularly admitted. In the history book just cited, we read that in the late nineteenth century "Americans in the Western states objected to unrestricted Chinese immigration." Reality was far less bland. In California during the 1870's there was a real danger of anarchy as white workers agitated for an end to

Chinese immigration; taking matters into their own hands, mobs terrorized Chinese laborers (who were accused of unfairly lowering wages). It should be remarked that many American histories —such as the widely read *Pocket History of the United States* by Allan Nevins and Henry Steele Commager (New York, Washington Square Press, 1967)—pass over the entire affair in silence.

As soon as we look behind the civics-course façade of peaceful accommodation and progress, a surprising number of similar incidents come into sight. Going back to early colonial times, it becomes apparent that violence has had a persisting influence in our society, and that it may have been a necessary precondition for the kind of free government we take for granted.

The early settlers lived with their guns at hand not merely because hunting was good, but because defense against Indians was necessary. One must admit that the Indians were not always—or even essentially—the aggressors: from the seventeenth century to the nineteenth, our society's expansion could in part be seen as a lengthy process of expropriating their lands. Although Americans fought a long series of wars with various Indians tribes, from the Pequot War of 1637 (in which the tribe of that name was virtually annihilated) to the post-Civil War campaigns that opened up the last frontier, it is curious that the best-remembered engagement is Custer's Last Stand (1876). Why have Americans glorified this atypical example of an Indian victory, and forgotten the Seminole Wars, the bloody Black Hawk War and the brutal expedition of the "Missouri Legion" in 1823? Is it because we are now ashamed of our victories?

To gain access to Indian lands, violence was not always necessary; our practice was to acquire them by treaty or bribe when possible, by force when threat failed. Moreover, such a recourse to military action became habitual whenever our Manifest Destiny seemed thwarted by *any* unreasonable people on our frontiers. The War of 1812 (triggered by the demands of War-Hawk Congressmen from the West), the Mexican War of 1846–48 and the Spanish-American War of 1898 reflected a tradition of armed

39

self-help inherited from the early colonists. When the contested frontier between Canada and Alaska was referred to an arbitration commission in 1903, Teddy Roosevelt did not hesitate to threaten the use of force should the award go against the U.S. And not only T.R., but William Howard Taft and Woodrow Wilson as well, intervened repeatedly in the Caribbean, sending armed forces to Panama (1903), the Dominican Republic (1904 and 1916), Nicaragua (1912), Mexico (1914) and Haiti (1915).

The extralegal use of force to expand our territory has, to be sure, often been hotly debated. The New England states threatened to secede during the War of 1812, the Mexican War was opposed by many Northerners and the Treaty of Paris ending the Spanish-American War was ratified by a mere two votes (reflecting the distaste for the acquisition of "imperial" territories). After the Marines were illegally used to establish an American protectorate over Hawaii in 1891, President Cleveland refused to accept the *fait accompli* and annexation had to wait until 1898, when McKinley's scruples were overcome by the obvious economic and strategic advantages of American control.

Here again, popular histories often show an unmistakable prudery when referring to extralegal violence committed by Americans. For example, Nevins and Commager do not mention that American planters forcibly imposed a republican constitution on the islands in 1887, and that Queen Liliuokalani's attempt to revoke it was put down by military intervention; Cleveland's refusal to accept a protectorate over Hawaii is simply mentioned, with the explanation that "he rightly thought that the methods used were improper."

On the whole, Americans have never hesitated to use force, regardless of treaty commitments, whenever it seemed necessary to secure their interests. The behavior of the original colonists in revolting from the British Crown was, in this respect, imitated by American settlers in both Texas and California. Just as Hawaii was annexed after our settlers had used force to set up an independent republic, Texans rebelled against Mexico in 1835 and the Californians revolted in 1846 (with the aid of Captain Frémont of the United States Army). Curiously enough, we tend to forget this forcible establishment of independent republics by American settlers who could thereafter apply for annexation; popular mythology glorifies the Alamo (a defeat), not the formation of the Lone Star and Bear Skin republics. And who today talks about the abortive attempts of Southern soldiers of fortune to establish new slave states in Cuba or Nicaragua in the 1850's? Recent American intervention in the Dominican Republic and Vietnam corresponds to a custom, not merely to the will of an atypical administration.

External expansion and even aggression need not imply, of course, that extralegal violence is either condoned or typical within a society. But just as the use of force on the frontier was a reflex of the early settlers that became a national tradition, so certain forms of violence characterized the internal life of the colonies and have recurred since.

It would be a grave misreading of history to believe that because the Pilgrims signed the Mayflower Compact, they were ideal democrats in the modern sense. Since they attempted to establish a religious community subjected to a kind of Protestantism that was rejected by the Church of England, these early settlers punished local residents whose beliefs or conduct seemed sinful and irreligious. Such majority repression of minority views characterized the subsequent Puritan colony of Massachusetts (which expelled "subversives" like Roger Williams and Anne Hutchinson, required church membership as a condition of voting and hanged some nineteen supposed witches); in other colonies as well, those who rejected the prevailing consensus were often subject to varying forms of coercion.

To cite but one example from the 1630's, a Virginian named William Claiborne settled on Kent Island in Chesapeake Bay, within the territory granted to George Calvert (Lord Baltimore). Since the Calvert family sought to establish Maryland as a Catholic colony, Claiborne—a vigorous anti-Catholic—was forcibly evicted. Ultimately, both in Maryland and elsewhere, re-

41

ligious toleration became the rule in the colonies, but the term "witch hunt" did not thereby disappear from our political vocabulary.

When the Quakers of Pennsylvania refused to participate in the Revolution on the grounds of pacifism, they were ostracized —and some of their leaders illegally arrested. After independence, popular distrust and repression of minorities often caused violence as citizens took justice into their own hands. In the 1830's, Mormons led by Joseph Smith were forced to move from New York to Illinois; after they established the city of Nauvoo on the Mississippi River, antipathy led to rioting and eventually to the lynching of Smith and his brother.

This willingness of Americans to use force on a dissenting minority cannot be easily dismissed, for it has too often occurred— on both sides of a given issue. Abolitionists, themselves subjected to mob violence (like the murder of Elijah P. Lovejoy of Alton, Illinois, in 1837), did not hesitate to riot when the illegal operations of the Underground Railroad were interrupted by the seizure of runaway slaves. The vigilantes of the frontier, lynchings in the South and persecution of Oriental immigrants in California all conformed to this pattern of popular impatience with legal niceties when pressing "injustices" or "intolerable" practices seemed threatening.

Frequently, of course, a majority can exercise extralegal coercion without resorting to bloodshed; social ostracism and unequal enforcement of the law has been a more typical reaction to minorities than the lynching of eleven Italians suspected of Mafia activities (New Orleans, 1891). Non-lethal Ku Klux Klan activity in the Reconstruction era and the "Red Scare" of the early 1920's are good examples of communal passions which, since colonial days, have occasionally transcended legal procedures. Senator Joseph McCarthy was not the first American to whip up popular sentiment in support of charges that could not be proven in the courts, and crosses were burned to terrorize Negroes before they tried to move into the white suburbs of Chicago.

* * *

No society is entirely free from outbursts of majority coercion of the type just described. Perhaps more important in the American context is a tradition of violence and rioting by the discontented poor. Bacon's Rebellion (Virginia, 1676), Shays's Rebellion (Massachusetts, 1786) and the Whiskey Rebellion (Western Pennsylvania, 1794) are well-known examples of early frontiersmen who found existing conditions unbearable. Slave uprisings like Nat Turner's Rebellion (1831), or John Brown's raid on Harper's Ferry (1859), or marches on Washington by unemployed workers, like Coxey's Army (1894) and the Bonus Expeditionary Force (1931), were similar explosions of despair.

These scenes of violence were not carefully planned social revolutions, but rather spontaneous expressions of a sense of fundamental injustice. As Nevins and Commager remark concerning one of these quickly suppressed uprisings:

> Shays's Rebellion . . . was in the tradition of earlier agrarian uprisings—Bacon's Rebellion, for example, or the Regulator outbreaks in Western North Carolina on the eve of the Revolution; it was not so much a revolt against government as a violent protest against conditions that had become intolerable.

Like recent Negro rioting, earlier Americans who formed isolated and depressed minorities have reacted violently when the avenues of individual betterment, characteristic of our society as a whole, seemed unfairly closed to them.

Here at last one begins to see more clearly the unique function of violence in American society. Both explosions of minority discontent and nonlegal coercion by local majorities have had a common element: they have been *social, economic* or *religious* rather than political. Whereas the French revolutions of 1789, 1830, 1848 and 1870 were attempts to change the political organization of the society, violence in the United States has normally been addressed to preserving the way of life of a majority or improving the condition of a minority. Such uses of force are

43

political only in a secondary sense, for the participants have been animated by specific grievances within the existing Constitutional system, not by political principles that require the creation of a new regime.

While the repeated political revolutions in modern French history created social cleavages that have weakened democratic institutions, violence in American life has paradoxically strengthened our democracy. The reason is that the American willingness to ignore legal processes has reflected the individualistic assertiveness of our national character. It may be precisely because we have been *more* willing to use force than the subjects of most European societies, that discontent has usually been dissipated relatively quickly. Because conflict has tended to come to a head on a *local* scale, grievances have not had time to accumulate into national movements dedicated to the overthrow of the Constitution.

This aggressive spirit explains why American political rhetoric in the nineteenth century was so passionate. It also explains why private violence was so widespread in the settlement of the West (armed conflicts between cattle ranchers and rustlers, sheep-grazers or farmers), in the repeated and often murderous attempts to suppress labor unions (such as the Homestead Massacre of 1892, when three hundred private detectives of the Carnegie Steel Company fought a pitched battle with striking workers), and even in competition between rival businessmen (the 1882 "War of the Copper Kings" in Montana, the use of coercion to drive out competitors in the creation of monopolies like the Standard Oil Company and so on). Although big business was sometimes reinforced by governmental authority, as in the great railroad strikes of 1877 and 1894 (both put down with the aid of troops), labor agitation was frequently broken by more or less illegal means (notably in the strikes organized by the Knights of Labor in the 1880's, by the IWW or "Wobblies" after the turn of the century, and by the CIO in the 1930's).[1]

[1] In Europe, heads of state have rarely been assassinated by discontented indi-

Yet the willingness to use force if need be to secure one's "rights" has not destroyed American institutions, because there has been surprisingly little disagreement as to what these rights—in the broadest sense—were. All have tacitly agreed that the fundamental object of human government is to provide a framework in which citizens can gain material wealth and happiness. With agreement on the ends to be pursued, political conflict has focused on the proper means. Hence the Populists sought to change our monetary system, not our Constitution.

Because Americans have not usually endured injustice patiently, on the assumption that a paternal government will one day correct it, their recourse to violence has been directed toward the pursuit of specific individual or group demands, and *not* to the overthrow of our system of government.

Violence has therefore reflected the same self-reliance required for the operation of our democracy, reinforcing it instead of undermining it. As Rousseau put it: "A little agitation gives energy to the soul, and what makes the species truly prosper is not so much peace as freedom."

Without endorsing or condemning violence, it is important to *understand* it as part of our tradition. The contemporary assumption that American politics is essentially pacific and legal is quite misleading. We have indeed achieved a government of laws, but men have greatly contributed to its vitality by their resort to nonlegal methods. This conclusion poses two questions: First, why do we now tend to forget the role of violence in our past? Second, will the present upheaval in our cities paradoxically contribute to the resolution of Negro despair and strengthen our society (as similar events have done in the past)? The answers to these questions are closely related.

---

viduals; regicide has usually been connected with a fundamental political revolution (Charles I in England, Louis XVI in France, Czar Nicholas II in Russia). Only in America have discontented office-seekers, bitter partisans of a defeated cause, or psychotics made it a habit to attack the President in the delusion that, *without changing the Constitution*, they could thereby rectify injustice.

45

Many times in our history, the majority has repressed those who held "subversive" views; the desperate poor have on a number of occasions exploded with angry violence, only to have their uprising put down by force. Hitherto this was rarely critical in the United States: farmer discontent was undercut by the continual opening of new lands to the west, and worker discontent by the continual influx of new immigrants. And since the development of the West and the immigration of new unskilled labor made for almost unbroken economic development, the only unresolvable social conflict in our history was created by slavery.

Even the Civil War was beneficial for the victors, for it spurred the industrialization of the North and gave rise to the rapid economic growth of the late nineteenth century. The formula for American democracy can therefore be stated as follows: repress minority violence or fundamental dissent by peaceful means if possible and organized force if necessary, and then wait for prosperity to solve the social conflict painlessly. Since even discontented groups eventually profited from our growing wealth, they were sooner or later absorbed in the "melting pot" (which was always heated by violence or the threat of violence, and in any event has produced more of an "Irish stew" than the homogeneous, classless society we think we have).

Although the attempt to unionize American industries was still causing bloodshed on the eve of Pearl Harbor, the United States came of age during World War II. After the war, we had two decades of relatively constant economic growth, during which organized labor was finally accepted as legitimate and domestic violence was relatively rare. This interlude created the impression that our political system always resolves internal conflict by legal means; for the present generation of Americans, our national life is viewed as essentially peaceful.

This temporary decline in violence and coercion explains the current tendency to overlook the importance of such methods in our history. But it also raises a serious problem. The parallels between previous violence and the explosive discontent of the

46

Negro are striking; like former groups of disadvantaged poor, Negroes may learn that delicate mixture of aggressiveness and lawfulness characteristic of our democracy. But an ominous question remains: will the formula for channeling the use of force so that it strengthens our institutions work as well in the immediate future as in the past? It is not just the Negro who must learn how to combine self-assertion with restraint.

As a mature society, the violence that characterized our history has largely been sublimated into popular culture; now that the gun-play of the far West has ceased to be an actual practice, it has reappeared on movie and TV screens. Although modern suburbanites like to feel that they are law-abiding citizens, they enjoy watching Batman take the summary execution of justice into his own omnicompetent hands.

While our culture has continued—and perhaps even increased —its emphasis on vicarious aggression, violence and self-assertiveness, most of our citizens believe that such extralegal action is illegitimate. Nor should this be surprising considering the unprecedented affluence of the last twenty-five years. The ethnic working class of the New Deal era has been transformed into a property-owning lower middle class that seeks to protect its acquisitions. No longer tempted to change the *status quo*, the children of Irish, Italian or East European immigrants can proclaim their attachment to lawful political processes that often frustrated the ambitions of their parents or grandparents.

The danger in all this is that after a certain point, a majority newly accustomed to law and order will repress Negro discontent with even more brutality than past majorities vented on the farmer and worker. In this case, after all, class conflict is simultaneously racial conflict, and local minorities are simultaneously a national minority. If violence continues in our cities, the white community may become more extremist, the ghetto increasingly isolated and radicalized, and a continuation of violence more likely. And since this vicious circle is more difficult to break in the case of Negroes than for other ethnic or religious

47

minorities—if only because Negroes have been repressed by coercion and violence for some three centuries—the ends of the American regime may themselves be brought into question.

Extremist students, repelled by the war in Vietnam and frustrated by persisting domestic injustice, are attracted to direct action justified by a revolutionary ideology. Established Negro leaders are frequently outflanked by young radicals for whom violence is the only solution to racial inequality and poverty. Already the slogan of Black Power is beginning to be merged in the public mind with support for Castro, North Vietnam and communist principles.

White liberals are increasingly torn between their devotion to the cause of racial equality and their fears or disorder in the streets. Past violence was generally localized, and hence only once broke the Constitutional fabric. If the confrontation between the Negro minority and the white majority takes on the character of a national test of strength, there is little doubt that the majority will be victorious. But at what cost to its own ideal of a government of laws?

GEORGE GALLUP

The Failure of
Leadership

"People have improved; their leaders
. . . have not."

*If the problems that beset American democracy are finally to be
understood in terms of concepts and attitudes, their symptoms
may nevertheless be objective and amenable to mechanical solutions. One such problem is that of the relative wisdom of the
electorate and their representatives. Dr. George Gallup maintains that the Millsian prophecy has been sustained by history—
that the competence of the electorate has risen—but that the
competence of their governors has not kept pace. For this incongruity, he suggests, there may be some practical remedies.*

A T N O T I M E during recent decades has there been such
widespread disillusionment with government nor such
skepticism about the functioning of the democratic process. This
does not mean that people have lost faith in themselves or in
democracy. They have become disenchanted with the compromises men make to attain public office, and the compromises
they are ready to make to stay in office.

Americans are less pragmatic, more idealistic than they were a
generation ago. The wheeling and dealing practices of politicians
once regarded as the nature of the game today give offense to the
typical citizen. One reason is that the American public has meas-
urably improved through the years. It is more enlightened, more
compassionate. Despite the impression that might be gained

49

from riots, increasing crime and drug addiction, people throughout the nation are less prejudiced and have a deeper concern for the poor, a greater urge to help the underprivileged of other nations and a burning desire to find a way to prevent wars.

In short, people have improved; their leaders in government have not.

In the first years of the Republic it was assumed that men of ability would seek public office even if this entailed great sacrifice on their part. An amazing number of brilliant men did enter public service, considering the very small population from which they were drawn. Politics was then the province of the amateur and not the professional—as is still true of the mother country, England.

As America grew and prospered, those who in an earlier age might have devoted at least part of their lives to public service turned to more lucrative pursuits. Men of lesser ability took over the task of running the government. When Alexis de Tocqueville viewed the American scene he was struck by the lack of men of stature in public office. He observed: "On my arrival in the United States I was surprised to find so much distinguished talent among the subjects, and so little among the heads of government. It is a well-authenticated fact that at the present day the most able men in the United States are very rarely placed at the head of affairs; and it must be acknowledged that such has been the result in proportion as democracy has outstepped all its former limits. The race of American statesmen has evidently dwindled most remarkably in the course of the last fifty years."

It was the year 1831 when Tocqueville came to observe the workings of democracy in the United States. Some fifty years later, James Bryce arrived in America bent on the same purpose. He, too, was shocked by the low caliber of men whom he found in government office. In *The American Commonwealth* he reported: "The American statesman is apt to be timid in advocacy as well as infantile in suggestion."

I am certain that if an observer with the insight of Bryce or

Tocqueville were to visit the United States today, some eighty years after Bryce, he would discover that the situation has not changed. The quality of our elected leaders has not appreciably improved. The professional politician still rules the day. Since politics is his career he sees to it that he is well paid. In England, where politics has retained its amateur status, a member of Parliament receives only £1,700, or roughly $5,000 a year. He does not have a highly paid staff; in fact, he does not even have an office, a secretary or a telephone. He is limited to an expenditure of $450 of his own money for election campaigning, and he must account for every cent that is spent by his friends in helping to elect him. Government service is performed usually at a real sacrifice, but it is still an honored calling that attracts the finest of the university graduates.

The American congressman, by way of contrast, has a suite of offices and an annual salary seven times as great as his British counterpart's. He has a dozen or more members of a staff paid for out of government funds. He can, and often does, employ members of his own family. He enjoys under-the-table benefits that are hard to ferret out of government expenditures and that are zealously kept from public scrutiny.

Quite naturally, the congressman's first concern is to keep his job. And for this reason a large part of his time and energies is devoted to mending political fences and to serving as a kind of glorified errand boy for his constituents. Virtually all requests for help could be handled better by a central bureau set up by the government for this purpose. But the congressman is loath to give up errand-running for fear of losing some of the votes which he may gain by doing personal favors for his constituents.

The congressman knows that well-organized minorities and pressure groups can play an important role in his reelection. So he gives his attention to those who make the loudest noise. A powerful group, such as the gun lobby, can keep him so cowed that he is even afraid to pass legislation to keep machine guns out of the hands of children, criminals and the insane.

The assumption, widely held, that congressmen have to be sensitive to the will of the people, since they have to face elections at regular intervals, has not proved to be valid. Except in closely contested districts, or states, a congressman need pay little attention to majority opinion. He needs only to stand in well with the party machine. Typically the individuals who control the machine are far less interested in responding to the public's wishes than they are in their own political fortunes. From time to time, of course, even those congressmen who represent "safe" districts may be swept out of office when voters lose confidence in the President and his Administration. Only rarely is the congressman defeated because of a failure to follow majority opinion on major issues.

Observers of the political scene often equate congressional action with public opinion, under the mistaken notion that Congress does accurately reflect public opinion. Even as astute a student of public affairs as Walter Lippmann falls into this error. In *The Public Philosophy,* he wrote:

> Mass opinion has acquired mounting power in this country. It has shown itself to be a dangerous master of decisions when the stakes are life and death. The unhappy truth is that the prevailing public opinion has been destructively wrong at the critical junctures. They have compelled the governments, which usually know what would have been wiser, or was necessary, or was more expedient, to be too late with too little, or too long with too much, too pacifist in peace and too bellicose in war, too neutralist or appeasing in negotiation or too intransigent. When the world wars came the people . . . could not be aroused to the exertions and sacrifices of the struggle until they had been incited to passionate hatred, and had become intoxicated with unlimited hope.

Were it not for the public-opinion surveys that have encompassed every major issue and problem of the last three decades, this indictment of Lippmann's might go unchallenged. The truth, which can be documented with a mountain of facts, is that the public has behaved in an exemplary way. Lippmann's strictures should be directed not at the people, but at their legislative representatives.

To cite some evidence from the records of the Gallup Poll: in the mid-1930's the public was much more alert to the threat posed by Hitler than was Congress. Large majorities called for a big arms program with special emphasis on building a large air force. Congress did nothing until we were thrust into war in 1941. Voters wanted the embargo provisions on the Neutrality Act lifted some nine months before Congress acted. The public favored peacetime conscription before the possibility of such a measure was even discussed in Congress. When war came the people were in favor of making far greater sacrifices than they were called upon to make. And, when the war ended, it was Congress and not the public that demanded the boys he brought home in a hurry.

At about this same time, Dr. Robert Millikan, then president of the California Institute of Technology, made these observations in a public address:

> One may be discouraged about the administration, about the Supreme Court, about the racketeering of labor leadership, about political corruption, about many ominous tendencies in American life, but he cannot be discouraged about the way the common man seems to be understanding and correctly appraising, on the average, the American situation . . . If all of this does not show that the average American has more intelligence and more conscience than his political leaders, then I don't know straight thinking and straight social morals when I see them.

In many areas of public life, reform is desperately needed. The public approves of these reforms, but Congress is reluctant to vote for change, particularly in those areas that concern election to office. We still have no intelligent way of selecting candidates for office. We leave this to the machine, which means we leave it to the boss; and we leave it to anyone who wants to throw his hat in the ring, no matter what his competence. No one in his right mind would choose the president of a university in this manner, or the president of a business firm. Only in politics do we have no plan for inducing our outstanding citizens to stand for office, and if we did the problem of financing their campaigns might abort the whole effort.

The amount of money required to campaign for high political office has reached the proportions of a national scandal. Astronomical sums are needed by a candidate seeking the Presidency. Even to run for a seat in the House of Representatives requires a sum of money that only a very few can afford. It is generally conceded that to contest the seat of an incumbent in Congress at least $100,000 is necessary. Which means that unless something is done about this situation, only a rich man can afford to enter politics, or a poor man who is willing to do "favors" and "work for" those who put up the money. The public could stop this nonsense by putting a top limit on the total amount that can be spent—as is done in Britain.

The evil effects of large campaign expenditures are far-reaching. Since so much money is invested in attaining office, it is only to be expected that a congressman will try in every way to keep his job and safeguard his investment. One way is to get for his constituents all he can out of the national grab bag—everything from roads, public buildings and army installations to a multitude of other benefits, whether or not these are needed or deserved. Undoubtedly this wins votes and influences those constituents who are asking not what they can do for the country but what the country can do for them. In essence this practice is a kind of bribery that voters should learn to distinguish and to resent just as deeply as they would an offer in cash to buy their votes.

The view, widely accepted, that a congressman's chief function is to get as much loot out of the U.S. Treasury as he possibly can has contributed to the cynical attitude many hold toward the whole business of politics. And when a group of log-rolling congressmen jointly raid the Treasury for their mutual benefit, the cost can soar to fantastic amounts. A conservative estimate is that one tax dollar in every four is spent needlessly and almost solely for the purpose of reelecting congressmen to office.

One way to cure this evil, or at least to mitigate it, has been advanced by two presidents—Truman and Eisenhower. Both have suggested that the term of office of senators be limited to two six-year terms. President Eisenhower would also place a limit of twelve years on members of the House of Representatives. The present two-year terms would be extended to four years, and the limit would be set at three terms. Voters of the nation, I think, agree with these proposals, but Congress will always fight any such plan. "A priesthood never initiates its own reform."

Limiting the term of office of congressmen, in Eisenhower's words, would create a situation in which the member of Congress "would tend to think of his congressional career as an important and exciting interlude in his life, a period dedicated to the entire public rather than as a way of making a living or making a career of exercising continuous political power. Possibly each would spend less time in keeping his eyes on the next election and more on the good of the nation. A more rapid turnover of the membership in both Houses, with its constant infusion of new blood, would largely eliminate the career politician in Congress."

It can be argued that experience in Congress is of great value, just as it is in every other field. Experience in administration is undeniably important; the country needs highly trained, talented and experienced civil servants who make government service their career. But in policy-making positions, such as those filled by the congressmen, experience can often be as harmful as it is valuable. Eisenhower has this to say on the point: "Many argue for the value of long experience in Congress. Admittedly, experience may produce greater skill in political maneuvering in the legislative process but [such experience] does not produce better statesmen." This view agrees with that held by Thomas Jefferson, who believed that a system of rotation that brought new men into office was desirable because the newly elected were more responsible to the wishes of the people and freer of the corruption and indifference that comes from long-continued officeholding.

No person who believes in the democratic process could possibly justify the autocratic power that chairmen of the committees of Congress have arrogated to themselves. These chairmanships, it should be emphasized, are assigned on the basis of seniority and not ability. Seniority is gained usually by representing districts or states that are dominated by one party. It is in these constituencies where democratic principles are most likely to be ignored that the same man wins election after election. Solely by right of seniority, committee chairmen can stop legislation and thwart the will of the people for often trivial reasons.

American democracy, fortunately, is virile enough to move ahead despite the little men who guide its destiny. Eventually the will of the people does prevail in most areas. When the public is fully informed about the dangers of the present system and how it tends to defeat true leadership, then we can hope that it will insist that the system be changed. America will then reach a higher level of democracy, politics will command the high respect it deserves, and men of stature will be attracted to public office.

I I

American
Foreign Policy

ASSUMPTIONS

Democracy is the most desirable form of government for any nation capable of maintaining it.

Among the world's existing or aspiring democracies (called, for convenience, "the Free World") there exists a fundamental consensus as to ends and means. Thus relations within the Free World tend to be peaceful and reasonably harmonious.

America has both an interest in and an obligation to assist the development of viable democracy within the Free World. Conversely, America has a moral obligation to help defend the Free World from enemy attack, since a threat to any part of the Free World is a threat to all of it—a threat to liberty itself.

HENRY STEELE COMMAGER

Myths and Realities in American Foreign Policy

> "Only a people infatuated with their own moral virtue . . . could be surprised that they have forfeited the respect of much of mankind. . . ."

In recent times, public debate about American foreign policy has become widespread and sometimes superheated. Nearly everyone has been obliged at least to review the traditional assumptions that are presumed to define the role America plays in the world; and in the process, nearly everyone has experienced something of the difficulty involved in trying to reconcile the claims of national security, political idealism and unyielding morality. The well-known historian Henry Steele Commager is one who regards the evolution of our foreign policy as a nearly straight-line development from innocent origins to moral ambiguity. If there is such a thing as moral law, says Professor Commager, we have broken it; if not, we should stop invoking it.

TWO PERVASIVE and persistent assumptions have conditioned, if not dominated, much of American foreign policy from the beginning of national self-consciousness—a period which began even before 1787—conditioned especially the philosophy of American relations with and attitudes toward other peoples and countries. First is the assumption, or the myth, of American uniqueness—a myth which justified and encouraged the habit of isolation. Second is the assumption of the political, social and moral superiority of America—a myth which rationalized Mani-

59

fest Destiny, mission, imperialism and, in our own time, the imposition on the rest of the world of something that can be called, without stretching analogies too far, a *Pax Americana*.

These two assumptions had a common origin and have had a parallel history. For almost two hundred years they have continually interacted on each other, and their consequences, too, have been intertwined. Once we recognize the similarity, even the identity, of these assumptions, we can more easily reconcile what appears on the surface to be a conflict between isolationism and interventionism or—to put it historically—between the stance which the United States adopted through most of the nineteenth century and that which it assumes today. Isolation and superiority are rooted in a common attitude toward the Old World and in a common body of philosophical convictions about the character of the New World and the destiny of the American nation.

What is the origin of these myths and what is their rationale? What shapes do they assume, what directions do they pursue, what attitudes do they encourage, what prejudices do they foster? How are we to explain their origins, their character and their vitality through the vicissitudes of our own history and the history of the modern world?

The notions of uniqueness and of isolation—two sides of the same coin—were born out of geography; not just the simple geography of the Atlantic and the Pacific acting as all but impassable barriers—that was obvious enough—but the larger geographical circumstances of the discovery of the New World. We quickly become hardened to words and deaf to their meanings, and it takes some stretch of the imagination for us now to remember that for almost three centuries the New World was indeed *new*—new, strange and inexplicable. It was new in nature, new in history, new in its people; and no military conquest, no royal decrees, no papal bulls, no literary gestures, no scientific theories even could assimilate it to Europe.

Where, after all, had the New World been all this time? Why had God chosen to hide it from the eyes of Christian men; why had He peopled it with men who were scarcely human and who were certainly heathens? There were giants in the New World; there were pygmies; there were men with one leg, and men with their heads on their chests; there were men with one eye in the center of their foreheads, and men with scales or feathers, like beasts or birds; there were Amazons; there were hermaphrodites. Even more marvelous was the natural world—the world of gigantic serpents, of alligators, of sea monsters, of clouds of mosquitoes who darkened the skies—the world of tangled jungles and fetid swamps, of deserts that stretched into infinity, of mountains that towered fifty miles into the air and lakes as big as oceans.

Where had it been all this time, and why was it unveiled now, five thousand years after creation? Clearly it was reserved for some special destiny, though whether for weal or for woe only the future would reveal. What was unmistakably clear was that the New World was not just an extension of the Old; as it was different in nature and in man, so it had a different history and a different destiny.

It was in the English colonies that the notion of uniqueness and of special destiny caught hold and flourished, and this even though the differences in nature and in man that distinguished the two worlds were far less ostentatious in the English than in the Spanish colonies. But it was not nature that proved decisive; it was history. The Spaniards, the Portuguese and the French who came to the New World carried their state, their administration, their armies, their church and their land systems along with them, and transplanted them as nearly intact as could be managed. Threatened as they were by the immensity and the hostility of nature in their regions of America, they clung all the more ardently to what connected them with Spain and France. But the English colonies represented a genuine transfer of population. The settlers along the shores of the Chesapeake or of

61

Cape Cod were not the creatures of their home governments; they came pretty much on their own. Nor were they fearful of being overwhelmed by or absorbed by the native population. "We hope to plant a nation, where none before hath stood" wrote the author of *Newes from Virginia*, and that is what, eventually, they did. For it was not only the Indian of the New World who was different; in the end it was the European in the New World who was different, and that was far more important. As Stephen Vincent Benét's Dick Heron said:

> This is a world where a man starts clear
> Once he's paid the price of getting here.
> For though we be English, true and staunch,
> We'll judge no man by the size of his paunch. . . .
> For here is a knight, and a Newgate debtor,
> And which of the two will prove the better
> Can you read the riddle? I will not try.
> But we live under another sky,
> From the men who never have crossed the seas.
> I thought I came for a lump of gold,
> But I shall die like a squire of land
> With my sons about me, hardy and bold
> And something my own that I never planned. . . .[1]

British America was, in a sense, independent long before the Declaration of Independence, and would have been independent without it. She was independent because she was different, and the difference had already put its stamp on her character and isolated her from her mother country—which was not really England, but Europe.

It was, properly enough, not an English American, but a son of Normandy, Jean de Crèvecoeur, known appropriately enough as "the American Farmer," who saw this and explained it for posterity to read. He saw that the American was indeed a "new

[1] From *Western Star* by Stephen Vincent Benét (Holt, Rinehart and Winston, Inc.). Copyright 1943, by Rosemary Carr Benét. Reprinted by permission of Brandt & Brandt.

man"—the American from England and Scotland, from Holland and Baden and France, it made no difference—for *ubi panis ibi patria*. He was a new man in that he did not pull his forelock to his betters. He was new in that he owned land and could pass it on to his children. He was new in that children were not a curse, as elsewhere in the world, but a blessing, for he knew that there would be meat and drink for them, clothing and shelter and material well-being. He was new in that he could worship as he pleased and govern himself.

The American was not, to be sure, wholly a new man, for being an American was a complex business long before Henry James observed that it was a complex fate. The American spoke the English language, observed (or refused to observe) English law, lived under English forms of government; and England was the mother country even for those not of English extraction. But all that made the struggle for independence even more compelling, and its achievement more complex and comprehensive. It meant that political independence would never be enough.

For political independence was not enough. The Great Declaration said as much when it invoked the necessity of assuming "among the powers of the Earth, the separate and equal station to which the Laws of Nature and Nature's God" entitled them. The crucial word, for our purposes, is "separate." Americans had to prove, and have always been busy proving, that they are indeed separate. With Americans of the Revolutionary generation, independence was far more than political. It was religious, for it repudiated the religious establishment and substituted in its stead voluntary churches and the separation of church and state. It was economic, for it provided the largest and richest area on the globe for an experiment in agrarian democracy, and dedicated that vast area to free trade. It was social, for it did away with traditional class structures, abolished the familiar categories of aristocracy, bourgeoisie and peasantry (not, alas, of slavery) and inaugurated a far-reaching experiment in social equality. It was geopolitical—if that is the proper term—for it turned away from military solutions for colonialism, rejected entangling alliances and embraced geographical and political isolation. And it was moral, in that it repudiated the moral standards and malpractices of the Old World and set up a society which was to have new moral standards.

Nor was all this merely a matter of repudiation, for independence was not negative, but creative. It was creative politically. Americans were the first people in modern history to repudiate a "mother country" and "bring forth a new nation," and that gesture inaugurated the era of modern nationalism. Since the Americans established the precedent in 1776, some ninety colonial peoples have broken with their mother countries and set up on their own. It was creative politically, too, in that Americans "realized the theories of the wisest writers" (the phrase is John Adams') by institutionalizing what had heretofore been merely philosophical precepts. They answered the question of how men make government with the Constitutional Convention. They answered the question of how power can be limited with a written Constitution, separation of powers, checks and balances and judicial review. They answered the question of the relation of mother country to colonies by abolishing colonies and substituting in their stead territories and states, all the way from Ohio to California. It was creative in religion and philosophy in that it legalized religious equality and laid the foundations for universal education. It was creative socially in that it ended formal class distinctions among whites. It was creative economically in that it made possible widespread land ownership, raised standards of living and threw open jobs and professions to all men indiscriminately.

Certainly the deep sense of separation and uniqueness which independence inculcated was positive rather than negative. No conviction was more widespread, among the Founding Fathers, than this: that the Old World was corrupt and decadent and that the New World must, at all costs, avoid contamination from the Old.

64

"Blest in their distance from that bloody scene," wrote Philip Freneau of the relations of Old World and New, "Why spread the sail to pass the Guelphs between?"

Why indeed? Why risk infection in these

Sweet sylvan scenes of innocence and ease . . .
Where Paradise shall flourish, by no second Adam lost
No dangerous tree or deathful fruit shall grow
No tempting serpent to allure the soul
From native innocence. . . .

So, too, said Washington's favorite aide, David Humphreys, who likewise described the happiness of America in terms of isolation:

All former Empires rose, the work of guilt,
On conquest, blood or usurpation built.
But we, taught wisdom by their woes and crimes . . .
Fraught with their lore, and born to better times,
Our constitutions form'd on freedom's base.

Dr. Benjamin Rush, who had studied in Edinburgh and London and then settled happily in Philadelphia where he practiced medicine, founded schools, guided the destinies of the Commonwealth, wrote essays on all subjects and became a Founding Father, never ceased to preach the danger of contamination from abroad. "America," he said, "should be greatly happy by erecting a barrier against the corruptions in morals, government and religion which now pervade all the nations of Europe."

No one was more insistent on the necessity of separation of the New World from the Old than Thomas Jefferson. A true cosmopolitan, he delighted in the music, art, architecture, literature and society of the Old World, and he was never happier than when visiting the bookshops along the quays or sipping chocolate in the salons of Paris. But Jefferson never for a moment thought that the pleasures and advantages which the Old World offered to its upper classes were worth the price exacted of its lower—worth the price in poverty, misery, ignorance, su-

65

perstition, tyranny and war—and he knew that America had the best of it. To his old mentor George Wythe he wrote in 1786:

> If all the sovereigns of Europe were to set themselves to work to emancipate the minds of their subjects from their present ignorance and prejudices, and that as zealously as they now endeavor the contrary, a thousand years would not place them on that high ground on which our common people are now setting out. Ours could not have been so fairly put into the hands of their own common sense, had they not been separated from their parent stock, and been kept from contamination, either from them or the other people of the old world, by the intervention of so wide an ocean.

And seventeen years later Jefferson confided to his friend the Earl of Buchan, "I . . . bless the almighty being who, in gathering together the waters under the heavens in one place, divided the dry land of your hemisphere from the dry land of ours."

As Secretary of State, Jefferson had supported—though with some misgivings—Washington's Proclamation on Neutrality, the first of its kind in history. When he himself assumed the Presidency, his disillusionment with France was as deep as had been his earlier disillusionment with Britain, and it was his Inaugural Address that promised "honest friendship with all nations, entangling alliances with none." His embargo was a daring but desperate device to avoid war with Old World nations, a device whose potentialities were probed, but not exploited. The War of 1812 confirmed Jefferson in his passion for isolation, and in 1820 he assured his old friend William Short:

> The day is not distant when we may formally require a meridian of partition . . . which separates the two hemispheres. . . . and when, during the rage of eternal wars of Europe, the lion and the lamb within our regions shall lie down together in peace. . . . The princi-

ples of society there and here are radically different, and
I hope no American patriot will ever lose sight of the essential policy of interdicting in the seas and territories
of both Americas the ferocious and sanguinary contests
of Europe.

"Both Americas"! Here, quite clearly, is the principle which
was to emerge three years later (and with Jefferson's formal
blessing) as the Monroe Doctrine. What it meant then— and
since—is that Europe and America were two different "systems";
that they had different interests, characters, civilizations and destinies; and that they should leave each other alone. This is the
most deeply felt, if not the most faithfully observed, of American
articles of faith. Implicit in it are both the great myths which
have inspired American foreign attitudes and policies for a century and a half: the myth of uniqueness, which emerged as isolation; and the myth of superiority, which emerged as mission, and
eventually as imperialism.

Even before the Monroe Doctrine, isolationism took on continental dimensions, and for no one more fully or uncompromis-
ingly than the isolationist Jefferson. The Master of Monticello
had from the beginning looked westward across the Alleghenies
and all the way to the Pacific. He was the chief architect of those
land policies which were to open up the West to settlement by
farmers, and he strove—in vain—to banish slavery from all the
territory west of the mountains. As early as 1793 he had planned
to send out André Michaux on a quite illegal exploration to the
headwaters of the Missouri; that expedition did not materialize,
but ten years later the expedition of Lewis and Clark did. Meantime Jefferson had doubled the territory of the United States by
the purchase of Louisiana and had ousted the Spaniards from
West Florida—a process which his successors were to continue
until all the Floridas were part of the United States. James K.
Polk, who accentuated isolationism and added the first "corollary" to the Monroe Doctrine, was also the President who pre-

sided over the "reannexation" of Texas and the "reoccupation" of Oregon. Meantime the Russians had been persuaded to give up whatever claims they may have had south of Alaska, and there were threatening gestures toward the British in Canada.

Thus, within a quarter century, the Monroe Doctrine, whose original purpose was to proclaim isolation, had come to be identified with the principle of United States hegemony in the American continents. During the next eighty years that principle was to take on both larger implications and broader authority, assuming protean form in Pan-Americanism; Cleveland, Roosevelt and Lodge "corollaries"; and Wilsonian intervention. In our own day the principle has provided a rationale if not a justification for return to a unilateral application of the principles of the Monroe Doctrine and for the most miscellaneous kinds of intervention in the internal affairs of Latin American states. "Communism" has now taken the place, in the American imagination, of the "Holy Alliance." Just as President Monroe charged that "the political system of the allied powers is essentially different . . . from that of America" (and therefore irreconcilable with it), so his modern successors, Eisenhower, Kennedy and Johnson, have found "Communism" to be "essentially different" and therefore incompatible with the principles of the Great Doctrine. Just as earlier Presidents intervened in the affairs of Venezuela, Mexico, Nicaragua and the islands of the Caribbean, so their present-day successors intervene in Guatemala, Cuba, Santo Domingo and, through the Central Intelligence Agency, in many other South American nations.

The principle of isolation was by no means confined to the application of the Monroe Doctrine in these shifting shapes. It conditioned American policy toward the Old World during the entire century from the Treaty of Ghent to the First World War. At the outbreak of that war it counseled "neutrality"; and though the United States abandoned neutrality in 1917, once the war was won, neutrality and isolation revived and flourished, dictating the rejection of the League of Nations and the precipitous withdrawal of the United States from the affairs of Europe and Asia. Disillusionment with the First World War took overt form in the neutrality legislation of the thirties, and encouraged in many Americans a kind of xenophobia. Charles A. Beard was the intellectual spokesman for this policy. Like Jefferson he was sophisticated and cosmopolitan; and, like Jefferson, his isolation was rooted not in ignorance nor in vainglory, but in a conviction of the uniqueness of America and the corruption of Europe: if America allowed herself to be caught up in the ancient quarrels and wars which for centuries had made a shambles of the Old World, then she might lose her special character and her special virtue.

Isolationism, or the doctrine of American uniqueness, functioned not only in the political arena, but in the social and cultural too. Perhaps most remarkable in the social arena was the attitude toward immigration and emigration. The United States was the first major nation to throw its doors open indiscriminately to all comers; the first to challenge the traditional notion of the immutability of national allegiance and encourage the transfer of allegiance; the first to place naturalization and citizenship within the reach of all newcomers. For over a century it lived up to the promise so eloquently proclaimed by Emma Lazarus's poem on the Statue of Liberty. Americans were able to welcome, altogether, some forty million immigrants, because they were confident that these could be assimilated, because they knew that what Crèvecoeur had said back in 1780 was true:

> In this great asylum the poor of Europe have met together. . . . Urged by a variety of motives here they came. Everything has tended to regenerate them: new laws, a new mode of living, a new social system; here they are become men; in Europe they were as so many useless plants. . . . they withered and were mowed down by want, hunger and war. What then is the American, this new man? *He* is an American who, leaving

behind him all his ancient prejudices and manners, receives new ones from the new mode of life he has embraced, the new government he obeys, the new rank he
holds. He becomes an American by being received in
the broad lap of our great *Alma Mater.*

And Crèvecoeur added, prophetically:

Here individuals of all nations are melted into a new
race of men, whose labors and posterity will one day
cause great changes in the world. Americans are the
western pilgrims, who are carrying along with them that
great mass of arts, sciences, vigor and industry which
began long since in the east; they will finish the great
circle.

In short, the millions who fled to the New World did so because they wished to separate themselves from the Old. They
came here because they wished to be new men, and their identification with America was their regeneration. Migration did not
cease with the arrival of the European on the western shores of
the Atlantic. It continued all the way to the Pacific, for the West
was to America what America was to Europe—with the fundamental difference that while emigration from Europe constituted a repudiation of the Old World, migration into successive
wests constituted a vote of confidence in the New.

It was natural that, as Americans welcomed immigration, they
looked askance at emigration. That some newcomers were disappointed in the United States and returned to their old homes;
that others were ungrateful and went back with the money they
had earned, to buy land or a shop in their native lands—these
things were to be expected. But that native-born Americans
should migrate to other countries seemed like a betrayal. This
double standard for immigration and emigration applied with
equal force to naturalization. Immigrants who did not at once
give up their native citizenship and embrace American citizenship were denounced as "hyphenated" Americans—and to be

hyphenated was to be disloyal. But it was taken for granted that Americans who settled abroad—in the "colonies" in London, Paris, Florence—proudly retained their American citizenship to the end of their days.

Culturally as well as socially the American asserted that he was a "new man." No sooner had the Declaration separated America from Britain, than Americans threw themselves, almost convulsively, into the task of creating, or vindicating, an American culture. As Thomas Paine wrote, "A new era for politics is struck, a new method of thinking hath arisen." Now there was to be an *American* culture, an *American* language, *American* philosophy, *American* law, *American* art and letters. "America is an independent empire," wrote young Noah Webster, "and *ought* to assume a national character," and he urged his fellow-countrymen to "unshackle your minds and act like independent beings." Soon two pioneers of mathematics, Erastus Root and Nicholas Pike, were contriving an *American* mathematics; soon Jefferson had substituted the decimal system for pounds, shillings and pence; soon the Reverend Robert Davidson and the Reverend Jedidiah Morse were describing an *American* geography; soon one Amelia Simmons brought out an *American Cookery* "adapted to all grades of life." Meantime almost every man of letters turned resolutely to the creation of a literature which would be truly American. It took almost a century to achieve that, and it cannot be said that the other hopes or ambitions were ever truly fulfilled, but what was important was not the ultimate achievement but the philosophy and the passion that animated the attempt. America had to have a culture of her own because America was *different*.

It is abundantly clear that the myth of uniqueness carried with it, and all but required, the myth of superiority. For if the explanation of the uniqueness of America was to be found in geography and history, her character was to be explained, rather, in terms of philosophy and morals.

Doubtless the origins of the doctrine of American superiority can be traced to the Puritans, and to the commonwealth they established in Massachusetts Bay. That commonwealth was a New Jerusalem, it was Zion, it was a City set upon a Hill, and its people were the Chosen People, for "God sifted a whole nation, that he might send choice grain over into the Wilderness." It is a sentiment that echoed down the corridors of history. "What great things has the God of Providence done for our race," said the Reverend John Rodgers in 1784. "By the revolution we this day celebrate he has provided an asylum for the oppressed . . . and in due time the universal establishment of the Messiah's kingdom." And there is more than a hint of the sifted-grain theory in the motto of the California Society, that "the cowards never started, and the weak died on the way." Nor was it the Puritans alone who could claim to be a community of saints, but all who sought out a wilderness for righteousness' sake from Plymouth and Massachusetts Bay and the Providence Plantations to New Harmony and the Amana Colony and the new commonwealth of the Latter Day Saints in distant Deseret. But it was not merely the religious or the utopian communities that were Holy Communities. Was not all of America a Holy Commonwealth? So Americans could believe, and so many did.

As, over the years, the religious justification for separatism and saintliness evaporated, it was replaced by secular arguments grounded on fact and experience rather than on faith. *Amerika du hast es besser,* wrote the aged Goethe, and that was a visible fact that almost every white American could accept as the common sense of the matter. For it was obvious that America was better than Europe, her soil more fertile, her climate more favorable, her resources inexhaustible, her expanse limitless. Clearly, too, the government and society of the New World were more enlightened, more benevolent and more humane than anything the Old World had to offer—at least for those lucky enough to be white. Every schoolboy could recite the catalog of American virtue and good fortune: no kings, no aristocracy, no established church, no Inquisition, no faggot, no rack, no standing armies, no wars, no useless riches, no hopeless poverty, no dark ignorance, no flaunting vice. And these were merely the negative manifestations of good fortune—and good sense. Put it all positively, and the argument is even more impressive: instead of tyranny, self-government; instead of the Inquisition, religious freedom; instead of poverty, a general well-being; instead of classes, equality; instead of ignorance, universal education; instead of vast armies living on war, universal peace; instead of great cities with fetid slums, a boundless expanse of virgin land; instead of vice rioting in every street and flaunting itself in every salon, virtue and innocence. These were all articles of faith. There were other tests, no less persuasive. There was the test of progress—that was one everybody could understand. Americans gave to progress a new definition and a new meaning: improvement in the material welfare of the average man. There was the visible fact of population growth. Where, in the Old World, population barely held its own, in the New World it doubled every twenty-five years. That was true of the eighteenth century; if the nineteenth closed the gap between Old World and New in this matter of natural increase, it gave America a new advantage through large-scale emigration; and all through that century the young United States overtook Old World nations, one after another. Or there was the phenomenon of expansion more rapid than that of any other nation, expansion not merely through territorial conquest, but by occupation. No wonder Americans came to assume that it was their Manifest Destiny to occupy the whole of North America. There was even the test of economic wealth and industrial might that the ebullient Andrew Carnegie celebrated in his well-named *Triumphant Democracy:* "The old nations of the earth creep on at a snail's pace; the Republic thunders past with the rush of the express."

There was exaggeration in all this, to be sure, exaggeration and a willful ignoring of slavery and racial prejudices, and much else besides. And there was self-deception as well. But there was still enough reality to give some substance to a myth of superiority

73

which flourished for almost two centuries. What insured vitality to this myth was that by a natural, almost an inevitable, association, the superiority of the New World rubbed off on those who were fortunate enough to be part of it—not only the "huddled masses yearning to breathe free" who had deliberately chosen America, but the native-born as well. They took credit not only for the superiority of government and institutions, but for the superiority of nature, and complacently regarded the peace, prosperity and progress of the New World as somehow a tribute to their own wisdom and virtue.

The principle of the moral superiority of the American people found most eloquent expression in the doctrines of mission and Manifest Destiny. The notion of mission began, naturally enough, at the time of independence, and hints of it can be found in the most famous of all documents. It is "all men" who are created equal—not just Englishmen—and who are endowed by their Creator with "unalienable Rights." The Great Declaration appealed irresistibly to European *philosophes*, as did the constitutions and bills of rights of states like Virginia and Massachusetts. Soon Turgot was writing:

> This people is the hope of the human race. It may become the model. It ought to show the world by facts that man can be free and yet peaceful, and may dispense with the chains in which tyrants and knaves of every color have presumed to bind them. The American should be an example of political, religious, commercial, and industrial liberty.

The Americans rejoiced in the role which history had thus assigned them, and prepared to play it. They held out—somewhat tentatively to be sure—the hand of friendship to the revolutionary leaders of France. They encouraged, though they did not aid, revolution in Latin America, and were the first to recognize the independence of Spain's former colonies. Latin American revolutions owed less to the American than to the French Revolution,

74

and Latin American independence less to the Monroe Doctrine than to the policies of George Canning; but Americans liked to think that theirs was the flame and the inspiration.

The American mission was to spread the principles of democracy and of freedom throughout the globe; the method was not force, but example; and leaders of revolutions in South America, Greece, Hungary and Ireland who counted on more than sympathy were speedily put right. Not indeed until 1898 did the United States intervene actively in support of a revolution against a European "tyrant," and then (as in 1941) it was fortuity rather than principle that cast the decisive vote.

Manifest Destiny was another matter—the manifest destiny of the American nation to spread westward to the Pacific and—if the cost was not excessive—northward and southward as well. The story is familiar enough and need not be retold: the purchase of Louisiana; ousting the Spaniards from the Floridas; the annexation of Texas followed by war over a boundary dispute which ended with the annexation of over half a million square miles of Mexican Territory; maneuvering the Russians out of the Pacific Northwest, and then the British and then the purchase of Alaska; establishment of hegemony in the Caribbean and the acquisition (annexation is too rude a term) of the Panama Canal territory. Here is a story of expansion, conquest and aggrandizement without parallel in modern history; yet to this day most Americans are convinced that American expansion was peaceful, and that only Old World nations—and now China, of course— were guilty of aggrandizement, conquest and imperialism.

Manifest Destiny and mission converged in what has been called The Great Aberration, but what was really a logical product of both: the Spanish and the Philippine wars. Ever since Jefferson's day the United States had cast covetous eyes on Cuba, and fear that Britain might extend her sphere of influence over that island played some part in the formulation of the Monroe Doctrine. Thirty years later the Ostend Manifesto asserted boldly that "from the peculiarity of its geographical position . . .

75

Cuba is as necessary to the North American republic as any of its present members, and belongs naturally to that great family of States." The Grant administration witnessed abortive attempts to annex both Cuba and Santo Domingo. In the nineties the spectacle of Cubans struggling heroically against their Spanish rulers touched the sympathies of Americans and added humanitarian to political and strategic considerations to dictate intervention. In a lightning war, they ousted the Spaniards from Cuba and assured that island independence—of a sort; in the process they picked up Puerto Rico in the Caribbean, and the Philippine Islands off the coast of China, while a willing Hawaii fell into their convenient lap. Annexation of the Philippines was not permanent, but historically it was the most significant product of the Spanish War.

Myth and realism had united to bring about annexation of the islands. No one (unless Theodore Roosevelt or Admiral Mahan) had thought that the Philippine Islands were a logical part of an American empire, chiefly because no one had thought much about an American empire. But when, on that May morning of 1898, the islands fell to Admiral Dewey, and when the Filipinos under the patriotic Aguinaldo joined with the Americans to overthrow Spanish misrule and win their own independence, President McKinley and the American people were confronted with a wholly new problem. It is probable that President McKinley decided on annexation before he hit on its logic or justification; but when he did formulate this, it so happily combined mission and Manifest Destiny as to satisfy all but the most intransigent. "We could not turn the islands over to France or Germany, our commercial rivals—that would be bad business and discreditable. We could not give them back to Spain—that would be cowardly and dishonorable. We could not leave them to themselves—they were unfit for self-government. . . . There was nothing left for us to do but to take them all, and to educate the Filipinos, uplift them and Christianize them." Business, strategy and mission, with education and religion thrown in as a bonus—here they are, all jumbled together; and they have been jumbled together ever since.

There was an added complication when it was discovered that the Filipinos did not really want to be an item in American Manifest Destiny, and fought for three years for their independence. "Beneath the starry flag, civilize them with a Krag," American soldiers sang as they proceeded, with their new Krag rifles, to give the Filipinos a foretaste of what the Vietnamese would get sixty years later when they, too, proved impervious to the claims of American benevolence.

The curious interplay of uniqueness and superiority emerged a decade or so later with the outbreak of the Great War in Europe. President Wilson met the challenge of that war with a proclamation calling upon the American people to support isolation. He permitted his party to campaign for his reelection on the program that "he kept us out of war"; he called for "peace without victory"; and he announced, on the eve of our entrance into the war, that there was such a thing as being too proud to fight. From 1914 to 1917 isolation was cherished and observed, because it was based, ultimately, on moral considerations. But when the nature of the war changed, a new set of considerations came into play—considerations not alone of strategic security, but of moral security. Now moral arguments rationalized what strategic arguments necessitated and gave to the enterprise of war an exalted moral character. "It is a fearful thing," said President Wilson, "to lead this peaceful people into war. . . . But the right is more precious than peace, and we shall fight . . . to make the world itself at last free." It was Germany's unrestricted U-boat warfare that was the legal *casus belli*; but the war was not merely to restore international law. Rather, it was "to secure the rights of nations, great and small, and the privilege of men everywhere to choose their way of life and of obedience," for "the world must be made safe for democracy."

Thus, to preserve isolation, Wilson led his nation into a crusade which took on global dimensions. The crusade was successful enough in the defeat of the Central Powers; but it was not successful in its moral aims, and its failure to achieve these led, ineluctably, to the revival of isolationism. That the isolationism of the twenties and the thirties had strong moral overtones is notorious. Animated by the noblest of motives, fired by the most ardent zeal, Americans had launched a crusade to make the world safe for democracy. They had won the war; but, confronted by the wily diplomats of the Old World, by secret treaties, by selfishness, ambition and greed, they lost the peace. How familiar it all was: American innocence confronted by European depravity! In righteous indignation Americans rejected the treaty which their President had negotiated, because it was a treaty flawed by greed and vindictiveness. They rejected the League of Nations too, because it threatened both their isolation and their Monroe Doctrine and because it threatened to involve them, willy-nilly, in the future quarrels of the wicked Old World. So once again Americans retired into isolation. They had been, for a time, too proud to fight; now they were too proud to be associated with nations whose standards of honor were less exalted than their own.

Isolation and the consciousness of moral superiority persisted all through the thirties, even in the face of totalitarian aggression in Europe and Asia; and they account for the tardiness of American participation. The overwhelming majority of Americans were deeply shocked by the wickedness of the Nazi and Fascist regimes, but the majority of them denied responsibility and feared involvement. "We told you so," they seemed to say to the quondam internationalists. "This is what you must expect from the corrupt and decadent peoples of the Old World. Let us have no part of it. Let us be an island of civilization in an ocean of anarchy, so that when the holocaust is over, there will survive on this continent one nation that has not been physically or morally exhausted, and that will be able to restore civilization in a stricken globe." And notwithstanding that President Roosevelt moved steadily toward a working, and even fighting, arrangement with the Allied powers, neutrality remained the official and the popular American position until Pearl Harbor settled the issue once and for all.

These myths of innocence and of superiority were, almost from the beginning, battered by reality. For the United States was never really isolated—not geographically, politically, socially, or economically, and certainly not culturally. No sooner had the Treaty of Paris been signed, in 1783, than the new United States had to vindicate her territorial integrity from Spain and from Britain. She was caught up in the French Revolution, and when political parties emerged, it was to take sides on that conflict. She was threatened by Napoleon in the Caribbean and in Louisiana. She was assailed on the high seas by both the great contending powers, and in 1812 she had to fight once again to vindicate independence. The War of 1812 cleared the air politically, and thereafter for almost a century the United States enjoyed immunity from more overt involvement in European wars. But there was still the problem of clearing the continent of foreign rivals— the Spaniards, the British and the Russians—and not until 1867 could it be said that the United States had all the territory she had any right to expect! Economic involvement, too, was continuous, for the United States depended on Europe for markets and for credit. Socially the connection was massive, for every immigrant brought with him part of his own culture—his language, his religion, the habits he had acquired, the skills he had learned and the resentments he nursed. This applied with special force to Negroes from Africa or the West Indies, and their descendants have to this day retained some of their Old World culture. Needless to say, the cultural involvement of the United States with Europe was complete, for culturally the United States was, until just the other day, a parasite nation. Every time an American speaks his "native" language, every time he worships in a Christian church or a Jewish Temple, every time he makes a legal contract or draws a will or serves on a jury, every time he builds a

Gothic cathedral or a Roman post office or a Georgian house, every time he makes a mathematical calculation or studies flora and fauna, every time he hangs a reproduction of an Old Master or listens to chamber music or reads the *Christmas Carol* to his children, he is acknowledging the persistence and power of his cultural involvement with the Old World.

Isolation is, and has always been, a myth. So is American innocence and moral superiority. It has always been difficult to take seriously the American claim to innocence, for as long as slavery persisted the doctrine of moral superiority could not stand up to serious examination. Yet during much of the early history of the Republic, Americans were in fact not so much innocent as free from the temptations that assailed less fortunate peoples. They were immune from religious wars and from the worst excesses of militarism; they did abate the acrimony of class conflict; they were able to provide material well-being for unprecedentedly large numbers of their people.

But gradually the Old World sloughed off many of its vices and inhumanities and overcame many of its handicaps, while the New World acquired some of all of these for itself. If the relative positions of the two societies were not wholly reversed, they were, after a fashion, brought into equilibrium. Old World monarchs were no longer absolute, and in time most European governments could claim to be at least as democratic as the American. The Inquisition disappeared and so, too, religious intolerance; and if anti-Semitism lingered on in parts of Europe, racism lingered on in all of America. The lines between the classes were blurred, and heavy taxation closed the gap between the rich and the poor; but Americans developed their own version of class consciousness and dug a gulf between rich and poor as deep as any in Europe. In the more ostentatious tests of morality there was, on the whole, little to choose between Old World and New. Certainly the American lost whatever innocence he might once have displayed, and by the time Henry James got to *The Ambassadors* (1903), he stood on its head the theme of New World

virtue and Old World corruption which he had announced in
The American (1877) and *Daisy Miller* (1878).

It takes a long time for changes of this nature to reveal themselves and for an awareness of them to percolate down to the
mind of the average American—changes in America of which he
was only dimly aware, changes in Europe of which he was quite
unaware. Millions who had been born to the older myths were
not prepared to abandon or to reconsider them; other millions
who had embraced the myth as part of the process of Americanization persisted in the conviction that they had made the right
choice, and handed on that conviction to their children. So the
myth of New World superiority survived and flourished long
after it had served whatever purpose it may have had.

It required the agitation, the turmoil, the violence and disillusionment of the 1950's and 1960's to dramatize the anachronistic
quality of these myths, In these decades blow after blow rained
down upon the American consciousness, dissolved American superiority, dissipated confidence and shattered complacency. In
the sixties—it can almost be dated from the assassination of
President Kennedy—Americans awoke with a sense of shock and
incredulity to the discovery that the American Dream was largely
an illusion. Twenty million Negroes were second-class citizens—
or worse. Thirty million poor made a mockery of the proud
claims of an affluent society. For 200 years Americans had laid
waste the exceeding bounty of nature, cut down the forests, destroyed the soil, polluted the rivers and the lakes, killed off much
of the wildlife and gravely upset the balance of nature; and now
at last an outraged nature was revolting. Cities everywhere were
rotting away; crime flourished not only on the streets but in high
places; the supposed demands of security had qualified the institutions of democracy and of constitutionalism, and permanently
shifted the balance in the relationship of the military to the civilian power. The nation which had invented revolution had become the most powerful bulwark against revolution; the nation
which had fought colonialism and imperialism had become, in

81

the eyes of much of the world, the greatest champion of both; the nation which Jefferson had dedicated to peace had become the most militaristic of great powers and was waging a pitiless war of aggression on a distant continent.

Yet notwithstanding reality, the myths of isolation and of superiority persist; they still condition, if they do not dominate, much of our foreign policy.

We are no longer isolated, but connected with more nations and organizations than any other power. We boast military establishments in some sixty nations, and a CIA operating in at least that number. We are an American power whose word, we like to think, is fiat in this hemisphere. We are a European power, and NATO is not the sole instrument of and the monument to the principle that we are legitimately in Europe. And now we assert that we are an Asian power.

Clearly all this is the very opposite of, and negation of, isolation; but it is, just as clearly, a re-emergence of the ancient notion of the uniqueness of America. For now once again, as in the eighteenth century, we are prepared to go it alone. There are other powers, to be sure—Britain and France, for example—but they do not really count, and when the going is tough we do not bother to consult them. We did not consult them at the time of the Cuban crisis, which might have plunged them into an atomic war; we did not consult them at the time of our intervention in Vietnam, which came in defiance of the Geneva agreements. In New York City there is, to be sure, a United Nations which we were largely responsible for setting up, but we do not take it very seriously or permit it to function in matters we consider vital to ourselves. No, we are the one true world power; we are the spokesman for the Free World; we are prepared to respond—so says our Congress—wherever freedom is threatened by Communism or subversion. And that is what we have done, though not, it must be confessed, very consistently or with a very careful definition of what constitutes a threat to freedom: witness the

Truman Doctrine, the Eisenhower Doctrine, the Lebanon venture, the domination of Western Germany, unilateral intervention in Latin America and unilateral intervention in Asia (for SEATO, which is designed to provide a cloak of respectability to our venture in Vietnam, is of course our creature).

And paradoxically, American power acts as American weakness once acted: to exempt us from the ordinary relationships and responsibilities that burden other nations, to encourage us to set standards to which we expect all other nations to conform.

Thus as we have become the greatest of world powers, we have achieved a new isolation that is positive rather than negative: a moral isolation. In the first century of our history we isolated ourselves because we would not accept the moral standards of the nations of the Old World. Now we isolate ourselves because we have formulated and unilaterally apply political, military and moral standards that the nations of the Old World would not accept. Not our lack of power, but our abuse of power, has isolated us.

The second great myth—moral superiority which sets us apart from the power-hungry nations of the Old World, with their armies, their conquests and their empires, and their disregard for the sanctity of law and of treaties—is now relied upon to justify an almost limitless exercise of power by the United States. In the past this consciousness of superiority enabled us to indulge in conduct which in other nations was odious, because our purposes were benevolent and our hearts were pure. Today it underlies and rationalizes an excercise of power in every quarter of the globe that is quite unprecedented in history. Because now, as in the past, we are confident that we represent freedom, law, order, justice and the wave of the future, we feel justified in policies of intervention, subversion and aggression which we have always judged to be reprehensible in others. We acknowledge the United Nations but assert, nevertheless, that on us alone rests ultimate responsibility for keeping the peace and for preventing aggression. We recognize the binding character of treaties, and even multiply them, but we do not in fact feel bound by them if they get in the way of saving the "free world." We are unqualifiedly dedicated to the search for peace but carry on that search with the heaviest military arsenal that any nation ever possessed —or used. In the name of defeating "aggression" and achieving "peace," we pour onto one small country a heavier tonnage of bombs than we dropped on either Germany or Japan during the whole of the last war. We plead for the peaceful use of the atomic weapon and tremble with indignation when China detonates her own atomic bombs, but we do not choose to remember that we are, so far, the only nation that ever used atomic weapons in war; nor do we seem to find it odd that our own military and political leaders threaten to use atomic weapons again if they think the situation requires it.

It is this deeply ingrained notion of the moral superiority of the United States, and the superiority, too, of her institutions and her way of life, that enables us, with straight face and even with straight conscience, to maintain a double standard of morality in international relations. Thus communism is by very definition aggressive, but not capitalism: intervention in Hungary proved that, and intervention in Santo Domingo proved nothing. China is not "peace-loving" and cannot therefore be admitted to the United Nations; but we—even though we ring both the Soviet Union and China with air bases, armies and navies—are by definition "peace-loving." When Communist countries carry on clandestine activities abroad, their conduct is subversive, and indeed they are engaged in an "international conspiracy"; but when our CIA engages in clandestine activities in sixty countries, it is a legitimate branch of foreign policy. North Vietnam, when it had less than a thousand soldiers in the South, was "an aggressor nation"; but half a million American soldiers in Vietnam, the largest fleet in the world off Vietnamese waters and daily bombings of the North did not make us an aggressor nation. The Soviet Union has puppet states, and we look upon them with justified contempt; but our own puppet states—South Korea,

Taiwan, Vietnam, Thailand, even, in a sense, the Philippines
—are merely showing how enlightened they are when they cooperate with us. We do not permit a sovereign Cuba to invite
the Soviet to establish military installations on its island; but we
think it entirely proper that an independent Thailand should
invite us to establish what is the world's largest airfield in their
territory, and see no reason why China should take this amiss.
If Russian or Chinese planes should fly over American soil we
would regard that as an intolerable violation of international law;
but we make daily flights over China without troubling ourselves
about the law. When, in an undeclared and illegal intervention
in Guatemala some twelve or thirteen years ago, we established
an illegal blockade and bombed a British freighter which failed
to recognize that blockade, no one supposed that Britain would
retaliate by bombing New England; when, in a war in which we
were not as yet involved, the North Vietnamese fired at—but did
not hit—one of our cruisers escorting enemy gunboats, we made
that a *casus belli* and retaliated with years of ceaseless bombard-
ment. When, in the last war, Germans destroyed villages because
they had harbored snipers, we were justly outraged; but any Vietnamese who so much as fires a gun at one of our planes invites
the instant destruction of his village by our outraged airmen. We
looked with horror on the concentration camps of the last war;
but we set up "refugee" camps in Vietnam which are, for all
practical purposes, concentration camps. And we have driven as
large a proportion of the Vietnamese people from their homes,
destroyed as much of their forests, their crops, their dams, their
villages, as did the Germans in the Low Countries or in France in
the last war.

We have long known that "power corrupts"; but we do not
think that power corrupts us or can ever corrupt us, because we
always wield it for the benefit of Mankind.

Only a people infatuated with their own moral virtue, their
own superiority, their own exemption from the ordinary laws of
history and of morality, could so uncritically embrace a double

85

standard of morality as have the American people. Only a people whose traditions of isolation have made them immune to world opinion could be surprised that they have forfeited the respect of much of mankind by their misuse of power throughout the globe.[2]

---

[2] This was written in the dark days before President Johnson announced his decision to limit bombing of North Vietnam and before the beginning of the peace talks in Paris. It was written even before the "McCarthy miracle" had begun to take form. There is, after all, a reserve power in the American character which enables our people to reassert, in moments of moral peril, the simpler, sterner virtues of an earlier time. Yet our myths of uniqueness and superiority have carried us a long way and done us much harm. Whether we shall now be able to rise above them still remains to be seen.

FRANK N. TRAGER

The Objectives of
American Foreign Policy

> ". . . I believe *intelligence* and *fact*
> are still on the side of the U.S. pol-
> icy. . . ."

*Diametrically opposed to the views of Professor Commager are
those of another distinguished scholar, Frank N. Trager. Both
men agree that American foreign policy has been reasonably consistent since the end of World War II, but that is perhaps the
only interpretation on which they do agree. Professor Trager
holds that, in general, our policy has been true to its professed
assumptions and that these assumptions are sound. Thus he sees
our policy not merely successful, but honorable as well.*

T HE STATEMENT of assumptions about American foreign policy which heads this section of the symposium
is, I believe, a reasonably fair, general expression of American
opinion. Yet, like all such, it requires close scrutiny.

That democracy is the most desirable form of government for
any nation capable of maintaining it is certainly an assumption
that most Americans today would accept. In an earlier time, for
example in the period dominated by President Wilson's second
term or in the anticolonial optimistic first flush of independent
states arriving on the scene at the end of World War II, uncriti-
cal American emphasis more frequently was placed on the desirability of democracy and less on the capability of maintaining it.
But the "Cold War," with all of its implications, changed this

87

emphasis. Beginning at least with Stalin's postwar rejection of President Truman's offer to continue the entente of the World War II allies, Americans began to understand the need for coupling desirability with capability.

Americans respond in varying tempers to the conduct of a De Gaulle—that "French ingrate"—or to other regimes in the Free World. However, I believe that most Americans do feel that there exists a community of interests among the world's existing or aspiring democracies and that therefore their relations tend to be peaceful and reasonably harmonious. Critical Americans recognize and acknowledge the evils and imperfections in the Free World, but they also recognize that peace and reasonable harmony are possible because within its orbit fruitful debate between, and recurring changes in, governments tend to substitute for aggression, that is, the use of force to impose policy.

I believe that Americans who think about foreign policy would assume that we have an interest and an obligation to assist the development of viable democracy throughout the world and to defend it from attack. But I think, in fairness, it should be added that many Americans are now sophisticated enough not to insist that democracy be defined solely in terms of the institutions of the United States of America and to accept those participatory or representative institutions of other societies whose indigenous and acquired cultures produce their own variants of human freedom. Freedom in a polity, after all, essentially means that the community has both the right and the means to alter its government—and even its system of government—while being assured of the continuing right and means for further change.

To sum up at this point, I think this a fair statement of the assumptions presently entertained by a majority of Americans. I think, moreover, that these assumptions, with careful qualifications, have actually provided the basis for American foreign policy since 1945, and that this policy has, in turn, been a generally faithful reflection of the assumptions. For my own part, I happen to feel that these assumptions, as modified, are correct and that they may serve as supportive foreign policy guidelines now and at least for the short-run future.

An appraisal of any foreign policy should take into consideration at least two of its main characteristics: (1) long-range, relatively constant objectives or goals toward which policy is aimed —for example, peace and the security of the state—and (2) shorter-range interests, such as peace-keeping arrangements and appropriate defense measures, which responsive policies should serve. Since time and circumstance condition both long-range goals and shorter-term interests, successful correlation between the two, however desirable and desired, may not always be achieved. Hence, the formulation and execution of American foreign policy will inevitably reflect any predicted or actual discrepancy between goals and interests. Thus, continuing debates about policy are to be expected. Peace is one of the major policy goals, but since World War II there have been some forty wars or armed conflicts in different parts of the globe. We have been involved in six of them (Cuba, the Dominican Republic, Lebanon, Korea, Quemoy-Matsu and Vietnam).[1] No one can deny that since the end of World War II there has not been a single year of peace in the world. Nor can anyone deny that the armed pursuit of power by Communist organizations (states, parties, movements) has been and continues to be a central—I would say, the prime—cause in the majority of crises in which armed conflict has occurred. This is not to exculpate non-Communist states, parties and movements from having resorted to arms to settle disputes.

We were the prime mover in bringing the United Nations into being in the hope of settling disputes among member states by pacific means. But the decline of such hopes in the late 1940's has brought into being an array of alliances—including an informal alliance of certain nonaligned states—to replace the waning effectiveness of the UN system.

[1] *Time* (September 24, 1965), p. 31, published such a list. Whether or not *Time's* list or its analysis is accepted by historians or other analysts is irrelevant to my argument.

In the remainder of this essay I shall treat American foreign policy entirely in the context of its post-World War II development. To do this in a brief space I shall present statements of the four postwar Presidents selected to illustrate our foreign policy objectives. This will be followed by an analysis of what these statements imply and a critical conclusion applicable, I trust, to the present situation and to the short-range future.

On October 27, 1945, President Truman (speaking on Navy Day from a battleship) summed up what he called the "fundamental principles of righteousness and justice [on which] United States foreign policy is based":

1. We seek no territorial expansion or selfish advantage large or small. We have no objective which need clash with the peaceful aims of any other nation.

2. We believe in the eventual return of sovereign rights and self-government to all peoples who have been deprived of them by force.

3. We shall approve no territorial changes in any friendly part of the world unless they accord with the freely expressed wishes of the people concerned.

4. We believe that all peoples who are prepared for self-government should be permitted to choose their own form of government by their own freely expressed choice, without interference from any foreign source. That is true in Europe, in Asia, in Africa, as well as in the Western Hemisphere.

5. By the combined and cooperative action of our war Allies, we shall help the enemy states establish peaceful, democratic governments of their own free choice. And we shall try to attain a world in which Nazism, Fascism, and military aggression cannot exist.

6. We shall refuse to recognize any government imposed upon any nation by the force of any foreign

power. In some cases it may be impossible to prevent forceful imposition of such a government. But the United States will not recognize any such government.

7. We believe that all nations should have the freedom of the seas and equal rights to the navigation of boundary rivers and waterways and of rivers and waterways which pass through more than one country.

8. We believe that all states which are accepted in the society of nations should have access on equal terms to the trade and the raw materials of the world.

9. We believe that the sovereign states of the Western Hemisphere must work together as good neighbors in the solution of their common problems.

10. We believe that full economic collaboration between all nations, great and small, is essential to the improvement of living conditions all over the world, and to the establishment of freedom from fear and freedom from want.

11. We shall continue to strive to promote freedom of expression and freedom of religion throughout the peace-loving areas of the world.

12. We are convinced that the preservation of peace between nations requires a United Nations Organization composed of all the peace-loving nations of the world who are willing jointly to use force if necessary to insure peace.[2]

Obviously, the USSR was included among "our war Allies," and Communism, either as an ideology or as a practical power issue, was omitted from the totalitarian afflictions that helped to bring on World War II. This prospect—maintaining the wartime alliance for postwar peace-making and peace-keeping—was shattered by the events of 1946–47. Here—and I put it dogmatically for reasons of space—the choice was made by Stalin based

[2] "Restatement of Foreign Policy of the United States," Department of State *Bulletin*, XIII (October 28, 1945), pp. 653–656.

on his views of how to advance Communism in Eastern Europe and Asia.[3] Subsequent to President Truman's decision to come to the aid of Greece and Turkey (March–May 1947) in the fight against Communist aggression and rebellion, one major effort was made to restore the wartime alliance. This occurred when Secretary of State Marshall proposed the plan for United States aid to European recovery (June 1947) and, specifically, left the door open for Soviet and East European Communist participation. In July 1947 Moscow slammed the door shut for the Soviet Union and the satellites.

Certainly, at least from this time forward, the Soviet Union and the other European Communist states clearly became the main adversary of American foreign policy. As the several Asian Communist parties won control in North Korea, North Vietnam, and Mainland China, they joined the ranks of what came to be called the Sino-Soviet Bloc. The "Cold War," euphemism for actual "limited" warfare and wars of "national liberation," was on. It caused President Truman to amend his principles in terms of a general policy of "containment" aimed at keeping the peace by preventing any further Communist encroachment in non-Communist states. The Cold War was considerably warmed up in a variety of crises involving the United States: for example, Quemoy-Matsu, Cuba, Laos. Korea and Vietnam became "hot" wars, and both continue at different levels of intensity today. In short, despite the sharp cleavage in Sino-Soviet Party relations, I

[3] See this author's "The Far East," in *National Security: Political, Military and Economic Strategies in the Decade Ahead*, ed. David M. Abshire and Richard V. Allen (New York, Frederick A. Praeger, 1963), pp. 327–363, 432–436; and "American Foreign Policy in Southeast Asia," in *Studies on Asia, 1965*, ed. Robert K. Sakai (Lincoln, University of Nebraska Press, 1965), pp. 17–59. A very small group of scholars have set out to prove that the U.S. was at fault or more at fault than the USSR in bringing on the Cold War. On this point see Arthur Schlesinger, Jr., "Origins of the Cold War," *Foreign Affairs* (October 1967), pp. 22–52. Though Professor Schlesinger and I part company on a number of contemporary issues (for example, our views on Russia today, and on American involvement in Vietnam), his rebuttal of the "revisionists" should be read. His research reaffirms the Russian origins of the Cold War based on such factors as "the intransigence of Leninist ideology, the sinister dynamics of a totalitarian society and the madness of Stalin." I would not use the word "sinister"—it is in this context redundant—nor do I know that Stalin was "mad" in 1945–46. But the three factors without adjectival benefits are eminently sound.

reject the assumption, made by some, that since the death of Stalin the Soviet Union has embarked on a policy seeking to establish a genuine form of peaceful coexistence. I agree with Professor Sidney Hook, who, commenting on the "anti-anti-Communists," writes:

> Among their major assumptions is either that the leaders of the Soviet Union and Mainland China are no longer Communist or that Communism has evolved to a point where it genuinely accepts a détente with non-Communist countries. . . . These possibilities, however remote, are not excluded. . . . But to base present policy on them is to lapse into the outlook of ritualistic liberalism—which may be most comprehensively defined as the view that it is possible to be liberal without being intelligent.

If we turn now to Presidents Eisenhower, Kennedy and Johnson to seek out their conceptions of basic American foreign policy goals we find what we should expect to find. The basic goals change slowly and only in response to major catastrophes such as Germany and Japan posed in 1939–41, and the USSR and the People's Republic of China pose in the postwar period. Despite variations in the so-called style of our Presidents, their conceptions on this subject are understandably similar.

President Eisenhower said in his first State of the Union speech, February 2, 1953:

> Our Foreign policy must be clear, consistent and confident . . . must be coherently global . . . dedicated to making the free world secure . . . [yet] no single country, even one so powerful as ours, can alone defend the liberty of all nations threatened by Communist aggression from without or subversion within. Mutual security means effective mutual cooperation. . . . Our policy will be designed to foster the advent of practical

93

unity in Western Europe . . . will recognize the importance of . . . equitable world trade. . . . Our labor for peace in Korea and in the world imperatively demands the maintenance by the United States of a strong fighting service ready for any contingency.

Later, on April 16, in a speech before the American Society of Newspaper Editors, President Eisenhower clearly recognized what President Truman had faced: the parting of the Allied ways shortly after World War II; the division of the world into two antagonist blocs; the need to contain any further aggression. But because Stalin had died the previous month, Eisenhower once again, as had his predecessor, held out an olive branch to the new Communist group in power. The olive branch withered.

President Kennedy proclaimed his stance in the well-phrased Inaugural Address, January 20, 1961:

Let the word go forth to friend and foe alike that the torch has been passed to a new generation of Americans . . . unwilling to witness or permit the slow undoing of those human rights to which this nation has always been committed and to which we are committed today at home and around the world. Let every nation know, whether it wishes us well or ill, that we shall pay any price, bear any burden, meet any hardship, support any friend, oppose any foe to assure the survival and success of liberty. . . . To those new states whom we welcome to the ranks of the free, we pledge our word that one form of colonial control shall not have passed away merely to be replaced by a far more iron tyranny. . . . To those peoples in the huts and villages of half the globe who struggle to break the bonds of mass misery, we pledge our best efforts to help them help themselves, for whatever period is required—not because the Communists may be doing it, not because we seek their votes, but because it is right. To our sister republics south of our border, we offer a special pledge . . . in a new alliance for progress. . . . Let all our neighbors know that we shall join with them to oppose aggression or subversion anywhere in the Americas. And let every other power know that this hemisphere intends to remain the master of its own house.

So, too, would President Kennedy "strengthen the shield" of the United Nations and "request" of our "adversary . . . that both sides begin anew the quest for peace."

President Johnson reiterated the goals of his predecessors when in his State of the Union Message of January 5, 1965, he said:

We were never meant to be an oasis of liberty and abundance in a worldwide desert of disappointed dreams. Our nation was created to help strike away the chains of ignorance and misery and tyranny wherever they keep man less than God means him to be.

We are committed to help those seeking to strengthen their own independence, and to work most closely with those governments dedicated to the welfare of all their people.

And perhaps more eloquently he returned to these themes in his Johns Hopkins speech on April 7. There he said:

This will be a disorderly planet for a long time. In Asia, and elsewhere, the forces of the modern world are shaking old ways and uprooting ancient civilizations. There will be turbulence and struggle and even violence. Great social change—as we see in our own country—does not always come without conflict.

We must also expect that nations will on occasion be in dispute with us. It may be because we are rich, or powerful, or because we have made some mistakes, or because they honestly fear our intentions. However, no

95

nation need ever fear that we desire their land, or to impose our will, or to dictate their institutions.

But we will always oppose the effort of one nation to conquer another nation.

We will do this because our own security is at stake.

But there is more to it than that. For our generation has a dream. It is a very old dream. But we have the power, and now we have the opportunity to make that dream come true.

For centuries nations have struggled among each other. But we dream of a world where disputes are settled by law and reason. And we will try to make it so.

For most of history men have hated and killed one another in battle. But we dream of an end to war. And we will try to make it so.

For all existence most men have lived in poverty, threatened by hunger. But we dream of a world where all are fed and charged with hope. And we will help to make it so.

The ordinary men and women of North Vietnam and South Vietnam, of China and India, of Russia and America, are brave people. They are filled with the same proportions of hate and fear, of love and hope. Most of them want the same things for themsleves and their families. Most of them do not want their sons to ever die in battle, or to see their homes, or the homes of others, destroyed.

Well, this can be their world yet. Man now has the knowledge—always before denied—to make this planet serve the real needs of the people who live on it.

I know this will not be easy. I know how difficult it is for reason to guide passion, and love to master hate. The complexities of this world do not bow easily to pure and consistent answers.

But the simple truths are there just the same. We must all try to follow them as best we can.

96

It would be difficult and not especially useful to calculate the number of words that our Presidents and the Secretaries of State and Defense—to name no others—have employed to state and restate the objectives of American foreign policy since the end of World War II. But it is not too difficult to summarize these words in two sets of somewhat overlapping and interdependent propositions which hold to the present:

1. American foreign policy is devoted to three basic objectives. It seeks to preserve and promote U.S. security and the security of friendly and allied states; to advance and enhance stability, defined as the rule of law and maintenance of order, among states; and to help improve the conditions of living for all peoples— within a context of freedom (as defined above, page 88).

2. American foreign policy is designed to prevent the further erosion of freedom anywhere, which means denying any territory and any people to the Communist or other totalitarian enemy; and to use our great resources to help freedom everywhere, using our resources to help newly independent countries as well as others establish and maintain, within a context of freedom, the kinds of polities that they want.

Though debate is welcomed and disagreement surely exists, I believe (apart from sheer personal reaction to Presidential style among the Kennedy myth-makers and Johnson-haters) that with respect to objectives there is wide, if confused, majority support for the "global" concern of the stated policy goals as above set forth. The residual and still persisting elements of American isolationism—be they presumably based on Washington's Farewell Address, historian Charles Beard's "Open Door at Home," "America First," "Fortress America," or even Western Hemisphere Defense—put forth at various times by conservatives and liberals, by Democrats, Republicans and Socialists, dead and living, are *not* prominently in the foreground of post-World War II debate on goals for American foreign policy. There seems to be a majority thrust for American involvement in *world* peace and security, stability and improvement in the conditions of living, with freedom for all. This thrust for involvement, in contrast to withdrawal, gradually matured in the second, third and fourth Roosevelt administrations. The position of leadership and responsibility, acquired after a debate about entering World War II that was probably as acrimonious as the one over Vietnam, has not been, could not be, easily put aside.

The difficulty of foreign policy arises when our "objectives," which always include normative and—to use a controversial word—ideological elements, are put to the test of any instant case. How do we assess what President Kennedy called the "price," weigh the "burden," suffer the "hardship" in coming to the "support of any friend" while opposing "any foe" to assure the "survival and success of liberty"? Does the instant case—a real event in an unpeaceful world—fall under or outside the umbrella of our expressed policy goals? That there are cases outside the umbrella most of us would agree. For example, whether Outer Mongolia remains loyal to Moscow or shifts its loyalty to Peking is most probably of no concern to us. Hence, though we have global goals or objectives, we are *not* necessarily involved in every case everywhere, every time. But what of the cases that presumptively fall within the framework of our objectives? Do we face them or change the objectives so as to exclude them? If we face them, how do we rank their priorities? Since slide rules, test tubes and other such scientific devices are not here the definitive tools of inquiry, what calculus of interest do we use? Do we have sufficient and available data for an informed foreign policy judgment? In our kind of constitutional "open society" what are proper criteria for holding back or revealing data on which foreign-policy decisions must be made and carried out and supported by a majority of citizens and their congressional representatives?

These are but a sample of the questions that condition our choice of objectives, our acceptance or rejection of their consequences, and the "stuff" of our foreign policy debates. Concern becomes infected at times with confusion when choices or decisions are required between ends and means; among good, evil and lesser evil; between the uses and restraints of power which we so amply possess.

Given these general considerations, let us see how they worked in connection with U.S. policy in post-World War II Asia (including Vietnam). What did we do with respect to the objectives outlined by President Truman and his successors?

After the war, and until 1950, the United States largely withdrew from mainland and island Asia. We had in effect accepted the *fait accompli*—the Russian Communist installation of a puppet regime in North Korea as a consequence of USSR participation in the final assault on Japan. We regretted, but accepted, the failure of our policies of reconciliation as exemplified in the unsuccessful missions of General Marshall and General Wedemeyer (1945–47) to Mainland China. Yet, we were more hopeful about the rest of Asia. We were hopeful that, just as we gave up our imperialist past in the Philippines by a congressional timetable that provided for Philippine independence in 1946, so the other Western colonial powers would withdraw from Asia. Thus, there would be an end of Western imperialism and a beginning for newly independent states and nations freely joining the society of nations. In a measure, this came to pass peacefully as between the United Kingdom, on the one side, and Pakistan, India, Ceylon, Burma and Malaya. Thailand had never lost its independence. The Dutch were expelled from Indonesia by Indonesian arms, the United Nations and U.S. economic pressure. All these countries became UN members. The French, we believed or so stated—though it was not true then and did not turn out to be the case—were gradually preparing for the independence of the Indo-Chinese states (Laos, Cambodia and Vietnam) within some kind of French Union. This somewhat roseate and withdrawn view of Asia to which the containment policy applied in Europe had not yet been extended, was already dated when Secretary of State Acheson summed it up in his "Crisis in Asia" speech of January 12, 1950.

99

Three far-reaching events—the fall of Mainland China to the Communist Party (CPC); Communist aggression against Tibet and, more importantly, South Korea (the UN uniquely recognized "aggression" in the case of Korea); and armed Communist subversion, ideologically and otherwise initiated and supported by the Sino-Soviet Bloc against most of the newly independent states of Free Asia—brought about the change in U.S. Asian policy. In effect—to state it negatively—the U.S. extended its European policy of "containment" to Asia. In actual fact, United States Asian policy since 1950, despite errors of omission and commission, despite ignorance, but along with increasing knowledge, has basically sought to apply the objectives (in terms of each instant case) as summed up in the two sets of propositions on page 97.

The application of policy may be illustrated in a series of power moves made by Presidents Truman and Eisenhower, and supported or extended by Presidents Kennedy and Johnson, after the meanings of the three far-reaching events above mentioned had been digested:

1. We came to the defense of South Korea in June 1950 as the major part of the UN Command.

2. We signed bilateral security treaties with the Philippines (August 30, 1951), Japan (September 8, 1951), Korea (October 1, 1953) and the Republic of China (December 2, 1954).

3. We signed multilateral treaties with Australia and New Zealand (ANZUS, September 1, 1951) and with Pakistan, Thailand, the Philippines, the United Kingdom, France, Australia and New Zealand (SEATO, September 8, 1954). The latter treaty guaranteed the defense of Laos, Cambodia and Vietnam against Communist aggression.

4. We signed aid agreements (with or without a military component) with every government of then Free Asia beginning in the latter part of 1950 and continuing in greater or lesser degree through the 1960's.

5. We passed overwhelmingly (and later again overwhelm-

ingly rejected an attempt at repeal) the 1964 Gulf of Tonkin Joint Congressional Resolution supporting Presidential action in the war in Vietnam.

All treaty commitments were ratified by the U.S. Senate and all aid and related agreements were, and continue to be, authorized by the Congress. It should be noted that though these commitments are here listed in their garb of "law," they are clearly related to political, economic, military and socio-cultural elements that, so to speak, flesh out the anatomy of international relations.

One may argue that Presidents Truman, Eisenhower, Kennedy and Johnson should not have recommended all or some of these commitments; that at some stage these treaties and agreements should have been terminated or altered, as legally they may; and that the specific actions flowing from these instruments of policy should have been or should be suspended. However, no President and no session of the Congress have as yet taken any of these steps. On the contrary, each President and Congress has actually or tacitly reaffirmed the general validity of our commitments while making minor variations in their application. Certainly one may conclude that though a number of specific policy "errors"—an error, in the first place, is an act with which you disagree[4]—were committed under the framework of the above policy structure (any student of Asia can cite such errors), the generality of the applied policies, what might be called our short-range interests, generally conformed to the goals or objectives as presented to the American people and to the Congress by Chief Executives.

This, in the main, accounts for the large degree of political bipartisanship—with the exception of the Vietnam issue since 1965—in respect to U.S. foreign policy and its application since the end of World War II, more particularly since the late Sena-

[4] I highlight some U.S. "errors" in two recent publications: *Burma From Kingdom to Republic, A Historical and Political Analysis* (New York, Frederick A. Praeger, 1966), Chaps. 10, 13, 15; and *Why Viet Nam?* (New York, Frederick A. Praeger, 1966), Chap. 3 and elsewhere.

tor Vandenberg repudiated his former isolationist position in a memorable speech, January 10, 1945.

Because we are a free or "open" society we always have the opportunity to alter this posture. Herein, I have accepted the general posture as presented above. Those who disagree may seek to change it in terms of our institutional arrangements. I believe we have made mistakes in its application and that many of these mistakes have come about because we have wanted to believe or hoped that a change in the USSR was or is a change—a continuing "thaw"—for the long-range better. I find *no* convincing evidence that short-range changes in Soviet posture have, as yet, long-range probabilities—I do *not* say possibilities. This means that I believe *intelligence* and *fact* are still on the side of U.S. policy as it has evolved since we globally adapted to various cases the two sets of propositions as above indicated.

There remains for examination, albeit briefly, the case of Vietnam. It is not without significance that the so-called Vietnamese debate began only in the spring of 1965, long after the policies of Presidents Eisenhower and Kennedy served as the springboard for the quantitative—not qualitative—amplification undertaken by President Johnson. What is so offensive in the debate is the fact that many who call for "stop-the-bombing" or "de-escalation" do so only with respect to the side that has been the victim since 1954–55. They denounce the U.S. for bombing "civilians" though civilians who have been casualties have *not* been direct war targets. Whereas, they frequently fail to denounce the Communist North Vietnam, Viet Cong and National Liberation Front for planned terror and attack on civilians. They criticize U.S. "aggression" against North Vietnam since February 1965 when the bombing started. They seldom talk about the aggression and invasion of South Vietnam by North Vietnam that *admittedly* began long before 1965. Externally directed, controlled and supported Communist subversion against the newly independent government of the State of (South) Vietnam began in late 1954 or early 1955. They ignore or downgrade or belatedly condemn the existing treaty obligations undertaken since the U.S. Senate ratified the Manila Pack and SEATO-creating treaty of September 1954.

What is relevant here is not the Vietnam debate as such but rather that the issue of Vietnam has only infrequently been discussed either by those who favor or those who reject present U.S. policy in Vietnam in terms of U.S. stated objectives and interest *in the area as a whole.* To argue *now* that we *should not* have been there in the first place is historically irrelevant to the fact that our objectives called for our presence, and our actions did conform to these objectives. The position that we should withdraw wholly or partially (accepting in effect the proposition that a victory for the Communist North is a lesser evil, or even a good as compared to war) and let whoever wins win is now arguable, but then it contravenes the stated policy of the last four Chief Executives and of the Congress. So to argue in an "open society" is completely permissible. It is possible to change the objectives; or change the Executive and the Congress in order to bring about a desired result; or support the objectives but deny their application in the case of Vietnam; or some other variant of oppositional tactics. Then, however, the burden of "proof" is on the opposition, for theirs is the view that there must be an alteration in policy.

In attempting any or all of these "change" tactics, it would be honorable and accurate to take account of certain facts:

—Ho Chi Minh and his comrades are avowed Communists, that is, totalitarians who deny to non-Communists the right and the means to change the government and the system under which they live.

—The National Liberation Front and its controlling People's Revolutionary Party—the Viet Cong (abbreviation for the Vietnamese word for "communist")—are contemporary tactical names for segments of the Indo-Chinese Communist Party organized in Hong Kong in 1930 with Ho Chi Minh as its Moscow-designated leader.

103

—This Party, despite various changes in names and posture, has never given up its original aim to gain control by whatever means including force of all of Vietnam, Laos and Cambodia.

—As part of the process, it has tried since 1954 to subvert and take over the State (later the Republic) of Vietnam—South Vietnam—that by treaty became independent of France in April–June 1954.

—Whether we approve or disapprove of South Vietnam it had at long last rid itself of French colonial sway and had become a sovereign state before the 1954 Geneva Conference ended its charade.

—The Geneva Declaration, figuring so prominently in the debate over policy, is a declaration signed by *no* government at that Conference; and the Geneva cease-fire agreements are signed documents between North Vietnam and France—obviously conferring on the latter no rights with respect to a non-signatory state, the State of Vietnam (i.e., South Vietnam).

—Finally, the sovereign State of Vietnam refused to sign either the Declaration or the cease-fire agreement because its views (rejecting the partition of Vietnam at the 17th Parallel and calling for free elections in 1954 supervised by an international organization) were completely disregarded by all governments present at Geneva excepting the United States.

It is, of course, possible that one may admit the relevance of the foregoing facts and yet argue that South Vietnam for domestic reasons or for other reasons is not an "appropriate" case for which U.S. objectives should be invoked. Again, the burden of "proof" would be on those who so argue. Here, briefly, I reply that South Vietnam has in fact kept open the probabilities for participatory change—witness, among other items, despite some irregularities, the five stages of elections since 1965 (district councils, village and hamlet officials, constituent assembly, senators, president and representatives). No such national electoral event has been available to the North Vietnamese. Thus, at least because of the foregoing facts, the United States is honorably and, in the main, helpfully carrying out the application of policy to which it has subscribed since President Truman's administration.

Though Vietnam is not the focus of this chapter, it gives point to my concern for U.S. foreign policy in general and Asia in particular. When President Johnson addressed the National Legislative Conference in San Antonio on September 29, 1967, he quoted various Asian and Pacific Ocean leaders whose governments and armed forces have been carrying out policies akin to our own in Vietnam. These included (in the order of the President's quotations) the Philippines, Thailand, Australia, Korea, Malaysia, New Zealand, Singapore. Rarely do American communications media cite or chronicle the policies and contributions of these friendly or allied countries to the war in Vietnam. By contrast, the anti-American or anti-Vietnamese writings and words of the French (from De Gaulle, Lucien Bodard, Philippe Devillers, Jean Lacouture and others) have received considerable attention both in the editorial and news departments of those media who oppose present U.S. policy—for example, *The New York Times, Washington Post,* Channel 13 in New York City, CBS TV, etc.

Frankly, though I do not appreciate what they say, I feel that because of the controversy about Vietnam we—government and people—may take a fresh look at our objectives and their potential application for the next period ahead. We may begin to learn something about the Asians' effort to help themselves through the UN ECAFE, the Mekong River Valley Development, the Asian Development Bank, the organization of regional cooperative effort through the revived Association of Asian States (ASA), the new Asian and Pacific Council (ASPAC), the newer Association of Asian Nations (ASEAN) and similar enterprises (these latter three are candidates for a "merger" in the next five-year period). It is instructive to note that South Korea, Japan, the Republic of China, the Philippines, New Zealand, Australia, Indonesia, Malaysia, Singapore, South Vietnam, Laos, Cambodia, Thailand, Burma, India, Pakistan are actual participants in one or more of the above listed Asian organizations. ECAFE, the Asian Development Bank and the Mekong River Development Project may be regarded as largely or wholly economic. But the others, ASA, ASEAN, ASPAC and SEATO, are more than that. For most of their members have in one way or another acknowledged that if they are to retain a free role in the arc of Free Asia, they will have to cooperate in a variety of ways—cooperate to preserve their security and stability and to improve the conditions of living; cooperate to prevent the erosion of freedom in their part of the world and to use their resources to help extend freedom in their part of the world.

Since, as I have pointed out above, these are also the objectives of the United States, there is every reason to suppose that for the next period ahead this congruence of Asian and U.S. objectives may lead to a further enhancement of free societies everywhere.

WILLIAM PFAFF

The Problem of Motives

"To preach . . . the indivisibility of
freedom is to make a well-intentioned
declaration of permanent ideological
war against the world."

*William Pfaff shares both Professor Commager's dismay at the
delusional quality of American foreign policy and much of his
pessimism about its chances of success in the future. He criticizes
our actions abroad less in terms of their morality than in terms
of their realism, but his logic is remarkably similar to Professor
Commager's and his conclusions are equally chilling.*

I T M A Y B E that the United States is at a very dangerous
point in its history. The insecurities and discontents of life
within our society, intensified by the social and physical mobility
and innovation of the last fifty years, impel us toward some accomplishment sufficient to reconfirm our worth and meaning—
sufficient to restore to us identity and stability. The transnational
challenge of modern ideological politics, since 1918 undermining
the conventions and institutions of international relations, induce in us an equivalent disregard of convention and "legality"
in the pursuit of Great Goals or redemptive historical changes.
Our industrial and military power gives us a sense that anything
is, or could become, possible—if only we find the right techniques, the right "systems," the right alignment and use of our

power and knowledge. We *can* remake the world: this is the lure. And with so exalted an opportunity, what may not be, what will not be, justified? There is a profound externalization here of inner doubt: a displacement of our troubles from their real locus to an imagined—and thus less vexing—zone of national accomplishment.

Myth is indispensable to national action. Great gross formulations of idealism and concern unify a society and underwrite action. But there must be intellectual hardness and tension or we become the victims of myths. In the United States in the past two decades we have had too little of these qualities, and, instead, an indulgence—by leaders, by intellectuals—of what can only be called a liberal historicism improvised in imitation of our enemies.

Thus our security has become identified with a liberation of mankind. Our national purpose has become "a worldwide victory for freedom" (according to Mr. Rusk). Our power to accomplish this is seen as "unique in this world and unique in history" (according to Mr. Humphrey). We Americans are "in a position unique in world history" (according to Mr. George Ball). Thus do we confirm our insecurity: the very hyperbole of our language and extravagance of our self-congratulation betrays uncertainty about real and attainable objectives.

Our conviction is that American foreign policies can—and must—bring about fundamental and liberal change in the character of modern historical development. We are, according to public discourse in the United States, poised amidst dominoes—and our challenge is not victory or defeat in Vietnam or Cuba, but to achieve order in history, or the "success" or "failure" of the Third World, or the creation of a "peaceful revolution" in international society ending the era of despots and radicalism. This clearly represents the enduring effect of Wilsonianism in our political thought, but it also responds to a deep American (and human) desire to make of our actions and sacrifices great events. We thought it ignoble to intervene in World War I to restore a balance of power; accordingly we did it to end war—and this has been our purpose in every war since 1918. Today, as our wars come more often than ever, some of our leaders warn that the great enterprise of ending war may demand of us a decade or a generation of Vietnam-like struggles. Hyperbole of purpose—historicism, an historical messianism—now threatens virtually to institutionalize for us the very thing we would eliminate from history.

The practical historicism of American foreign policy ignores the serious difference between historical contingency and cause. We act in the present as though our actions were within a dialectical process that produces identifiable progress toward an identified conclusion; yet at the same time we reject Marxism, or any other closed system of history. But only a closed conceptual system can make possible a reliance on the remote consequences of political action. Impressed by what national power and action have done in the past to change history, we translate this to the future, making the observation into an expectation.

The problem of American foreign policy is crucially a problem of intelligence, of intellectual leadership. Can idealization and rhetoric be adequately cut away from truth (or its fair approximation)? Nearly every serious person knows that the assumptions stated at the beginning of this section are either untrue or inadequately true. They state what Americans *want* to be true, and they rationalize what we are doing in the world. We indulge them and shrink from attacking them in part because they obviously express intuitions of truth—that freedom is precarious, that the existence of a Third World of Bolivian tin miners and famished Indian peasants and distraught and detribalized African laborers reproaches us as human beings—and threatens us with a revenge. The injustice of the world frightens us when it does not enlist our compassion. The injustice of the world abroad is at the same time easier to contemplate than the injustice of America—the existence of brutalized and virtually disenfranchised classes of Americans. This latter is unmanageable reality. We need a myth of justice accomplished—or accomplishable. Thus we want to believe in the efficacy of social and economic development programs abroad; we want to believe in the inevitability of progress.

That is part of it. But a society, as W. H. Auden once remarked, is a system which loves itself. What is our norm of progress? Ourselves. The generalization of America to the world is the implicit objective of American foreign policy. We understand this as benign, and we thus blind ourselves to ourselves. The objects of our benevolence see menace in this ambition of ours and in the power which lies behind it. The United States obviously is a conglomeration of decency and injustice, of goods bought at a price we prefer not to calculate. But that our evangelism of ourselves can dismay others should hardly be a surprise. What is unusual is that we should seriously—if tacitly—assume that the generalized qualities of America really are relevant to the world as a whole. Here seriousness fails us, and we are victims of a pernicious sentimentality about ourselves. Our proclaimed objectives of foreign policy rest upon the assumption that, nearly everywhere, men's dominating ambitions and essential values are identical to the professed beliefs of the American progressive middle classes.

The American people simply have no real understanding of the precariousness of our liberty, how special were the conditions which created it, how utterly dependent it is on our own qualities and our willingness to practice it. The internal peace which this country has enjoyed since 1865 makes us think that ours is the norm of human society, not a colossal exception. In the lifetimes of living Americans, their fathers and their grandfathers, there is no experience of collective tragedy. In the last sixty years alone mankind has experienced the most immense upheavals, disasters, betrayals, genocides—and we Americans have directly shared in none of it. We have been insouciant adventurers in foreign wars, willing to believe that Belsens and Vorkutas and Stalingrads— and plagues of communal slaughter, institutionalized sadisms and hysterias—really exist, but with no experiential grasp of what they mean. Our emotional knowledge of modern history extends only to depressions and Pearl Harbor and now a televised Asian war directly involving a few thousand American families. Thus in a real sense, contemporary history, the precariousness of life and social institutions, is incomprehensible to Americans. This explains how we can be so surprised, so casual, so optimistic, so enthusiastic, so confident that mankind can be converted to our norm—so certain that freedom, our freedom, is indivisible.

At home, in domestic politics, we understand the limits of responsible action and reasonable accomplishment. Foreign policy takes us into a different dimension—that of world history—which began in metaphysics and ends in eschatology. This is where the apparent possibilities of action can intoxicate us. Why not save the world? It is a task commensurate with the power we already have to destroy it—and acquiring thermonuclear weapons systems was only a splendid engineering feat. History is the dimension of ultimate national meaning and accomplishment, and now—we are assured—is America's moment in history. We have had to learn from Lenin and Mao Tse-tung, and they are committed to the possibility of saving the world and stopping time.

We half believe these possibilities and half scorn them. We believe that we ought to be pragmatists, and we adduce arguments of practical national interest and national security for what we are doing, but—as in Vietnam—these usually come after the fact, and if they are tangible arguments they also are insufficient to explain the facts. Neither a plausible fear for our national survival nor a plausible imperialism put American power on the mainland of Asia—it was idealism.

No political action is pure. This is part of the reason for the transparent contradictions of American policy in the 1960's—illiberalism practiced for liberal reasons, interventionism practiced out of isolationist fears and longings. This is tolerable, predictable. It is less easy to admit the next level of motivation: the secret love for Russia, for example (and Russia's for us), which underlies our great rivalry (if it were not for Russia what would we be? where would we have found greatness?); the atavistic fears which are shadowed in our official proclamations about revolution in Asia; the intuitions of impotence and of omnipotence, the self-hatred, expressing themselves in our controversies over national policy.

Yet national introspection no more easily or reliably produces candor than personal introspection. The layers of motivation are lifted away to disclose new impulses—or dreams, or fears. Politics is like poetry in its density of entangled reason, emotion and intuition. Like poetry, political action would reconcile the unfreedom and disorder of a universe of unique phenomena. But poetry attempts this by analogy, politics in historical action. Politics must, then, ultimately fail; its successes are necessarily provisional, conditional, elusive and paradoxical.

Is democracy desirable for any nation capable of it? Obviously —if one believes that individual men should have a voice in what happens to them. But what is it that they, acting democratically, may seek? The answer must be: to survive, to possess wealth, to live decently with one another, to have their way, to exalt their society . . . to make war. It is credulous to believe that all men want peace—or want it at a sacrifice to other things that they want. War can be sweet; adventure, domination, power, sacrifice —these are men's motives too. Men are idealists. And the abyss, the extinction of desire, is an ideal.

The blindness of ambition, the obscurity and contradiction of human motivation, are truisms of literature and politics but find no place in the American ideology of universal democracy. We do not admit that Hitler or Stalin may have been, in a meaningful sense, "democratic" leaders—which is to say, valid representatives of a national will. We resist admitting that Mao Tse-tung or Ho Chi Minh may at the same time be the popular and "democratic" heads of state their admirers say they are, and the ruthless zealots of their enemies' accusations.

Freedom, political liberty, is no more indivisible than peace. Again, the proposition asserts a wish, not a fact. Not only do men fear freedom as well as seek it, it is self-evidently divisible. If it is indivisible then it has never existed. To attempt to extirpate the divisions between freedom and unfreedom is a reliable way to give unfreedom the victory.

The institutions of civilization are man's self-defense against himself, the fortifications thrown up to prevent us from doing the things we know ourselves to be capable of. To fight to preserve those institutions where they exist—democratic or parliamentary government among them—is a meaningful thing. To undermine or disregard them in the cause of perfecting or surpassing them is a momentous contradiction, perhaps a sanguinary one. To preach in national policy the indivisibility of freedom is to make a well-intentioned declaration of permanent ideological war against the world. Such may be necessary for an individual, but it is folly for a state.

It comes down to this: the United States is a very lucky country, but the luck can run out. Our political institutions made—and make—a very big difference in modern history simply by existing. They were an innovation in the conduct of civil society; they demonstrated that something could be done which had not before been done. The precedent was, and remains, important.

But to establish a precedent does not confirm a nation in success. Others may adopt and adapt what we have designed and make more of it than we have yet done. At the same time we can fail as a nation, lapsing into social and political sterility, whatever our institutional structure, or attenuating or debasing our past accomplishments of civil liberty. This society is neither so stable nor our institutions so resilient as we indulgently think; and our predominant impulses today are directed abroad, to tasks in which—as we define them—we are certain to fail. We are so ambitious—and yet so evasive with ourselves—as to appear to dread reality: we search to justify ourselves and transcend reality with lies about history.

RUSSELL KIRK

The African Example: American Ritualistic Liberalism in Action

". . . the American Constitution is not for export."

Dr. Russell Kirk is well known for his articulate adherence to the principles of political conservatism. His views on foreign policy would not, therefore, necessarily be expected to coincide with those of Messrs. Commager, Pfaff or Stillman. Yet on the important question of whether American policy should accept as an assumption that our own social and political institutions may be used as desirable models for less developed countries, all four men substantially agree.

PROBABLY the simplest test of American foreign policy in recent years may be made in Africa. Over the past fifteen years, the United States has established an elaborate diplomatic apparatus in the new African states, and has expended great sums in economic and military aid to those governments. The authors of American policy apparently have expected to advance the interests of the United States in that continent, and indeed to assert there much of the leadership and authority formerly possessed by European powers.

This whole concept was intertwined with the American assumption that the "emergent nations" could and would embrace

American political forms, American economic methods and American public and private objectives. I mean to suggest below that this belief was an illusion, and that it has enfeebled whatever American influence might have been exerted upon Africa.

In both America and Africa, this confusion of aims and possibilities was made worse by a loose and often demagogic employment of such terms as "freedom" and "liberal democracy." In Africa, the "freedom" sought had next to nothing to do with American Constitutional liberties, but was rather the political independence of former colonial territories; while "liberal democracy" (a body of institutions of nineteenth-century origin, almost peculiar to Western Europe and the English-speaking nations) was both incomprehensible and impossible in the new African regimes.

These illusions and misunderstandings strongly affected many of the principal architects of American policy and many of the principal molders of American opinion. It would not have been possible for the American government to have acted on the basis of these fallacies, nevertheless, had not the American public generally been in vague sympathy with the notion of Americanizing Africa and most of the rest of the world. Only since the ineffectuality of American measures for Africa has become manifest have we seen any widespread doubt of the assumptions to which I referred above. Until quite recently, Washington's African policy, if not clearly popular, at least obtained public acquiescence from the great majority of American citizens.

When the emergent nations—encouraged, in several instances, by American public and private manifestos—threw off European political domination, few voices were raised against the thesis that the new African states would emulate American society. The diplomatic, economic and even military policy makers of Washington seem to have taken it for granted that emergent Africa was a *tabula rasa*, upon which Democracy and Progress, American style, might be writ large. But nothing of the sort has occurred.

So far as a consistent American policy toward Africa may be discerned, that policy has failed. Given its premises, it could not have succeeded. The fallacies which led to that failure are the illusions of "ritualistic liberalism."

It was Professor Sidney Hook, I believe, who coined the term "ritualistic liberalism" to describe the condition into which much of American "liberal" opinion is fallen nowadays: an infatuation with old liberal slogans untempered by any prudential examination of the exigencies of our hour, an ideological fidelity to the liberal letter that forgets the liberal spirit. Dr. Hook was referring primarily to the attitude which many American liberals exhibit toward the Communist movement. A similar ritualism, I believe—a like confidence that mere repetition of liberal formulas and evocation of god-terms can suffice for dealing with our present discontents—may be found in the concept of American foreign policy entertained by many liberals. And this infatuation with yesterday's abstractions is clearest where Africa is in question.

One encounters the roots of such attitudes and aspirations toward Africa in the advice which Colonel House gave to President Wilson—but which Wilson had no opportunity to act upon. One sees the development of such ideas in President Franklin Roosevelt's cloudy African ambitions—which, again, were not then fulfilled. And from the Truman years to the present, Washington's African policies have been governed by "ideals" never to be realized.

There has existed in this country no widespread enthusiasm for American intervention in African affairs: most citizens have been indifferent to such concerns, while most members of Congress have been suspicious of American involvement. Yet powerful elements in the State Department and in other branches of the Executive Force, certain pressure groups (ethnic and economic) and a good many publicists have advocated African undertakings which, sporadically, the American government has embarked upon. The results must be disappointing to the advocates of these designs.

A decade ago, this body of "progressive" doctrine applied to Africa was most loudly enunciated by Mr. Chester Bowles. (Of recent years, in New Delhi, Ambassador Bowles has been relatively silent on African concerns, with reason.) As representative of a school of thought, the Bowles dogmas deserve reexamination.

In 1956, Mr. Bowles delivered both the Godkin Lectures at Harvard and a somewhat similar series at the University of California, Berkeley; these addresses soon were published under the respective titles of *American Politics in a Revolutionary World* and *Africa's Challenge to America*. Chester Bowles spoke as a thoroughgoing utilitarian and political universalist, convinced that all societies ought to be reconstituted in the American image—if necessary, at American expense. Though he went farther in his recommendations than would most American citizens, still he appealed to certain public prejudices that are general enough, and particularly to the dominant climate of liberal opinion at American universities.

By an American-sponsored industrialization of "underdeveloped regions," under forced draft, he would have Americans out-materialize the Soviet materialists. The world should become one immense copy of American society, repeating the phrases of Jefferson and F.D.R., adopting American technology, imitating our manners and institutions and presumably inheriting our problems and afflictions. Mr. Bowles' brand of One-Hundred-Percent-Americanism may be imposed quite simply, with equal facility, upon the ancient civilizations of India and the primitive peoples of central Africa.

Here I interject a general proposition of mine bearing some relation to American foreign policy. It seems to be a law governing all life, from the unicellular inanimate forms to the highest human cultures, that every living organism endeavors, above all else, to preserve its identity. Whatever lives tries to make itself the center of the universe; it resists with the whole of its power the endeavors of competing forms of life to assimilate it to their substance and mode. Every living thing prefers even death, as an

117

individual, to extinction as a distinct species. So if the lowliest alga struggles fatally against a threat to its peculiar identity, we ought not to be surprised that men and nations resist desperately —often unreasoningly—any attempt to assimilate their character to that of some other body social. This resistance is the first law of their being, extending below the level of consciousness. There is one sure way to make a deadly enemy, and that is to propose to anyone, "Submit yourself to me, and I will improve your condition by relieving you from the burden of your own identity and reconstituting your substance in my image."

Yet just this is what Mr. Bowles and Americans of like mind, with goodwill and innocence, proclaim as a rallying cry for American policy makers in a revolutionary world. To be sure, they do not use precisely these phrases, and they really seem to be unaware of the grand assumption behind their own humanitarian projects; yet naïveté does not alter the character of the first principles upon which the design is erected.

"The most powerful ideas and principles in the history of man are closely linked with the evolution of American democracy," Mr. Bowles writes in *American Politics*. "Today it is *our* revolution for self-determination, for human dignity, and for expanding economic opportunities which is alive and marching in Burma, India, and the Philippines, in Nigeria, the Sudan, and Tunisia, indeed throughout the non-communist world."

In both these books, Ambassador Bowles repeatedly implies that modern revolutionary movements—except for Marxist undertakings—have been inspired directly by knowledge of the American Revolution. *Africa's Challenge* concludes with "the fervent hope that we shall soon come to view the Soviet challenge not negatively as a mortal danger, but positively as an opportunity for which the continuing political, social, and industrial revolution of Jefferson, Lincoln, and Henry Ford has equipped us as no other people on earth." Revolutions are made, he informs us, out of devotion to the writings of "Locke, Rousseau, and Jefferson." A revolution of rising expectations, founded upon American theory and experience, "shapes the attitudes and aspirations of the one and a half billion people of India, Africa, and South America," and its objectives are "freedom from foreign domination, political or economic; a full measure of human dignity regardless of race, religion or color; and increased economic opportunities, broadly shared." In Africa, as elsewhere, independence was sought "in the name of liberal democracy."

Such are the foreign policy postulates of an advertising man. But these also are the convictions of certain decision makers in Washington, and of eminent gentlemen of the press. They have had their consequences in Africa.

In truth, the African revolutions of our century were not in emulation of the American Revolution, but were accomplished out of very different circumstances and materials: so far as African leaders were conscious imitators of earlier upheavals, they looked to the French and Russian revolutions. What lip service these latter-day revolutionaries have paid to the American experience has come after the fact of their own revolutionary triumph —in well-founded expectation of American largess. The African independence movements owe much more to the London School of Economics, or to the Sorbonne, than they do to the Declaration of Independence; and we ascend into a Cloud-Cuckoo-Land of political fantasy if we pretend that American Constitutionalism was the inspiration of Jomo Kenyatta (who does seem to have read Hegel), Kwame Nkrumah or the present masters of Nigeria, Algeria and Egypt.

Still, historical facts are of no primary significance to the ritualistic liberal; approximations will suffice. Of the Abyssinians, for example, Mr. Bowles writes in *Africa's Challenge*, "Their religion is Orthodox of the same strain as the Coptic Christian Church of Egypt." Neither the Coptic nor the Abyssinian church is Orthodox, actually: they are Monophysitic. But what does religion matter? Hydroelectric dams are what Africa needs. Only the future is the concern of Mr. Bowles; and if he, and a number of people in Washington, know Africa only by brief speaking junkets—why, James Mill was ready to give laws to India without ever having set foot there.

Africa's future must be governed by "self-determination." This is an end in itself, because Woodrow Wilson employed the term. Nothing must be permitted to stand in the way of immediate self-determination throughout Africa. "When harried American policy-makers suggest that under present-day conditions such principles as self-determination are valid in some years and not in others, or that they apply to white Poles but not to dark-skinned Africans, the disillusionment of the people in Asia, Africa, and indeed throughout most of the world, is profound."

Well! In our century, fanatical insistence upon self-determination, down to the tiniest "cultural group," has been tremendously destructive. But Mr. Bowles and his friends ignore this—and do not remark how self-determination has been advantageously employed by the tyrants of our age. Full speed ahead! The world must become one vast America—plus the welfare state—before the decade is out: so Mr. Bowles told us ten years ago. But the world in general, and Africa in particular, have been disobedient.

Although American society and the American economy, and a peculiar ideology of Americanism, compose Mr. Bowles' nominal pattern for a universal order, still this ideal has curiously little resemblance to the existing American social structure. In Mr. Bowles' writings one finds next to nothing about order and justice; while by "freedom" he usually means national self-determination, not private rights. What he seeks is conformity to an abstraction called "liberal democracy," egalitarian and industrialized. And this liberal democracy does not mean to Ambassador Bowles the conditions which America has known for the past century. His liberal democracy exists in a utopian future. He expresses some contempt for Britain and France, in their present difficulties with liberal democracy and the welfare state, and he waxes impatient with Americans because of their stubborn attachment to prudence in politics. Where, then, are we to find our models for the future liberal democracy of Africa? Why, as Mr. Bowles tells us in *American Politics:* "In other democracies —Germany, India, Israel, Burma—where there is basic agreement upon a worthy national purpose *yet to be achieved*, there is no failure to mobilize the necessary energies and resources through the mechanisms of democracy."

Whatever doubts one may feel concerning these four states as models for emergent Africa, in any event the Africans have not imitated them, either. Having thus solved Africa's difficulties, however, Mr. Bowles utters an exhortation against catch-phrases —more particularly, the slogans of the Eisenhower administration: "Some insist that we can afford to put up with this political *sloganizing* in foreign policy. After all, they say, the Republic has thus far survived similar sloganizing on domestic policy questions. . . . Foreigners, however, cannot reasonably be expected to play by American ground rules. . . . These calculated phrases, in my judgment, have cost us dear throughout the world—far more than we can easily afford."

But after this sagacious platitude, Mr. Bowles proceeds to enunciate as shopworn a set of slogans as ever was employed by anyone discussing American foreign policy. "In this Nuclear Age," says Mr. Bowles, "without such a vision—the people perish." Without such a vision? Or because of it?

Ten years after Bowles' two little books were published—a decade during which the Bowles attitudes strongly influenced Washington's measures toward Africa—American objectives for Africa must be judged a thorough failure, if Bowles' ideals are accepted as the general policy. Africa has obdurately insisted upon being Africa.

Not one liberal democracy exists in "emergent" Africa, nor is there any prospect of such development.

The United States is denounced in many African countries as the great new imperialist power.

Self-determination becomes the splintering of the artificial African "nations" into tribal and ethnic fragments, as in Nigeria.

Where a possibly viable self-determination has stirred, it has been put down by the United Nations, the United States and the African radicals, as in Katanga; or ignored, as in the slaughter of the separatist Negro Christians of the southern Sudan.

No large-scale industrialization has commenced, but in much of Africa the agricultural and extractive industries have declined.

Many of the African leaders admired by Mr. Bowles have been devoured by their own revolutions, or have degenerated into squalid oligarchs.

Constitutionalism is a sham in Africa: the dictator, the tribal chief, the military junta and the unitary, repressive party are triumphant.

The most nearly stable African governments are those least influenced by Mr. Bowles' ideals—hereditary monarchies like Ethiopia and Morocco.

The African states most eager for planning and development, *à la* Bowles, suffer from the highest rates of unemployment in the world: Egypt and Algeria.

Not only have the Africans experienced fierce disappointments, but it is difficult to perceive how American interests or American ideals have been advanced by Washington's African policies. Most American economic aid has been squandered, as in Ghana, and American flattery of African emergent politicians generally has been repaid by the irresponsibility of the African bloc in the United Nations. Nkrumah and Nasser, long maintained in power by American economic aid, presumably are not quite Mr. Bowles' liberal democrats.

As Secretary Rusk acquired some mastery over his own department, a degree of realism crept into America's African policies. The American ambassador to the United Nations may continue to give lip service to the demands of African nationalists, but there will be no American crusades against South Africa, Southwest Africa, Rhodesia or the Portuguese provinces. Nevertheless, inconsistent meddling in African affairs continues to produce more mischief than good.

Consider President Johnson's dispatch of three transport

planes and a small body of troops to the Congo, in July 1967—a measure promptly denounced by many leading Democrats and Republicans, liberals and conservatives, in Congress. The Department of State believed it necessary to shore up General Mobutu's dictatorship—but to shore it up against whom? Not against Communist influence, but against its domestic opposition and against mercenaries previously useful to Mobutu himself. The apologists of the State Department were confused. America had intervened in the Congo twice before—why not now, even if circumstances had altered? The United States, it was said, had the obligation to "preserve the territorial integrity of the Congo." But by what treaty had the United States assumed so heavy a responsibility? By what authority of the United Nations? Nothing was done to preserve the territorial integrity of Nigeria, simultaneously in peril. Does some obligation exist to preserve the territorial integrity of all African states—Egypt, perhaps, and the Republic of South Africa?

By such well-meant interference, great states create empires in a fit of absence of mind, as did the Roman Republic. Garrisons are quartered in the most remote regions, and resources are dissipated; "overextension" becomes a running sore. Within the United States, foreign policy is monopolized by the Executive, while the Senate is not expected to advise and consent even after the event.

And African cultures and peoples, told to conform themselves to the American liberal democracy, react as any human community must react against an alien intrusion—even the most humanitarian intrusion. In the Congo, the Belgians may be recollected with nostalgia; or men may look with some hope to the counterbalancing power of the Soviet Union or of Communist China. The humanitarian improvers from across the ocean soon will appear as hypocrites. What liberal democracy was being preserved in the Congo—the regime of Mobutu, bent upon the judicial murder of Tshombe, Mobutu's predecessor in power and sometime ally?

Order in Africa, and America's African interests, cannot be secured by the visionary recommendations of Mr. Bowles and his school. The Williams slogan of "Africa for the Africans" needs to be taken more literally, and not in the sense intended by Mr. G. Mennen Williams.

African political patterns will not and cannot resemble those of the United States. Chieftainship, old-style or new-style, will assert itself, no matter how much America intervenes.

African economies will not and cannot be formed upon the American model. So far as Africa can attain prosperity, it will be found in revival and expansion of agriculture and mining, not in neo-mercantilistic nationalism and grandiose industrial gestures financed by the American Treasury.

African peace cannot be achieved by American encouragement of fanatic nationalism and "anticolonialism," which mean internecine war and the destruction of European guidance. The fundamental need is for cooperation among the African states, and for friendly relationships with the former colonial powers and the remaining European settlers.

Neither Soviet Russia nor Communist China is strong enough to penetrate effectively into Africa—unless the United States, with all the cordiality in the world, awakes bitter African resentments by desultory interference. As Mr. Arthur Krock remarked of American action against Katanga, there we did Soviet Russia's work for her—at the cost of not a single ruble to Moscow.

It remains true, as Edmund Burke argued, that sometimes a policy of salutary neglect is the best means by which a great power can deal with distant and irascible commonwealths. Certainly the attempt to clap a vague ideology of Americanism upon Africa must be ruinous. As Professor Daniel Boorstin puts it, the American Constitution is not for export. And where the European powers, after generations or even centuries of experience, failed to make Africans into Europeans, the United States cannot expect to create a liberal democratic suburbia.

SENATOR GEORGE McGOVERN

Today and Tomorrow

"While the Cold War weighs less heavily on the world, a new polarization is shaping which will increasingly dominate the future."

Senator George McGovern agrees with several other contributors in saying that our Cold War-bred preoccupation with national security has distorted the balance of values in our foreign policy. But looking ahead, he sees a new, even more menacing challenge arising. If we meet it intelligently and in time, he says, we may yet be able to achieve that fusion of conscience and self-interest that has sometimes eluded us in the past.

A T NO OTHER TIME in our national history has it been more important than now for Americans to take a new, long view of the role which we can and should play in world affairs.

In this "winter of our discontent," we need to reflect, with considerably greater care than we normally permit ourselves, about what is important to us and also what is consonant with our American character and values.

This kind of reflection seems to be particularly difficult in Washington, where both the Administration and Congress are usually under the gun of a host of problems requiring immediate action. The pressure of acting quickly, without adequate time or information for basic considerations, is probably a major reason for our dilemma in Vietnam—and for other, briefer ventures such as the incident at the Bay of Pigs and the recent intervention in Santo Domingo.

I think it is a fair statement that most members of Congress and most Americans have until recently accepted the step-by-step progressions which have carried us ever deeper into the war. But now we are increasingly appalled by the cost in lives and money, disturbed by the war's effect on relations with our allies and troubled by the never-distant danger of finding ourselves propelled into a nuclear war.

If we had it to do over again, most of us probably would resist becoming so deeply involved militarily and politically in an obscure little jungle ten thousand miles from our shores—a part of the world of which we know and understand little—with U.S. soldiers supposedly protecting one group of Vietnamese against other Vietnamese in a costly struggle of doubtful objectives. I suspect that 95 percent of Americans would agree that they want "no *more* Vietnams," even if they differ on how best we should extricate ourselves from the present struggle.

This is the wisdom of hindsight, of course. But there *is* wisdom in being able to say meaningfully, "This is a mistake we will not make again." Men of experience are usually candid enough to admit that they learn more from their mistakes than from their successes, and this is true of nations, as well.

But it is not enough to *say* we want no more Vietnams and thereby believe that we have immunized ourselves against the danger. The great power and momentum of the United States and the complexity and volatility of the world situation are such that there is no easy formula for staying out of future quicksands.

A key question is whether or not our present assumptions about the world will help us avoid the danger of getting involved in other Vietnams, while advancing the security and well-being of the United States. Are there policies and programs more likely to achieve these ends?

American foreign policy in the years since the end of World War II has been based on the assumption that the chief threat to our security and to world peace is an international Communist conspiracy directed from Moscow and backed by Peking and other Communist capitals. Anti-Communism has been the touchstone of our policy, especially in Asia.

For the most part, we have acted on the assumption that any regime hostile to Communism—no matter how corrupt or unrepresentative—was worthy of our support; conversely, any regime friendly to Moscow, or even neutral in the Cold War struggle, was regarded as an enemy. We have poured out billions of dollars in economic and military assistance to unpopular dictatorships, provided only that they sounded the proper anti-Communist notes. Batista in Cuba, Trujillo in the Dominican Republic, Rhee in South Korea, Chiang Kai-shek in Formosa and Diem in South Vietnam are only a few of the more illustrious of our allies who have been recipients of American favor because of their anti-Communist orientation.

If we search for the basic motivation behind our policy in Vietnam since the end of the World War II, we shall find anti-Communism at the center. The same holds true with reference to our China policy and our general stance in Asia and the world as a whole.

Yet, the two most powerful forces moving in Asia and the developing world since 1945 have been not Communism, but nationalism and the "revolution of rising expectations." With the collapse of the old British, French, Dutch and Japanese imperial systems during and after World War II, Asia was convulsed by revolutionary forces aimed at throwing off outside control and securing a better life for the people.

Our own revolutionary, democratic tradition enabled some Americans to understand these fundamental forces. Believing that Western imperialism had run its course by the end of World War II, our government encouraged the British to liquidate their Asiatic colonial system; we insisted that Japan surrender her imperial holdings; we brought considerable pressure on the Dutch to withdraw from the East Indies; and we granted full independence to the Philippines.

But in China and Vietnam, the revolutionary leaders were

Communists, which automatically made them the enemy in American eyes. To our policy makers, especially after the bitter experience of the Korean War, Mao Tse-tung and Ho Chi Minh were part of a worldwide Communist monolith bent upon global conquest. We seemed ready to ostracize any Communist government, no matter how strong its base of local support, and to embrace any ally, no matter how odious and ineffective, provided he carried an anti-Communist banner. Having substituted Communism for the devil, we felt sufficiently free from sin to rebuke those who failed to enlist on the side of right. Although we had followed a policy of avoiding involvement in European alliances of the nineteenth century, Secretary of State Dulles regarded neutralism as "immoral" when practiced by the newly emerging governments of the post-World War II period. Forgetting that what we are *for* has been the source of our strength more than what we are *against*, we made anti-Communism the guiding principle of our policy.

Thus, although Ho Chi Minh had stood with us in the war against Japan and saved American pilots shot down over the jungle, we backed the French effort to crush the Vietnamese independence struggle led by Ho. This action ran counter to President Franklin Roosevelt's view that Indochina should be placed under a United Nations trusteeship and prepared for independence. "France has milked it for one hundred years," Roosevelt said. "The people of Indochina are entitled to something better than that." But with his death, that view faded, and two billion dollars in American aid went to the French effort which ended in defeat at Dien Bien Phu in 1954.

Ho Chi Minh emerged as a victorious hero from the eight-year war against France—not because he was a Communist, but because he tapped powerful forces of nationalism and popular revolution as a counter to a crumbling colonialism and an inept puppet regime. The evidence is convincing that if we had accepted Ho and permitted the Vietnamese to work out their affairs free from American involvement, North and South Vietnam would have united under Ho. Such a regime might have served as a more effective buffer against Chinese penetration of Southeast Asia than the divided and warring two Vietnams which we helped initiate and which have been the occasion for so much grief over the past decade.

We have supposed that the number-one enemy of Asia was Communism and that any sacrifice to contain it would be popular, but few Asiatics share our obsession with Communism. The bad memories that fester in Asian minds are associated not with Communism, but with Western imperialism, human misery and corrupt local hierarchies. The exploitative capitalism Asiatics have experienced bears little resemblance to the enlightened economy and public policies that have served America so well. So, while anti-Communism has been an effective rallying cry to secure congressional authorizations of American military and financial aid for compliant regimes in Saigon and elsewhere, it has not been in tune with the strongest aspirations of the people of Asia. Too often we have become identified with corrupt, stupid and ineffective dictators who made the Communist revolutionists look appealing by comparison.

The obsession with Communism that pulled us into the Vietnamese struggle has even more clearly dictated our policy toward China for the past two decades. In spite of the enormous power of the United States and the relative weakness of China, anti-Communism has been a blinding light that has led us to aggravate the very dangers we ought most to diminish—the increased belligerence of China, the disruption of normal communications and a growing military involvement on China's border that could ignite a third world war.

It is becoming increasingly clear that anti-Communism is not an effective policy to promote the security of the United States and the peace of the world; it is rather a negative, emotion-charged ideology that leads us into bankrupt alliances; ill-advised military ventures; and the neglect of genuine dangers, problems and opportunities that are crucial to our survival. The old Cold War slogans no longer fit the real world.

Present-day realities no longer conform to our assumptions

about Russia, "international Communism" and America's proper role in the world. We are no longer in the days of the Berlin airlift, or of Stalin, or even in the days of Khrushchev. The ideological and messianic fires of the Russian revolution have burned low, and the Soviet Union, while still capable of considerable mischief—as in the Middle East—is essentially not a revolutionary force in world affairs today. Recently we have witnessed the extraordinary spectacle of the Soviet leaders snubbing Fidel Castro because he pursues a militant policy of trying to overthrow Latin American governments by Communist intrigue and force. When the Russians recently celebrated the fiftieth anniversary of their revolution, our ambassador and our Secretary of State attended the celebrations and joined in the toasts. Communist China, on the other hand, boycotted the observances and issued a blast accusing the Russians of having sold out the Revolution. In 1965, when India and Pakistan were at war over Kashmir, with Peking cheering from the sidelines, Moscow intervened as a peacemaker and helped to settle the conflict at the Tashkent conference.

No longer are we confronted with a unified, centrally directed international Communist monolith. The Communist powers are so divided among themselves that any effort to deal with them as a unified bloc is almost certain to misfire. Indeed, Russia's so-called satellites in eastern Europe have been demonstrating growing independence of Moscow during the past twenty years.

Nor can we assume that the so-called Free World is united behind Washington, as witness the recent behavior of French President de Gaulle. The old fear of a Moscow conspiracy which once held the Western Alliance together is beginning to dissipate. Few people outside of the United States any longer see the Cold War between Washington and Moscow as a matter of great importance.

But while the Cold War weighs less heavily on the world, a new polarization is shaping which will increasingly dominate the political and economic future.

The important fact of the latter third of this century is not the gap between Washington and Moscow, but the growing gap and the alienation between the rich countries of North America and Europe and the poor countries of Asia, Africa, much of Latin America and the Middle East. This polarization is not just economic, though this would be serious enough. It is also racial and psychological. The growing alienation is between the poor and *colored* countries of the southern half of the globe and the rich and *white* people of the northern half.

The far-reaching danger of this should be obvious, but it is not without a certain historic irony. For the Soviet Union, like the United States, has now reached a sufficient level of prosperity so that it is viewed by the poor countries as being nearly as much a white—a "have"—nation as the United States. The revolutionary leadership has passed on to Peking and Havana, and it is not without a considerable amount of truth that the Red Chinese accuse the Russians of being apostates to their own doctrine. Nor should we underestimate the powerful psychological appeal which the Peking line can have in much of the world. The momentary internal troubles of the Chinese should not blind us to the fact that their battle cry in Asia, Africa, the Near East and Latin America against the wealthy white "exploiters" is capable of attracting millions of recruits if the present situation continues or worsens.

It seems almost unbelievable to the average American, for example, that over 50 percent of the world's people live in countries whose per capita income is less than $130 a year, and that three-quarters of the world's people live on less than $190 a year, as contrasted with the United States average of $2,600 yearly. Nor can even these stark figures quite convey the fact that the average American lives thirty-five *times* better than the average Asian. In poor countries, the great bulk of a family's income goes into food, yet even with this, their diet is in shocking contrast to ours. For example, the average American eats 219 pounds of meat a year, while the average Indian has only 4 pounds;

the American has 39 pounds of eggs yearly, the Indian has a half pound; the American eats 213 pounds of vegetables yearly, while the Indian makes do with 6 pounds.

This is what Henry George meant by the "open-mouthed, relentless hell of poverty"—a short, brutish existence in which malnutrition deforms and vitiates, in which illiteracy and ignorance perpetuate poverty and malnutrition. And while it is true that such poverty has long existed in the world, and that there has always been a disparity between the wealth of some nations and others, there are nonetheless important differences between the present situation and that which prevailed in the past.

First of all, the gap in income and living standards has never been so great as today. Secondly, this gap is growing rapidly.

In the single year 1966, for example, the per capita income of the 196,000,000 people of the United States *grew* by $157 to nearly $2,600. This is a marvelous achievement, but few of us fortunate Americans are aware that this gain in one year is as much as the *total* per capita income of seventy-five nations of Asia, Latin America and Africa. These countries, with 76 percent of the world's population, have an average per capita income of less than $190. Contrasted with our growth of $157, theirs increased an insignificant two or three dollars; some actually lost ground, sinking even deeper into poverty.

Today, four countries alone, with only 10 percent of the world's population have over 50 percent of the world's income; they are the United States, West Germany, Great Britain and France. On the other hand, over 50 percent of the world's people have less than 10 percent of its income; and by the end of the century, at the present rate, their share of the world's income may decline to 5 percent, while that of the wealthy 10 percent of the population may rise as high as 60 or 70 percent.

Yet, while this gap is growing so ominously, there is one immensely encouraging change from the past. For the first time in history, the world has both the technology and the capital resources to attack world poverty on a large scale, with excellent prospects of success. This being the case, the moral excuse of past helplessness is no longer available to us. The world *can* defeat acute poverty.

Another important change results from the revolution in communications. The ubiquitous transistor radio has reached the most isolated tribes of Africa, the most remote villages of Asia, the most distant herdsmen in the Andes. As a result, while three-fourths of the world's people may be desperately poor, they now know that such poverty is neither foreordained nor necessary. Not too surprisingly, they are in growing rebellion against their lot and looking for a solution which offers some hope that they, or at least their children, may know a life of some modest comfort and dignity, rather than the gnawing hunger, misery and fear which are now their normal companions. These three-quarters of the world's people, if allowed to sink further into poverty and hopelessness, are the tinder which Mao Tse-tung and Fidel Castro hope to ignite in a conflagration to consume the rest of the world in dozens of Vietnams.

Let me try to translate this into a domestic context. No American of conscience can view the recent riots in our cities as other than serious danger signals of the alienation within our own society of the Negro poor. But alarming though this alienation is at home, it is only a fraction of the polarization shaping up between the wealthy white countries and the poor colored countries.

In the United States, for example, 11 percent of the population is Negro, and by no means all of them are poor. Economic gap between the whites and Negroes is still unconscionably great; the per capita income of our Negro population in 1966 was $1,266 contrasted with $2,600 for the whites.

But against this background, let us try to visualize the global contrast. Think of the United States as having a colored population of 75 percent, with only 25 percent whites. Then imagine that the average annual income of the colored majority is only $190 while that of the white minority is $2,600. The explosive tension between the very wealthy minority and the desperately poor majority would be only too easy to visualize. And when you further imagine what would happen if the wealthy minority were becoming rapidly richer while the poor minority remained mired in misery and despair, the resultant explosive mixture would make Newark and Detroit seem like a Civil War cannonball alongside a monster H-bomb of today.

The basic fact of our time is emerging clearly: the challenge and danger to world peace is less and less likely to emerge from a military-ideological confrontation between the Soviet Union and the Western World, and is more and more likely to spring from the poverty and desperation of the colored three-quarters of the world. In the same way that Lincoln said that our country could not survive half free and half slave, it can be said today that the world cannot survive one-quarter rich and three-quarters impoverished.

No single question of foreign policy deserves as much thought and as high priority as this: how can the United States, in concert with other industrialized nations, reverse the present alarming trend, and thereby avoid further polarization into two widely divergent and antagonistic worlds? The future of peace turns on this factor more than any other.

What can we do about it?

There is a great deal we can do about it if we thoroughly understand the problem and have the will to attack it courageously in concert with both the rich and poor nations.

We all understand, of course, that the poor countries themselves must provide their own leadership and most of their own capital; and, in fact, they are already doing so. Any idea that the poor countries are not, as a whole, making a major effort is totally false. Since the early 1950's their annual rate of economic growth has surpassed 4.5 percent—a very impressive showing. And despite the fact that it is agonizingly difficult to accumulate savings for investment in countries on the borderline of survival, these same countries *are* providing 80 percent of their own investment capital. This has required sacrifice and self-discipline. But it is

134

not enough. The poorest countries also have the highest birth rate, so that even with an enormous effort, most of them are running very fast to stand still in terms of their per capita income. And the only way they can realistically break out of this vicious circle is by more outside capital and technical assistance.

Where will this come from? We Americans, with our own experience of the impressive generative powers of private investment, are prone to think that such investment may provide the answer abroad as well as at home. But unhappily the flow of American (and European) private capital to the poor countries is notably small, except to those countries which have been provident enough to endow themselves with substantial deposits of oil or industrial minerals. For example, private firms in the United States invested $769,000,000 in industrial plants and equipment in Canada (in 1964), but only $5,000,000 in Central America. Likewise, $501,000,000 went to Great Britain, but only $36,000,000 to India, though India's need was infinitely greater than that of Britain. The twelve million people of the Netherlands received $55,000,000 in American investment during the year; this was more than went to an aggregate sixty-four countries in Asia, the Near East and Africa, with a combined total population of 860,000,000. In other words, private investment goes abroad to highly developed or substantially developed countries, but almost never to underdeveloped ones, except in the extractive industries.

And what about bilateral governmental aid programs, and specifically those of the United States? The United States Foreign Assistance Act approved by Congress in 1967 was the smallest in years, amounting finally to an appropriation of $2,300,000,000. But even this small figure is illusory. When the catch-all bill is stripped of the military aid and the so-called supporting aid (mostly to Vietnam), and other extraneous matters, the hard core of what is really available for economic development is about $1,900,000,000. Out of our gross national product of nearly $800,000,000,000, the United States is contributing about one-fourth of one percent to development aid for poor countries, though it is committed before the United Nations to allocate one percent for this purpose. Moreover, this very modest amount is heavily concentrated in a small number of countries, so that the amount of aid which went to Negro Africa, for example, was only about $144,000,000 in 1967.

In terms of both the American capacity to aid the economic development of the poor countries, and of their need for this aid, the kindest thing that can be said is that our bilateral aid is inadequate.

But we are not alone. With a few notable exceptions, such as Sweden, most of the rich countries are contributing relatively little of their rapidly growing incomes to the needs of the poor countries. The net flow of official aid from developed to underdeveloped countries is about six billion dollars yearly, a level maintained since 1961. During this period, however, the rich countries have become considerably richer, so that the percentage of their income contributed has declined sharply. And since most of the flow is in the form of loans, the rising level of interest and amortization payments is such that they will eat up the entire flow of new capital in not too many years.

The poor countries, their credit largely exhausted, are rarely in a position today to consider "hard" loans from, for example, the World Bank. And the Bank's "soft" loan affiliate, the International Development Association, which is intended to make long-term loans on very favorable terms for countries of less than $250 per capita income, has exhausted its small loan funds, which it obtains by passing the hat periodically among the rich nations.

In sum, not only is private investment largely uninterested in poor countries, but bilateral aid is grossly inadequate and declining, and multilateral aid is now almost totally unavailable to poor countries on terms they can afford.

To make matters more difficult for the poor countries, their trade relations with the rich countries are also deteriorating. Their principal exports are commodities and raw materials whose prices are declining in relation to the industrial products which they must purchase. As a result, the poor countries must export more in order to buy the same amount of imports. In the process, their share of total world trade is declining; it dropped from one-third to one-fifth in the last ten years. A dramatic example is that of Latin America, which furnished 31 percent of U.S. imports in 1956, but now supplies only 15.8 percent—half as much as before. It takes a lot of Alliance for Progress aid to make up for this lost purchasing power through trade.

Nor is this all of the catalog of troubles afflicting the poor countries. One of the most severe problems is that their food production per capita is actually declining in whole continents, and the specter of hunger on a global scale is very real in a world which has seventy million new mouths to feed every year.

Latin America's food production per capita has actually dropped 7 percent since 1958, and Africa's has declined 6 percent since 1963. Major efforts have to be made to modernize the agriculture of the poor countries, but in the meantime they desperately need to import increasing amounts of food in order to buy time. Their need for food from the United States and other food-exporting countries is certain to be greater than ever before until they can win the battle of production on their own farms.

These hard facts obviously do not lend themselves to any easy or rapid solution. So long as the Vietnam war continues, moreover, it would be unrealistic to think that the United States could address itself meaningfully to a program of the scope and scale required. But we certainly can and should mount an adequate holding operation while we think through a new policy and program capable of grappling with this enormous challenge in the long run.

The alternative is to watch three-quarters of the world sink even deeper into stagnation, frustration and shattered hopes of the kind which breed despair and political chaos.

Our hardheaded objectives, I submit, should be twofold: (1) to strengthen the peace of the world and the security of our own country by helping the poor nations develop their economies at a rhythm and in a manner which most contribute to political and social stability and (2) by aiding their development, thereby also to stimulate the growth of expanding markets for American products.

These are the hardheaded reasons, and any nation must invoke them in policy matters. But I submit that there is another important reason of which we need not be ashamed. Our consciences, our Judeo-Christian ethic, our generous impulses, our heartache at the sight of human suffering—these are profoundly part of the American character which can and should enter into play.

At the time of the Marshall Plan, though the arguments mustered before Congress were largely those of self-interest, the deep impulse of the American people was one of wanting to help, far more than any hardheaded calculation. And seldom has a generous instinct been more profoundly right. There is no prouder or more successful accomplishment in American history than the Marshall Plan, conceived with great vision and executed with remarkable energy.

Today, the new challenge will call for at least as much vision, and for a great deal more energy over a much longer period of time. But it is essential that we address ourselves to it without delay.

Let me suggest a few guidelines that will be required to cope with the problem:

1. The United States should take the lead in mobilizing the wealthy industrialized nations to make a major and sustained assault on world poverty.

2. The wealthy nations should allocate an adequate amount of capital to provide the mainspring of the effort; a minimum of one percent of their gross national product to start, working up to 1.5 percent in five years and 2 percent in ten years.

3. The best instruments for channeling such funds are multilateral; organizations like the International Development Organization, the Inter-American Development Bank and the Asian

Development Bank are not only capable of administering such a flow, but they can do so without the political complications which too often mitigate the value of bilateral aid.

4. Finally, a special effort will be needed, in the framework of an overall program, to help feed the people of the poor nations on an adequate scale until their own agriculture can reach a greatly enhanced level of productivity.

These investments in a farsighted economic-development program will provide far more real security for the United States than much larger sums spent in military action in Vietnam or in many potential Vietnam-type tragedies which are now festering around the globe.

Instead of being frustrated by bands of hungry guerrillas in wars which we will almost certainly lose politically and morally even if we "win" militarily, let us tackle an enemy where we lead from strength. The war for humanity both at home and abroad is the right war for America to lead. It is a war where there need be no losers—a war aimed at victory for all mankind.

I I I

American
Economy

ASSUMPTIONS

*America's economic institutions are compatible with her free
political institutions. In practice this means a system of free enterprise, grounded on private ownership of property and subject
only to a necessary minimum of governmental regulation.*

*America's economic success may be taken as proof of the de-
sirability of its economic system.*

KENNETH E. BOULDING

America's Economy: The Qualified Uproarious Success

> "The mere fact that capitalism has been economically successful . . . is not a necessary guarantee that it will continue to be legitimate."

The American economy, says the eminent economist Kenneth Boulding, can only be described as an uproarious success. But that is not quite the same thing as saying that the ways in which we habitually characterize it are accurate or that it is as nearly perfect as it might be or that its form cannot change for the worse. Indeed, the very success of our economy may be one of the most dangerous things about it. And in order to understand how this may be true, says Professor Boulding, the first thing we must do is clear our minds of cant.

T HE ASSUMPTIONS listed at the beginning of this section reflect a vague sentiment that many people still feel about the American economy. But as useful descriptions of the reality, these assumptions are nearly worthless. They are worth little, too, as guide lines for the future, for in addition to being unspecific, they contain implications which we could accept uncritically only at our peril. There are, at present, ambiguities about the national economy that may be of the most fundamental importance, yet about which the old assumptions tell us next to nothing. It is vital, therefore, that we try to understand the real nature of our economic system without reference to slogans and that we try to anticipate as objectively as possible which current tendencies might develop into major problems.

The American economy is a segment of the total condition and activity of about 200,000,000 people residing within the geographic limits of the United States, plus a rather ill-defined set of activities of Americans residing abroad and of American organizations operating abroad. The first task in describing the American economy is to define the boundary that separates the economy from the other aspects of the total society. There is no absolutely clear line of division between what is inside the economy and what is outside of it. A rough division can be made, however, between those conditions and activities which are governed primarily by exchange and those which are governed by other relationships such as threat, fear, love, hate, identification and so on. Just as economics is the study of how society is organized through exchange, the economy is that segment of the total social system in which exchange predominates. It consists, therefore, in those activities that are directed either toward the production or use of exchangeables or toward the act of exchange itself. Because of the fact that by far the greater part of exchanges either have money as one of the exchangeables, or have exchangeables that can be measured in terms of money, it is only a slight poetic exaggeration to say that the American economy is everything which is stamped with a dollar sign either actually or potentially.

We begin describing the American economy, therefore, with the concept of the stock of objects which can be valued in terms of dollars. This is sometimes called real capital. It consists of the houses, automobiles, clothing, food stocks, inventories, factories, machines and so on which dot the landscape so plentifully. The total value of this stock is not regularly calculated but it may be estimated as between two and three trillion dollars. When we contemplate the capital stock we immediately run into a curious paradox. In the accounting system the capital stock does not ordinarily include people, especially in a non-slave society. Occasionally a human life is valued, as when a jury sets a sum of dollars as compensation for the loss of a breadwinner. Ordinarily, however, we do not put the dollar stamp on the capital value of a person, although we do on his income. Logically, however, the bodies and the minds of the human population are just as much part of the capital stock as the cows, sheep and machines; and the economy certainly cannot be understood without them. Indeed, some of the difficulties of the American economy arise because of the fact that whereas we have an elaborate and rather accurate accounting system for nonhuman capital, the accounting system for human capital is very imperfect. In understanding the American economy, we must realize that the capital value which a man has inalienably in his own body and mind usually exceeds by far the material capital that he works with, even though no dollar figure is usually put on it. Nobody has ever dared to put a figure on the total value of human capital, but under very modest assumptions it could very easily turn out to be from five to ten times the physical capital; yet it usually does not appear anywhere in our accounting systems.

As we turn from the stock of capital to the flow of income we pass from an area of surprising ignorance to an area of knowledge which at least in the past generation has become reasonably broad. The capital stock of both material and human capital has a "throughput." At one end it is consumed—that is, destroyed—by eating it; by wearing it out; by the sheer passage of time with moth, rust and decay; and through forgetting, aging and death. In order to maintain, and still more in order to increase, the capital stock, there must be *production*—that is, additions to the stock through building, weaving, tailoring, farming and through people being born and educated. The first, and almost the last, principle of economics is what I have elsewhere irreverently called the bathtub theorem: that the difference between production (what is added to the stock) minus consumption (what is subtracted from the stock) must be equal to the addition to the stock if these concepts are properly defined. One can divide production into *maintenance* and *investment*. Maintenance is the process by which consumption is simply replaced. These are the processes of homeostasis by which the erosion of the soil is replaced by adding fertilizer, by which the decay of buildings is replaced by repairs, and in which the cooling and tissue loss of the human body is replaced by eating and drinking. Production over and above maintenance is investment, which adds to the stock, whether of human population or of material capital. In the course of maintenance the stock can also be transformed. As housing decays, for instance, we do not merely replace it as it was before; we rebuild it in a new form. Similarly, horses are replaced by automobiles and clerks by computers.

National income accounts give us a great deal of information about the nature and dimensions of the processes of production and consumption, although they are often tantalizingly incomplete. Thus in 1966 the gross national product was about $743,-000,000,000 and for 1967 the preliminary figure is $785,000,-000. To understand the meaning of a figure like this, we first divide it by the population—now almost exactly 200,000,000. This arithmetic reveals immediately that the gross national product per capita is now about $3,900 a year at current prices. Not all of this is available as personal income. From the $785,000,-000,000 gross national product in 1967 we deduct capital consumption (67 billion dollars) and some indirect and direct taxes and transfers to get national income (650); more additions and subtractions give us personal income (626); subtracting personal taxes (82) gives us disposable personal income (545), of which we spend for consumption, expenditures, interest paid back by consumers, plus a few minor items, about $506,000,000,000. This still means that the average American has about $2,700 a year to dispose of, or nearly $11,000 for a family of four.

As an average this looks like a pretty good performance, whether we compare it with the past or with other economies around the world. In terms of the past, if we use per capita disposable income as the most significant measure of economic welfare, this has about doubled since 1929. We might say roughly that it has doubled in forty years. If we take out the Great Depression, it has doubled in less than thirty years, that is, in about a generation. A society in which the children are twice as rich as the parents is obviously not doing too badly. By comparison with other countries, the United States is, of course, the richest country in the world by almost any standards. Per capita disposable income even in Northern Europe, Canada and Australia—which are its closest competitors—tends to be about half what it is in the United States. In the socialist countries, per capita disposable income is probably about a third; and in the poor countries of the tropical belt, per capita disposable income is about one-twentieth of the United States level. Economically the United States can only be described as an uproarious success. If what follows sounds mainly critical, it has to be interpreted against this background of overall success.

Averages, of course, can be very misleading. We must look beyond a figure like that of per capita real income to the structure of the economy both in time and in space before it can be properly evaluated. In time, the critical problem is growth. There is a very fundamental principle of nature which states that everything is what it is because it got that way; in other words, we must look at the history of a structure before we can really understand it. If some countries have per capita real income of $100 a year and others of $2,500, this must be a result of a difference in their history. Rich countries are rich simply because they have been getting richer at a sufficiently rapid rate for a sufficiently long time. If we think of the process of "getting rich" as a process whereby per capita real income doubles in a certain period of years, it takes about five or six doublings to give us the difference between the poorest countries with about $50 per capita per annum and the richer countries with over $1,600. The doublings go $50, $100, $200, $400, $800, $1,600. With the kind of development which has characterized the successful countries in the

147

last hundred and fifty years, this has amounted roughly to a doubling of the per capita income every generation. A country that can keep this up for six or seven generations will end up being as rich as the United States is now, even if it starts from the barest subsistence. One of the most important questions about the United States economy, therefore, is why it has been subject to *sustained* growth over such a long period of time, for it is only this sustained growth which has made it as rich as it is now.

It is much easier to state this question than to answer it. Sustained growth at the doubling-every-generation rate has not on the whole been characteristic of human society. It is something, indeed, which has only come into existence in the last hundred and fifty or two hundred years. It is not just a matter of geographical expansion or increase in population; these will account for increase in the total product but not necessarily increase in the product per head. If we ask ourselves what element in society is capable of sustained growth of this kind, only one answer can be given: human knowledge. The growth of the United States economy, therefore, as with other successful economies, is primarily a result of the fact that the total social system encouraged the growth of human knowledge and the application of new knowledge to the techniques of production. Historically, we can distinguish at least two stages in this process. The first is the period before about 1860 when most of the new knowledge which was applied to economic life was what might be called "folk knowledge," the sort of thing one thinks of as "Yankee ingenuity." After 1860, we begin to see the science-based industries— chemical, electrical and, of course, in the twentieth century, the nuclear industry—which are based on the wide expansion of knowledge as a result of science. It may be that we are at the beginning of a third stage now with the development of computers and systems analysis, which represents, as it were, the application of the scientific method to the increase of science itself. It is too early, however, to know whether this really constitutes a major long-run acceleration in rate of development.

Another aspect of the position of the American economy in time is its position relative to other nations. At the moment the world can be divided pretty sharply into economically successful countries and economically unsuccessful countries, with the economically successful ones lying mostly in the temperate zone (plus one or two in the Caribbean), and most of the unsuccessful ones lying in the great tropical belt. Among the successful countries the rate of growth depends quite sharply on the existing per capita real income or per capita gross national product, with the poorer countries (like Japan) growing at a more rapid rate than the richer countries. This is not surprising, of course, for any growth process in nature tends to follow a pattern of declining rate of growth with increasing size. A boy that is growing several inches a year in his early teens is not necessarily going to be a giant when he is thirty. In so far as the economically successful countries are all growing in a similar pattern of development, we should expect the poor ones to grow faster than the rich ones.

The long-run effect of this, however, is that the successful countries will all become more similar. If present trends continue, by even the early part of the twenty-first century we should find that almost all the countries in the temperate zone have approximately equal per capita incomes. The world will then have separated out into a rather uniform rich belt around the temperate zone and a poor belt around the tropics. In the tropical countries there seems to be no relationship between the rate of growth and existing income. These countries may be expected to become more diverse, though as average rates of growth are low, they will remain poor.

One of the most striking facts about growth is that latitude seems to be a much more significant variable than the type of economic system. Both the socialist and capitalist countries of the temperate zone are all in the "successful" bracket, so that from this narrow point of view socialism seems to be almost irrelevant.

We should now take a closer look at the internal structure of

149

the American economy, not only because this is important in itself, but also because it may throw some light on the reasons for the success of the economy. The first thing to look at is the distribution of income. A high per capita income, as, for instance, in Kuwait, where statistically the per capita income is almost as great as in the United States, may hide very large inequalities. If income is very unequally distributed, no matter how high the per capita income of the economy, it cannot be given very good marks.

On this score the American economy has an oddly mixed record. On the one hand, it is clear that the American economy has not in the slightest degree followed the Marxist prediction that economic development would simply increase the income of property owners while the working class remained at, or even below, the subsistence level. In terms of the distribution between labor income and property income, the record of the American economy is impressive. The national income statistics themselves do not allow for an exact description of this distribution here, but a rough approximation can be made. At the present time the American economy distributes well over 80 percent of its total income to labor income in some form. By labor income I mean that which is derived from the sale of the activity of human capital. Probably not much more than 15 or 20 percent goes to the owners of material property as such. Thus, even judged by the socialist criterion of how much of an economy's income goes to labor, the American economy compares very favorably with any socialist state—especially when we recall that at any given level of technology, our economy is almost certainly substantially more efficient in producing income than a centrally planned economy. It is not surprising that under these circumstances Marxism has been so unsuccessful in the United States. In so far as it has any validity, it represents a special case which is irrelevant to most of the American pattern. Not only does the American economy return a surprisingly large amount of its income to labor, but historically this proportion has been increasing. It was probably something like 50 percent in the nineteenth century and 70 percent in the mid-twentieth century.

In spite of the success of the American economy in returning income to labor, there is a strange paradox: it has a persistent and intractable problem of poverty at the bottom end of the income distribution. The Bureau of the Census defines a poor family as one with a money income of less than $3,000 in 1966 prices. The proportion of total families that qualify as poor has fallen slowly from about 30 percent in 1947 to 14.3 percent in 1965. The absolute number of poor families, however, has not declined very much. The situation seems to be that while nearly 80 percent of the population—what might be regarded as "middle class" and above—have been increasing their incomes rather sharply, about 20 percent of the population have not been participating in this general increase. Here we have a pattern that is almost a parody of the Marxist model, in which 80 percent are getting richer and 20 percent are staying about where they are. This means that the relative position of the poor has been worsening—relative, that is, to the middle classes. A critical question, therefore, is the extent to which the poor represent a distinct "kith" in society, to use a technical anthropological term. That is, are the children of the poor themselves poor, or are there a fair number who rise out of the poverty and others who correspondingly fall into it? One suspects that in the United States, to a very considerable extent the poor are a "kith" in this sense, and that they do reproduce themselves genetically, if only because of the fact that Negroes and Spanish-Americans are so disproportionately represented in them, as are also poor Southern and Appalachian whites.

We do not really know the *extent* to which a "culture of poverty" exists, in which poverty perpetuates itself from parents to children for generation after generation. In so far as it exists, it is being eroded slowly as the numbers of the poor decline; but we certainly cannot contemplate this situation with any great satisfaction, especially as the poor are concentrated to such an extent in the central cities, the South and Appalachia. What is more, the poor are moving out of the South into the central cities. The social disorganization which results, as reflected in recent riots and burnings, can be attributed in part to a certain failure of the American economy—a failure at least to provide for a uniform rise in per capita incomes among all sections of the people.

The reasons for this partial failure are buried deep in the social structure of American society. One of the reasons, indeed, may lie in the nature of the developmental process itself. Economic development, whether of a whole country or of a segment of a country, is a process which involves profound cultural change. It means especially that the way of life of the children will be profoundly different from that of their parents. On the whole, the family is an institution for perpetuating the way of life and the values of the parents. The parents usually try to instill their way of life in the children, and often succeed in doing so even if they do not try. Cultural change from one generation to the next involves changes in values as well as in knowledge, and changes in values are often perceived as threatening our identity. Development therefore usually requires some agency beyond the family to break into the pattern of transmission of culture from parents to children. This always involves certain psychological costs.

In the United States our main agency of culture change has been the public school. At the level of the bottom 20 percent of the income scale, however, the public school system has not functioned effectively because of the local nature of its finance. Rural schools, Southern schools, Appalachian schools and central-city schools are notoriously below the level of our suburban schools. Thus finance is perhaps the most fundamental reason for this defect in the American economy. We must also recognize that the American problem in regard to public education is more difficult than it is in more homogeneous societies. Culturally the United States is a heterogeneous country with large numbers of cultural, religious and racial minorities. This makes the problem of the "culture of poverty" more intractable than in homogeneous societies such as the Scandinavian countries. Nevertheless, the resources which are needed to solve the problem are quite readily available; what is lacking is the political will and the institutional framework.

This brings us to the next question—that of the organizational structure of the economy. The main characteristic here is one of astonishing diversity if we include, as we must, the economic operations of government. The organizations of the American economy range in size all the way from the United States Department of Defense—which is essentially a planned economy with a gross product larger than that of the People's Republic of China—through a bewildering variety of semipublic and private organizations of all sizes. The gamut runs from General Motors, which has a gross product approximately equal to that of Brazil, down to the independent artisan, the family farm, the corner grocery and the boy with a newspaper route. Oddly enough there is no easily available breakdown of the product of the American economy by size of organization, but it is certainly safe to say that the American economy is dominated by large-scale organizations, both public and private. The largest of these is, of course, the federal government, which accounts for about 11.4 percent of the national product. Of this, about 9 percent is accounted for by the Department of Defense, which stands, therefore, as the largest single economic organization. The largest private corporation, General Motors, has total sales of about a quarter of the budget of the Department of Defense, and accounts for a still smaller proportion of the gross national product. If state and local governments are taken together they are almost as large a proportion of the gross national product (11 percent) as the federal government. This sector however represents a very large number of organizations—fifty states, over 3,000 counties, and about 35,000 townships and municipalities, not to count school districts and special districts of many kinds. The largest of these organizations, the state of California, has a budget of over $6,000,000,000 (only 8 percent of the gross national product).

153

However we look at it, the business of America is still business. Private business still accounts for about three-fourths of the gross national product (74.3 percent). Of the 22 percent or so contributed by government, about one half constitutes "government business," that is, activities of government which are really in the exchange sector of the economy. The contribution of households and farms to the economy is astonishingly small: about 6 percent of the gross national product.

TABLE I

PERCENTAGE OF U.S. GNP CONTRIBUTED BY VARIOUS SECTORS

	1929 (GNP = 103.1 billion)	1967 (GNP = 785.1 billion)
Government Total	8.2	22.5
Federal, Defense	} 1.3	9.3
Federal, Civilian		2.2
State and Local	7.0	11.0
Government (Non-Business)	4.2	10.9
Government (Business)	4.0	11.6
Business, Private	88.2	74.3
Business, Total	92.2	85.9
Business, Non-Farm	82.8	82.8
Business, Farm	9.4	3.1
Households	2.6	2.7
Rest of World	.6	.6

Table I shows these relationships and also shows changes from 1929 to 1967. If we were to characterize what has been going on in the structure of the American economy in this generation, we could summarize it in a single sentence by saying that the resources which have been released by the decline in the farm sector —a result of the extraordinary technological development in agriculture—have been almost entirely absorbed by national defense. In thirty-eight years the proportion of the GNP contributed by farms has fallen from 9.4 percent to 3.1 percent, whereas the proportion absorbed by national defense has risen by an almost equal amount, from something under 1 percent to over 9 percent. If we include government business in the total, non-farm business has hardly changed at all as a proportion of the gross national product, although government business has increased substantially. These figures throw considerable light on whether the United States is suffering from (or enjoying) "creeping socialism." It is pretty clear that the only place that socialism has crept very far in the United States is in the Department of Defense, which is, of course, the socialist organization next to the Soviet Union in size. Nevertheless, the private sector still dominates the American economy quantitatively.

Quantity, to be sure, is not everything. Qualitatively these figures unquestionably hide an increased role of government in the American economy. The Great Depression of the 1930's was a deeply traumatic experience for American business—indeed for the whole American society. It represented a massive failure for the existing system, a failure represented in quantitative terms, for instance, by a decline in the real national product by 30 percent in four years (1929–1933). This seemed like utterly meaningless poverty in the midst of plenty. The decline, furthermore, was very unequally distributed; and it was the productive members of the population who were particularly hard hit, both profit makers and the labor force. In the face of this massive failure of the Great Depression, the surprising thing is that so little structural change has taken place in the American economy. That little, however, has had a great effect, especially in the acceptance by government, in the Full Employment Act of 1946, of the responsibility for maintaining a reasonable stability in the economy. The success of this policy in the last twenty years unquestionably restored confidence in the existing system. If we want to devise a phrase to describe the American economy as it exists today, we could very well describe it as "Cybernetic Capitalism": a predominantly market type of private-property, private-enterprise economy, in which government plays an essential stabilizing role.

It now seems clear that the Great Depression, traumatic as it was, acted as a kind of shock treatment for American society. It broke it out of a box of complacency and put it onto a new track of development. In retrospect, indeed, the American economy in the generation before 1932 seems flabby and unprogressive. Per capita disposable income was not rising very fast, if at all. Our agricultural technology was relatively stagnant. The business cycle, even before the Great Depression, was a very serious problem. Social technology was primitive, there was little social insurance and old age and unemployment created unnecessarily severe hazards for large masses of the population. By contrast, from 1932 on, productivity in agriculture has increased spectacularly at nearly 6 percent per annum, social technology has undoubtedly improved and the business cycle has become a relatively minor element.

While a mood of mild self-congratulation seems to be in order, therefore, this mood should not divert us into neglecting the still unsolved problems of the American economy and the difficulties which it may run into in the future. Some of these have already been noted. For example, there has been the failure of the economy and its developmental process to reach the bottom 10 or 20 percent of the income distribution. This may well be the most serious of the unsolved problems. Nevertheless it is not the only one.

Another, the cumulative effect of which may be quite frightening, is the apparent inability of the American economy to achieve a satisfactory level of employment without running into a certain amount of wage and price inflation. In the fifties the fear of inflation dominated the policy makers, and we paid for this fear by a level of employment and operation of the economy which was too low to be satisfactory, though in no sense as disastrous as the Great Depression. On the whole, the level of unemployment in the fifties ranged about 6 percent of the labor force. If we take 3 percent as at least something to shoot at, representing what might be called reasonable capacity operation, this is a loss of about 3 percent of the product each year. Over a generation this amounts to a whole year's national product. In so far as the deflationary bias of the decision makers—the federal government and the Federal Reserve banks—discriminated against investment, the cost may be even greater in terms of growth. It comes as a shock to many Americans to learn that in the 1950's over forty-five countries had a higher rate of growth in per capita gross national product than the United States! It is a little unkind to call this the "Eisenhower stagnation," for the stagnation was only relative; but the implied criticism is not wholly unjust. Furthermore, the basic problem is still unsolved. It seems clear that even when unemployment gets down to 4 percent, there is a pretty sharp upward pressure on the wage-price structure. Surprisingly little effort has gone into thinking about this problem, even on the part of the economics profession. The most constructive suggestion, indeed, has come from Gardiner Means, who has proposed a discriminatory tax on rising money incomes, when the rise is a result of price or wage increases rather than a result of increased production or productivity.

The problem in a nutshell is that while it is fairly easy, especially through fiscal measures, to manipulate the money value of the gross national product, if the increase in the money value is a result of price increases, there may be no—or insufficient—change in the real product in which we are really interested. The problem then is how to create an adequate level of effective demand and at the same time prevent money, wages and prices from rising. The difficulty here is that there seems to be no way of controlling the general level of prices and wages without controlling individual prices and wages. Individual price and wage control, however, is anathema—and rightly so—in the American economy. It can be suffered only in times of extreme national emergency, for the administrative inefficiencies of any price and wage control system are so great that they could not be tolerated in reasonably normal times.

Another aspect of the American economy which gives cause for reasonable concern is the rise in the national defense sector which we have previously noted. This has implications for all aspects of American life. It has risen *not* primarily in response to economic needs or motivations, but mainly in response to threats from the rest of the world, especially, of course, from the socialist countries. There has also been a change in the national image itself—toward militarism and "national greatness," and away from isolationism and a modest appraisal of the national role in the international system. Whatever the reasons, the impact on the economy has been profound. There is indeed a military-industrial complex, against which President Eisenhower warned the country in his farewell address. The rise of the war industry is undoubtedly the most striking single change in the structure of the American economy in the past generation. It has consequences for the labor movement, for the educational system, for family life and especially for the young who are its principle victims. These consequences go far beyond the more than 9 percent of the economy which it absorbs. If we are not careful, it can become a cancer within American society. It represents an ethic, a state of mind and even a form of organization which is sharply at variance with the business tradition and the civilian culture of the society. It is ironic that we may be in danger of the same type of business-military alliance which essentially overthrew the business system in Nazi Germany. In fact, militarism in the United States is a greater threat to the business system than socialism. Businessmen seem singularly unaware of the essential inconsistency in their support of militarism.

There is a widespread myth in American society that it is only military expenditure which preserves prosperity and prevents us from having a great depression. This myth is widespread in both the business community and the labor movement. Like all myths, it has some foundations in the empirical world; the belief that it was Hitler that got us out of the Great Depression has some elements of truth in it. As our understanding of the economy increases, however, we should have growing confidence in our ability to insure full employment even when the level of the war industry is much less. If we compare the structure of the American economy in the 1920's with the structure today, we see that one of the major differences is the rise in the war industry and the fall in consumption as a proportion of the gross national product. The war industry, as we have seen, has risen from less than one percent to over 9 percent. Consumption expenditures by contrast have fallen from about 75 percent of the gross national product in 1929 to 63 percent today. The "bite" of the war industry comes almost wholly out of personal consumption. If the reconstruction of the international system permitted us to reduce the war industry to the 1929 level, with the application of our existing skills in fiscal and monetary policy to preserve full employment, American consumers would be about 15 percent better off. The view that the war industry creates prosperity can therefore only be described as an illusion.

From the point of view of long-run development, the situation may be even more serious, because the war industry absorbs a much larger proportion of what might be called the "growth resource" in the economy than the 9 to 10 percent which is absorbed out of the gross national product. There is indeed a "brain drain" internally into the war industry which is severely affecting the technical development of the civilian segment of the economy.

In taking a final long look at the American economy we must ask ourselves, "What are the underlying conditions in the total social system which are likely to affect its future?" We will confine ourselves here to two problems, both of them, however, of overwhelming importance when it comes to the future. The first concerns the kind of people which the society produces. At least three or four times in a century a new generation takes over the conduct of affairs. The people who are operating the American economy today will nearly all be dead or retired fifty years from now, and a completely new set of people will have taken over. This transference of culture from one generation to the next dominates the history of mankind. We noticed it earlier in the problem of the "culture of poverty." It may be a problem in a different sense for the "culture of wealth," for the culture of those who are economically most active and who comprise what is rather inaccurately called the "middle class." These are people characterized in a greater or lesser degree by a certain type of personality. They tend to be energetic, achievement-oriented, hard-working, with a strong image of the future and much activity directed toward the future. They are interested in economic calculation. They make decisions by some kind of cost-benefit analysis, however informal, and consequently they count cost; they ask for rewards, they save and invest. These are people dominated by what Max Weber called, rather unfortunately, the "Protestant ethic" (it has, in fact, been characteristic of American Jews and Catholics, and doubtless of many Japanese, for that matter), and which I prefer to call the "economic ethic."

The dynamic and developmental quality of the American economy has, for a number of generations, been the result primarily of the fact that the society produced the economic type of personality in large numbers, not only among those who went into business, but also in the labor force. Societies which do not produce this type of personality find economic development very difficult.

Among American young people today another type of personality seems to be on the increase. There is no very good name for this. We might simply call it the "non-economic" personality. This type is represented in its most extreme forms by the hippies, but one perceives it also among more conventional types. It is reflected in an increasing tendency, especially among able young people, to go into the professions rather than into business in general and the large corporations in particular. Whether this is a passing fad or whether it is the beginning of change in the character of American society, is too early to say. Nevertheless, it is clear that something is happening, and the future of the American economy depends a great deal on what it is. The personalities of adults are produced on the whole from childhood experiences. If, for example, there is any radical change in methods of childrearing, we may expect to find this reflected in the adult character of the population of the next generation. But of course early childhood experiences are not the sole source of adult character. There are also profound changes going on in school and adolescent experiences. How important this is quantitatively nobody knows, but it is about time somebody found out. We might be making a great mistake in projecting the habits and the character of the past generation into the future.

Somewhat related to this is a wide range of questions involved in what might be called the dynamics of legitimacy. Unless an institution can retain legitimacy both in the minds of those who operate it and in the minds of those who constitute its environment, it cannot survive. Legitimacy is intimately related to success, both in relation to power (threat capability) and wealth (exchange capability). Nevertheless, power and wealth do not create their own legitimacy, and the relationships are often unexpected. Thus the threat of socialism to capitalism is a threat to its legitimacy and to very little else. The mere fact that capitalism has been economically successful, as it has been in the United States, is not a necessary guarantee that it will continue to be legitimate. Within limits, failure and trauma often do more for legitimacy than success. The Great Depression, for instance, far from its shaking the belief of the American in his own system, reinforced that belief simply because the whole society had gone through a disastrous experience together. The very sacrifices involved may have reinforced belief in the system. Success might, therefore, possibly be more dangerous to capitalism than a certain amount of failure.

These are very tricky questions, and at the moment we certainly do not have any satisfactory answers. They must be asked, however, if only to prepare us for possible surprises. At times, though not always, it has been at the height of its success that an institution has suddenly lost its legitimacy and disintegrated. The very success of the American economy may be a reason for increased caution about the future. It is never safe to take the future for granted, least of all when one is successful.

161

ELSPETH DAVIES ROSTOW

The Political Economy of Partnership

> "The central characteristic of our political economy . . . is partnership."

Political systems imply congruent economic systems. Totalitarian governments have an affinity for statist economics and pure democracy would seem to call for an economy based on free competition. But terms such as "free enterprise," says Elspeth Rostow, no more accurately characterize the American economy than "pure democracy" describes our form of government. Our economic and political systems do, in fact, closely complement one another; and to understand either, it is necessary to understand the reality on which both are based.

FROM THE DAYS when Hamilton first challenged Jefferson's agrarian laissez-faire to our own time when Mr. Galbraith throws down his Veblenesque gauntlet before his theorist colleagues in Cambridge, Americans have debated about their economy. They have debated both about what it is and about what it should be.

Perhaps the most commonplace generalization about the nature of our economy is to speak of it in terms of "free markets" and "free competition." Or, as an economist might put it, "the best first approximation to an understanding of our economy is the atomistic competitive model."

In the face of this proposition critics took up their positions, some insisting that the economy is neither as atomistic nor as competitive as it should be, and others, contrarily, that atomistic competition cannot solve this or that specific national problem. From these two sides flowed prescriptions that public policy intervene in quite specific ways to correct either imperfections or inadequacies in the competitive system.

A great deal of American political history can be summarized in terms of the ramifications of this debate:

—Should we have free trade or tariffs?

—Should the federal government finance "internal improvements" (they would be called "social overheads" today)?

—Should there be slavery or freedom for the Negro?

—Should the federal government finance transcontinental railways, agricultural and technical universities and the diffusion of modern technology?

—Should the federal government control the railways and other inherent monopolies?

—Should the federal government control the central banking system?

—Should federal policy reflect the theorists' propositions about the diminishing relative marginal utility of money; that is, should we have a progressive income tax?

—Should federal legislation recognize the legitimacy of collective bargaining?

—Should the federal government assume responsibility for maintaining relatively full employment?

—Should the federal government subsidize health, education and housing for the less advantaged and structurally unemployed —and if so, by how much?

These familiar questions simply reflect the fact that we have passed through various stages of growth since 1787; each stage has thrown up characteristic economic and social problems; and we have grappled with those problems through our democratic political institutions as well as through the market mechanism. We have voted our tastes and judgments in both the market-place and at the ballot box—which is not surprising. Tariff policy and the scale of government investment in social overhead capital is an almost inevitable staple of politics in pre-industrial or early industrial societies, past and present.

As industrialization proceeded and the opening of the West tempted the North and threatened the South, we faced a unique passage in the struggle over slavery, which in strictly economic terms represented a gross distortion in a free labor market as well as, on a higher level, a violation of human freedom. (Earlier European struggles over the mobility of the peasant and the Russian freeing of the serfs belong in the same family of problems.)

At the end of the nineteenth century, industrial maturity brought with it the inevitable question of controlling the monopolistic and quasi-monopolistic institutions which the new technology fostered or made possible.

As men came to take advanced industrialization for granted, in the United States as in other nations, the political majority was prepared to balance its imperatives with legislation limiting hours of work and providing social security. The price was the revolutionary principle of progressive taxation of incomes. Many segments in a society based on high mass consumption revolted against the waste imposed by cycles in income and employment and were prepared to accept a wide range of indirect manipulations designed to sustain the rate of growth and the levels of real income and employment.

Like geological layers in a rock formation, this sequence of problems, the debates and their resolution, left their mark on contemporary national life, policy and institutions.

Setting aside any question of "should be" for a moment, what is our economy actually like today? The truth, of course, is that it is difficult, in any dogmatic terms to describe the structure of American political economy at a time when our society has these characteristics: (1) a gross national product moving toward $800,000,000,000, and a median family income of $7,000. Simultaneously, 16 percent of U.S. families with total money income of less than $3,000; voting, in the marketplace and by the ballot box, for rapid increases in education, health, the modernization of the cities and social justice for the poor and disadvantaged; (2) at the same time, in external affairs, the greatest power in an interdependent and contending world; and an engagement of something like 10 percent of our gross national product in military expenditures and assistance to other nations.

Yet one thing is increasingly clear: the central characteristic of our political economy, at home and abroad, is that of partnership, defined as voluntary agreements among legally independent units to achieve shared goals.

Since the mid-1950's, the pressure for expanded education, health and welfare expenditures has fallen, in the first instance, on state and local governments. Their disproportionate expansion has marked our society since that time; expenditures of states and localities have expanded from 8.5 percent to 11 percent of national output in the past decade. And because of the limited tax capacity of state and local governments, there has been a remarkable expansion in federal grants to the states, producing a new level of intensity and sophistication in the whole federal network of political life.

But the partnership goes beyond the heightened relations between Washington, the state capitals and the cities. The bringing in of Medicare, for example, required the linkage of federal policy and action to the private medical community of the nation, as well as to the intimate operation of hospitals at every level.

The expansion of expenditure on education in all its forms (with federal expenditures alone increasing at more than 15 percent a year) has woven a new fabric of voluntary collaboration between central government and educational institutions, public and private. Some have called the political innovations of the sixties "creative federalism"; the phrase is well chosen.

Similarly, the task of reconstructing the cities of the nation has forced a collaboration between federal, state and local government, on the one hand, and the leaders of the local communities, their educational institutions, insurance companies, etc., on the other. And so also with many aspects of the poverty program.

In an earlier time, when the economy's frontier was, typically, the progressive diffusion of the automobile, mass distribution of durable consumer's goods and the personal acquisition of a suburban house, the private enterprise sector could virtually carry the load. But when society self-consciously turned to improve its quality, taking its gadgetry largely for granted, its public and private institutions inevitably became engaged in new enterprises.

Typical of such enterprises are the massive and costly complexes that have arisen to sustain our military and space programs. These, in effect, are networks of intimate public-private cooperation. The same is true of foreign aid. It has been calculated, for example, that in addition to the flow of federal assistance to Latin America under the Alliance for Progress, "private" assistance from U.S. foundations, universities, church groups, states, cities, etc., reached a level something like $200,000,000 a year in 1965.

By the same token, the pragmatic partnerships mounted between public and private institutions at home to deal with the nation's problems have a counterpart in the international community. Within the past year, for example, several quite revolutionary adventures in partnership were launched: the Asian Development Bank, in which the U.S. capital share is a uniquely low 20 percent; the mobilization of resources from a dozen nations to deal with the second successive Indian drought; the agreement to create an international reserve unit to supplement gold; the Kennedy Round of tariff negotiations.

How, then, does this kind of partnership society—its private market mechanism hedged about with all manner of restraining or guiding forces, from tariffs to rent supplements, and evolving endless new variations of voluntary public-private collaboration —differ from socialist economies?

166

The first difference is, of course, that private ownership of the means of production and distribution still prevails. Despite the complexities of the modern corporate structure, this diffusion of power and authority is a central fact of our society.

Second—as a practical matter—none of the nations under Communist regimes has yet reached average levels of income which open the same possibilities and pose quite the same problems as those faced by the United States. The agricultural population of the Soviet Union is still more than 40 percent of the total; in the U.S., it is less than 6 percent. The Soviet Union and Eastern Europe may be on the eve of a mass diffusion of automobiles and durable consumer's goods, but the revolution has not yet occurred. Although these societies are moving out from the phase of heavy-industry domination, they have by no means adjusted to requirements of efficient production and distribution of modern consumer's goods and the consonant development of services.

The fundamental differences between the management of the American and Communist economies can be stated in general terms in the form of three propositions, all of which stem in one way or another from the basic differences between democratic capitalism and socialist one-party control.

First, of course, the Communist states are only slowly and painfully moving toward a relatively free pricing system, responsive to cost and demand. All manner of imperfections of competition, subsidies and taxes contribute impurities to the American price system; nevertheless, voting in the marketplace is so much more free here as to constitute a qualitative difference.

Second, the American economy, like American society, is made up of thousands of centers where people make those substantial public and private decisions that are rooted in the diffuse ownership of property. The centers for decision are far narrower in the Communist states.

Finally, and most fundamentally, the distribution of treasure between public and private expenditures, as well as its distribution among alternative public expenditures, is governed by a one-man, one-vote political process in the U.S., whereas it is determined by a self co-opting dictatorial leadership in Communist regimes. Those regimes may respond increasingly to pressures arising from public opinion, but there are no elected representatives of the people to create the tax system or pass on the national budget.

It is precisely these three differences which are now the focus of debate in Communist nations as they face the next phase of their development. It is becoming clear, for example, that a rational price system in itself does not solve the problems of stagnation or sluggishness in Communist economies—managerial skills and incentives are at least equally important; but the granting of the incentives and the freedom of action required to obtain efficiency seriously undercut fundamental social and political characteristics of a Communist regime.

Similarly, in the most advanced of the revisionist Communist states, Yugoslavia, the effort to move toward an efficient, modern economy is posing such searching questions as, what role, if any, does a Communist party have, and how does one move toward an alternative political framework if the Communist party is permitted to wither? One can be fairly confident that these questions will increasingly emerge elsewhere in the Communist world.

It is indeed true that the manager of a Soviet factory, or a Soviet teacher, has concerns, problems and objectives which are recognizably similar to those of their opposite numbers in the West. But the framework within which these counterparts operate remains radically different. Neither the complexities of the West nor transitional change in the East has yet washed out the simple basic differences between regimes of democracy and dictatorship.

Is our kind of system better than those of Communist states? The short answer—by conventional statistical measures—is yes. But one must take account of the fact that our industrialization, as well as that of other democratic societies of the West, began earlier than in Russia and most of the countries of Eastern Europe. Levels of economic and social welfare are related to the length of time since the beginning of takeoff and are related also to the building of compound interest into a society's institutions —including the capacity to save and to absorb modern science and technology.

Besides, the United States, with its abundant land and relatively modest population, has been the golden boy of economic history since the eighteenth century. High wages and a big market made us go straight for the best technology available.

But almost certainly the longer and more complex answer is also yes. By the values of most men, as they are being revealed with the unfolding of history, including the history of Communist societies, systems of diffuse power and authority, where the citizen can vote effectively both by the ballot box and the marketplace, are being judged superior to those where Father Knows Best (or pretends to do so). If such systems are to work, they require not only diffused power, but a widely diffused sense of communal responsibility.

These, surely, have been the dominant tendencies in the evolution of America's political economy. It has been a pragmatic evolution, piecemeal, dealing more or less directly with specific problems, never at any given moment corresponding wholly to anyone's ideal model of what it should be. Doubtless that is why it has always been so eminently debatable. But, to an extraordinary degree, history has confirmed both the propriety of our system's evolutionary tendencies and its great adaptability to further change.

The verdict of the foreseeable future appears to lie with an American political economy of partnership, reconciling diffused power and common purposes, freedom and responsibility.

HOWARD ZINN

The Politics of
the American Economy

"To judge ourselves by the rational and
human use of our resources, we are a
failure."

*As Kenneth Boulding has pointed out, the American economy
has encountered a "persistent and intractable problem" in its
inability to give approximately 20 percent of the population a
proportionate share in the increase of our national wealth. Professor Howard Zinn considers this our major domestic problem
and here suggests both why we have failed to solve it and what
we may yet do about it.*

W E O F T H E American illuminati have been extrava-
gantly, almost obsequiously, grateful for the New Deal
and its successors—from Truman's Fair Deal to Johnson's Great
Society. This gratitude has several sources: our failure to see to
what extent war and preparations for war have kept our economy
flowing; the carbohydrate prosperity of that class in the population—the middle class—which verbalizes gratitude best; the
drugged silence of the TV-watching, beer-drinking politically
cynical poor. There is also the continued refusal to see the world
as one, so that we toast our economy while two-thirds of the
world's people starve under the drone of tourist charter flights,
and some die in the explosions of our surfeit.

It is instructive to look at the New Deal and then at the Great Society and then back and forth again quickly, because the two rubbed together bring a small flash of understanding where separately they just shine dully, pleasingly. True, these are the 1960's (prosperity) and those were the 1930's (depression). But somehow, now as then, some among us live very high, and some live very low, and there is a chronic malaise—of lost opportunities and wasted wealth—in the economic air. Now, as then, in the distance (both very far and very near) there are tiny, incomprehensible cries that disturb.

The New Deal left unsolved—as the Great Society is about to leave unsolved—the major domestic problem (major because it is also the crux of the Negro's resentment) of our time. That is: how to bring the blessings of immense natural wealth and staggering productive potential to every person in the land. Also unsolved is the political corollary of that problem: how to organize ordinary people to convey to national leadership something more subtle than the wail of crisis. How can one (or rather, many) transform into a political fist the day-to-day ache felt, between emergencies, in garbage-strewn slums, crowded schools, grimy bus stations, overloaded hospital wards, Negro ghettos, rural shacks—the environment of tens of millions of Americans clawing for subsistence in the richest country in the world?

This is not to deny that the New Dealers were articulate, humane and on occasion profound. Their ideas fathered an unprecedented body of welfare legislation, and pulled the nation from the edge of economic disaster. Without clearly defined goals beyond getting over the depression, they found themselves creating new laws and institutions: the Tennessee Valley Authority, the social-security system, farm subsidies, minimum wage standards, labor relations boards, public housing. The New Deal refurbished middle-class America, restored jobs to the jobless and gave just enough to the lowest classes to create an aura of good will.

But when the reform energies of the New Deal began to wane,

171

around 1939, the nation was back to its normal state: a permanent army of unemployed; a poverty-ridden twenty or thirty million people effectively blocked from public view by a huge, prosperous, consuming middle-class; a tremendously efficient and wasteful productive apparatus—efficient because it could produce limitless supplies of what it decided to produce, wasteful because what it decided to produce was determined not by usefulness to society, but by profitability for business. That, we recognize with some reluctance, is a description of our nation in 1968, the Fair Deal, New Frontier and Great Society notwithstanding.

The word "pragmatic" has been used, perhaps more often than any other, to describe the experimentalism of the Roosevelt administration—the improvisation, the absence of long-range programs or theoretical commitments. Pragmatism, however, is a method; and experimentation can be guided by a variety of social goals. Understanding is better served by an inquiry into ends: in what direction is government willing to experiment? What goals, what ideals, what expectations direct its course? How far will it go?

New Deal measures were directed toward preventing depression, helping the poor, curbing ruthless business practices; and Roosevelt's speeches often had the flavor of a moral crusade. But F.D.R.'s aims were not sharply enough defined to prevent his shifting from one policy to another: from constant promises to balance the budget to large-scale spending in emergencies; from an attempt to reconcile business and labor interests in the National Recovery Act to belated support for the pro-labor Wagner Act; from special concern for the tenant farmer in the Resettlement Administration to generous price supports for the large commercial farmer in the Agricultural Adjustment Act of 1938.

The experimentalism of the New Deal, in short, had its limits: up to those limits, Roosevelt's social concern was genuine, his political courage huge, his generous spirit unfailing; beyond them, his driving force weakened. In 1938, with the nation out of the

worst of the depression, with the skeletal structure of social reform on the statute books, and with that year's congressional
elections showing a sudden waning of political approbation, the
Roosevelt program slid to a close. It left a mountain of accomplishment behind; and ahead, mountains still unclimbed. Many
millions—businessmen and professionals, unionized working-
men, commercial farmers—had been given substantial help.
Many millions more—sharecroppers, slum-dwellers, Negroes
North and South, the unemployed—still awaited a genuine
"new deal." The goals of the New Deal did not, in fact, much
exceed the restoration of the traditional structure of the American economy.

But why were the expectations of the New Deal so limited?
Why didn't the New Dealers simply declare that the government would *continue* spending, experimenting and expanding
public enterprise until no one was unemployed, until slums were
gone, until no family received below-subsistence income, until
adequate medical care was available to all, until anyone who
wanted it could get a college education? There were—and are—
political obstacles to such a program; but is not the first step
toward overcoming the obstacles an open avowal of the objectives?

Part of the answer, I think, is that humanitarianism can go
only so far in the redistribution of privilege; self-interest must
carry it further. In 1933 Paul Douglas, then an economics professor at the University of Chicago, wrote prophetically:

> Along with the Rooseveltian program must go . . . the
> organization of those who are at present weak and who
> need to acquire that which the world respects, namely,
> power. . . . Unless these things are done, we are likely
> to find the permanent benefits of Rooseveltian liberal-
> ism to be as illusory as were those of the Wilsonian era.

The groups that did organize—the larger farm operators, the several million industrial workers who joined the CIO—improved

their position significantly. The aged, with a push from the Townsend Movement, got a bit of help. But many others—tenant farmers, the unemployed, the service and domestic workers (that is, mostly Negroes)—were left behind. Reform from the top is humane but disinterested, and thus limited.

If it is only the underprivileged who can supply the driving force for a sharp change in their condition, then perhaps it is up to intellectuals to define expectations and work out programs. The New Deal experience indicates that the boldest programs, the largest expectations, come most often from intellectuals not closely associated with the White House, from those whose ideological reach is not impaired by their clinking glasses with the mighty.

John Dewey was one of these. An early American pragmatist, he believed, like Roosevelt, in moving step by step, but he proposed longer ones, taken two or three at a time. F.D.R. wanted to preserve the profit system. Dewey was willing to see it reshaped. Liberalism, Dewey said, "must now become radical. . . . For the gulf between what the actual situation makes possible and the actual state itself is so great that it cannot be bridged by piecemeal policies undertaken *ad hoc*."

Economist Stuart Chase, shrewdly looking beyond the question of ownership, suggested that old alternatives had been swept aside by the onrush of technology. There was a need, Chase said, for some uncategorizable collectivist society whose "general objective will be the distribution of the surplus, rather than a wrangling over the ownership of a productive plant which has lost its scarcity position."

William Ernest Hocking, the Harvard philosopher, asked for "collectivism of a sort" where "the totality of persons in a community . . . determine what is produced." Upton Sinclair talked of a cooperative society in which "every man, woman, and child would have the equivalent of $5000 a year income from labor of the able-bodied young men for three or four hours per day."

It was, all in all, a bolder dialogue than any we have heard since.

Although Roosevelt told students at Oglethorpe University during his 1932 campaign that he was in favor of "a larger measure of social planning," he was never willing to go as far as his own adviser, Rexford Guy Tugwell, to whom planning meant "something not unlike an integrated group of enterprises run for its consumers rather than for its owners." "Planning," Tugwell said, "implies guidance of capital uses . . . and there is no way of accomplishing this except through a control of prices and of profit margins."

Today, the vague goals, the limited forays of the New Deal, persist. We are not even talking the language of the bolder reformers of thirty years ago—Niebuhr, Dewey, Tugwell, Chase, Sinclair. If our perspective were as broad as theirs, the Johnson "war" on poverty, drawing on one-fifth of one percent of the gross national product (F.D.R. in 1938 was spending 3.5 percent of the GNP on public works), would get its rightful name: a feeble reconnaissance effort on a battlefield strewn with economic casualties. (The National Association of Manufacturers slyly argued against the Johnson poverty program by saying it didn't amount to enough to make any difference anyway, so why waste the money?)

We continue to analyze our economic performance in *gross* terms. We measure the magnitude of our production of goods and services (our gross national product has more than doubled, from about $350,000,000,000, in ten years) and then pronounce ourselves a success. But if we used as criteria, first, what we *do* with this fantastic productivity, and second, what is the ultimate distribution of wealth among the population, our assessment would be quite different. Our top twelve million families average $20,000 a year income, and our bottom twelve million families average $2,000 a year; we spend more money to buy whiskey than to build schools, more to advertise cigarettes than to do research on lung cancer; we construct magnificent towers of concrete and steel for insurance and advertising offices, while people sleep in cold, crumbling rat playgrounds.

To judge ourselves by the *rational and humane use* of our resources, we are a failure. But we conceal this failure with hoopla and gadgetry. History has never seen such squandering of resources, or such marvelous public relations.

When the headlines one day (January 27, 1966) can announce that the Johnson administration will "rebuild the slums" with an effort of about $400,000,000 a year, we have only proved that proper advertising can convert a pittance into a social revolution as easily as it transforms a mouth wash into a sexual triumph. Over eleven million families live in slum housing; they cannot afford the prices charged by private builders. Yet, the U.S. government over the past fifteen years has given money to subsidize less than thirty thousand units a year in public low-cost housing. This is not enough to match the rate of obsolescence, much less scratch the overall problem of urban slums.

Tokenism is the American way of reform, and it has become a national custom to happily celebrate gestures. In one year the increase alone in government tax receipts equals the total money spent for health, welfare, education, poverty programs. By turning over the added receipts to welfare purposes, in other words, the government could—but does not—double the available money with that one stroke. The surprised discovery of poverty led the President to allot $1,000,000,000 to attack it; in the same period, the discovery that South Vietnam was about to fall to the National Liberation Front led him to ask $12,000,000,000 for that. (In 1967, it was two billion for poverty, twenty-four billion for Vietnam.) And yet, every welfare bill signed by the President which makes another gesture is greeted with chiliastic fervor and an orgy of self-congratulation, and the eminences rush to the White House for the signing. In terms of today's needs, our welfare activities resemble Hoover's more than F.D.R.'s, and even the New Deal was bold only in relation to what went before.

Our feeling of beneficence is very much that of the white

South *before* the civil rights revolution, when every construction of a new Negro school was hailed as an act of grandeur. "We know the nigra problem, and we are working on it." The South was shocked when the ungrateful ones took to the streets. The nation is bewildered when a "well-off" Negro population like that of Watts in Los Angeles begins burning and looting, when other Northern cities follow and when "progressive" Atlanta goes a bit wild. Perhaps the nation's huge crime rate—a million crimes against property in a year—is a misinterpreted demonstration of distress, in a society where more constructive forms of social protest are too difficult.

When a nation has the total resources—in manpower, natural wealth, technique, productive plant—to feed, house, clothe, educate and keep in good health every single person in the nation and yet at least forty million people lack from one to all of these human requisites, the problem is clearly the *organization* of these resources. And we are practically bursting with organizational and administrative skills. Then what is wrong? It must be that we don't *want* to organize our national resources, because to do so would require discarding the "myths and symbols" which Thurman Arnold back in the thirties said stood in the way of practical steps to alleviate misery. It would also require, candidly speaking, cutting down on the possessions of that upper fifth of our population which owns 75 percent of the personal wealth of the nation, and reducing fat from the bulging middle.

We would need to adopt Tugwell's 1932 suggestion of national economic planning, to redirect our present huge production towards our most urgent needs, and to put our idle resources to work. We have, depending on who does the counting, three to eight million unemployed, but more important, 20 to 50 percent of our steel capacity unused, millions working at jobs that would be considered nonessential if we were really *at war* against poverty. A national planning body would mobilize that $35,000,-000,000 a year (estimated by the Council of Economic Advisers in 1960) which represents unused capacity, and find another

$50,000,000,000 to $150,000,000,000 out of our gross national product which now goes for less essential needs (speedboats, second cars, office buildings, beauty creams, advertising, overkill weapons).

Then, we could not only really begin to have an effect on poverty here, but also start to treat poverty in other countries as if it deserved equal attention with ours. Right now, the tiny amount of economic aid we give to the poorer countries is neatly balanced by the higher prices we keep charging them, and, often, the lower prices we pay. In 1958, for instance, the net loss from price decline *exceeded* the foreign aid received by countries producing primary commodities.

Why not tax the cigarette industry an amount equivalent to the money it spends annually on advertising (roughly $200,000,-000), outlaw cigarette advertising and spend the money on cancer research? We need not interfere with the private enterprise of a shopkeeper or a small farmer; but should we treat the American Tobacco Company as a disadvantaged part of the population? It is time to extend and firmly apply the doctrine declared back in 1877 in the Granger Cases where the Supreme Court found it legitimate to regulate businesses affected with "a public interest." All great corporations (150 of them, owning half the total manufacturing assets, dominate the economy) so affect the public interest that they need no longer be treated as private enclaves.

We have too many automobiles in this nation, and we keep producing more, while forty thousand people a year get killed on the highways and General Motors made $2,000,000,000 in profit in 1965. If we appropriated 75 percent of that profit, we could double the amount the federal government spent for education in 1965. If we extended the principle to other corporations, we could have $30,000,000,000, which might be used to add $3,000 a year to the income of the ten million families who now make under $3,000 a year. Inflation? We will need price controls for selected commodities.

During World War II the nation did not hesitate to tell people where to work, to tell industries what to produce and what prices to charge; the result was grumbling, but not rebellion. Of course that was *war*. Which only proves we have misnamed what is now being done about poverty. How strange that we should accept the right of the government to order young men to their death, and yet question its right to order the redistribution of wealth and the reallocation of productive activity.

The fear of "governmental control" is based on an ambiguity. National economic planning would increase control *over money*, but decrease control *over people*. Those who earn under $5,000 a year, and many who earn more, are already controlled by the circumstance of economic desperation. To raise their income, to provide medical care and education to all who need them, would decrease the extent to which people are controlled. Corporations are run by self-perpetuating directorates; to establish firm public control over them would extend the area of democracy in this country from the political sphere (where the "will of the electorate" is more ritual than reality) to the economic. This would not be a diminution of freedom, but its realization.

We learned in war—and in the experiences of the Scandinavian countries and England—that it is possible to have a much larger measure of economic direction without a corresponding loss in freedom of expression. The two seem to be rather independent variables: we hardly had fewer civil liberties under the rigorous conditions of wartime than in the days of free enterprise plus Senator Joseph McCarthy. But we persist in warning about "totalitarianism" as a concomitant of national planning when what we are really afraid of is inconvenience.

John Dewey spoke of a "planning" rather than a "planned" economy, because the latter seems to close off innovation and flexibility. A *planning* economy could create as much public enterprise as was necessary; it would direct resources from adults' toys to children's necessities. No preconceptions, whether socialist or capitalist, need be held; rather experimentation, to find the best means for ending poverty and deprivation in the United States.

This is utopian, of course. The Johnson administration no more set such goals and acted upon them than did the New Deal thirty years ago. It has even less reason to do so. This country is in the historically unique position of being able to give three-fourths of its people enough wealth to keep them quiet, and to dispense enough occasional food baskets to the other fourth (along with reminders of how well-off they are compared to the Indians and Chinese) to dull whatever pangs of resentment may arise. The poor are a conglomerate lot, in race and age, and are so isolated in hundreds of urban and rural ghettos as to make any national movement for redress extremely difficult.

Even in the crisis of the thirties, no truly national movement with broad social goals could get under way (although people like Governor Floyd Olson of Minnesota called for a third party with socialist-humanist aims). The Negro revolt of recent years had the special binding factor of race, as well as a grievance so intense it could not be soothed away. And there the success consisted only in winning the kind of legislative tokens which the New Deal gave to the poor in its day. (That is why we are now hearing shouts of "Black Power!")

Only the self-interest of the aggrieved themselves can provide the motive power to create that New Deal which neither F.D.R. nor J.F.K. nor L.B.J. gave us. National economic planning might one day be introduced with less humane purposes in mind, on behalf of war or privilege. It will take populist power outside of government, depending on the day-to-day politics of protest and demonstration rather than on the occasional use of the ballot, to ensure that the nation's wealth will be justly distributed. (The recent commandeering of an unused Air Force base in Green-ville, Mississippi, by hungry, homeless Negroes, is a tiny example.) What is a "just distribution"? It is impossible to say exactly. But we don't yet need to say exactly. The inequities now are so gross and so palpably unjust that we have much to do before we get to the really difficult questions of moral judgment.

The motive power for change cannot come from the present labor movement, headed by $65,000-a-year George Meany, or from those Negro groups which aim at little more than getting a few more Negroes into the circles of respectability. Conceivably, it could come from a combination of militant Negro veterans of the Southern campaign, together with organized groups of both races from the urban slums, along with high-school and college students who begin to resent being dispatched to neo-colonial wars. But only a series of uprisings from these groups—greater than those which have come these past few years from nonviolent armies of Negroes in the South and more disciplined than the recent urban rebellions—could move the nation on economic matters.

To predict that this will actually take place would be foolish. Social systems—no matter how unjust—have a huge capacity for self-perpetuation, and our system's capacity is larger than most. It is more likely that the shocks will come mainly from outside, from that three-fourths of the world which is hungry, colored and angry. Our nation has been determined to interpret those shocks as Communist conspiracies pure and simple, and to move against them with arms (as Alabama sent its deputies against the Negro, also seeing outside conspirators at work). But in the end, after who knows how much suffering, the world will change, and we will change with it.

As for academic intellectuals, they can no more provide the energy for social change in America today than Tugwell, Dewey, Douglas and others could in the days of the New Deal. What they *can* do, perhaps, is to hold up before society the utopian visions which quicken the pulse of those whose urgency is sharp and who have less to lose in making the pillars of society tremble. They can also affirm—using facts, figures and published plans— that the vision *can* be realized with available, though hidden, resources. And they can henceforth refuse to engage in the self-congratulation that accompanies token reform.

I V

American
Culture

ASSUMPTIONS

The distinguishing characteristics of American culture derive, in part, from the nation's political, social and economic systems. Thus, cultural values tend to be more subject to democratic and economic tests than to theoretical imperatives. This, coupled with a vigorous tradition of individualistic creativity, has lent increasing emphasis to cultural innovation. Electronic communications and other aspects of modern technology have served to accelerate the process.

In the critical field of public education, this innovative tendency has produced both a remarkable new wave of pedagogical experiments and some profound questioning about the true goals of education.

At worst, American cultural life appears protean and undisciplined; at best, dazzlingly creative and progressive. Unfortunately, few Americans seem altogether sure which is the more accurate view.

JAY MARTIN

American Culture: The Intersection of Past and Future

"Neither science nor art, then, has the power to protect its own integrity in modern culture."

No aspect of American life is more difficult to discuss than "culture." Its definition is not precise; the criteria by which it is judged are in dispute; and our assumptions about it tend, in many cases, to be inarticulate. Yet the need for better understanding the term is clear if we accept that "American culture" refers to the whole quality of our intellectual and creative life as a nation. This is the broad sense in which Professor Jay Martin treats the subject. He finds many anomalies and many disturbing tendencies present in our culture, but he also identifies some of the reasons why we may have hope for the future.

IN THE POEM "To a Historian," Walt Whitman well described two contrary impulses that are basic to the imagination. These are the personal and cultural yearnings for both the accomplished past and the uncreated future. The historian, Whitman says, is he "Who celebrates bygones"—"the surface of the races, the life that has exhibited itself," "man as a creature of politics, aggregates, rulers and priests." Whitman's own mission as poet-prophet, he announces, is quite the reverse: "Outlining what is yet to be / I project the history of the future."

Not Whitman alone, but Americans in general have been similarly compelled again and again to stand at this meeting place of past and future, celebrating (and sometimes lamenting) one and projecting (but often fearing) the other. They do this in order to understand the present, which has ever been their truest and deepest concern. As their concerns and conditions have shifted, of course, they have tended to pay more attention to one or the other impulse. Sometimes they have said that the past, through memory, is the only guide to conduct—our "only true possession," as Grace King wrote. At other times they have said that the concern for origins is fruitless and change essential. They have, on occasion, declared all projections of the future vain and impractical, even while they have devised the most practical of utopias. But whatever their memories or visions, they have unmitigatedly submitted themselves to the pleasures, and imaginatively dabbled in the delights, of the instant now. Thus, ultimately, they have asked even historians and poets, in their celebrations or projections, to give them a key to the present. For from the obvious multiplicity of American life, they have reckoned shrewdly that strains and inconsistencies are intrinsic not only to American society but to what lies behind it. They have asked for up-to-date guides to change and thus for maps of the ultimate context of change—their culture itself.

"Culture," as I intend to use it, is a metaphor for what is happening in the structure of human consciousness.[1] It is not sur-

[1] I have in mind here the distinction dramatized by Clyde Kluckhohn in *Culture and Behavior* (1962), p. 21:

The Economist: A moment ago you used the term "society." This brings me to a point which I have found confusing in certain recent more or less popular writings of anthropologists. Sometimes the terms "culture" and "society" seem to have been used as synonyms.

First Anthropologist: There would be fairly general agreement in our profession that this is undesirable. The terminology that has attained almost complete acceptance among us can be put simply, though not altogether precisely, as follows: A "society" refers to a group of people who have learned to work together; a "culture" refers to the distinctive ways of life of such a group of people.

The Philosopher: In my language, then, "a culture" is an abstraction, whereas "a society" is not?

Third Anthropologist: That is certainly correct in the sense that you can see the individuals who make up a society, while you never see "culture."

These views are shared by such anthropologists as Linton and Herskovits. See

prising that since our culture had been so marked by rapid, significant and confusing changes in its norms, interest in culture has been both continuing and intense among Americans. Collective introspection has been one of our most prominent cultural characteristics. Of foreign writers from Barbé-Marbois and Crèvecoeur onwards we demanded analysis; and if we made exiles or aliens of natives like Henry James, Henry Adams or Ezra Pound, who told us too much truth, we at last, when their truths are self-evident, reclaim them as prophets and read their books.

Americans have thus betrayed a fine instinct for self-preservation. For "culture" consists not of actions, but of acquired tendencies to react, habits of mind and feeling, assumptions which precede beliefs and emotions which lie behind motions. Culture, in short, is the ideational and generalized accumulation of the past, the abstraction lying behind government, religion, foreign policy and economic or military behavior. It is the intangible apprehended through these—what they all have in common, and what thus serves to explain their mysteries.

But where the human and natural environment changes rapidly, habits may become hindrances. In modern times the deepest tendency of culture (and the tendency which, indeed, defines it as specifically "modern") is to question itself. Obviously culture which "conforms" to the past through a belief in tradition may not well represent and accept facts of social change when the habits of culture are outdated by social novelty, when belief and custom draw further and further apart. At this point culture requires readjustment: new habit-patterns need to be created and old ones dissolved. And this must be done without either

---

M. F. Ashley Montagu, *Culture and the Evolution of Man* (1962), p. 39 ff.
"Culture" is a recent discovery: Perhaps it did not need to be named until it
was explicitly threatened. In 1871 for the first time, E. B. Tylor, in *Primitive*
"Culture" is a recent discovery: perhaps it did not need to be named until it
edge, belief, art, morals, law, custom, and any other capabilities and habits acquired by man as a member of society." But however recent its articulation,
man's desire to know and describe his culture is itself an aspect of the existence
of that "complex whole." Field ethnographers have repeatedly remarked on the
surprising degree to which even primitive peoples are aware of their culture, can
report in detail on its norms and are curious about their meaning.

surrendering the values of continuity to systemless novelty, or re-tarding the vitality of change in society. At its best, culture is the way of managing these tensions. Without contraries there is no advance—a maxim true for culture no less than for poetry. Our times dramatically provide us with the incongruous and ambiguous—the contradictory and problematic issues of the tensions which have grown up in the past century between habit and action.

The century between the end of the Civil War and our own time has been one of accelerating change in society and in the way we think about it. An increase nationally of both wealth and poverty; alterations in the human and natural environments made by technology; practical advances in science; the rise of the city; and the new laws, government and commercial activities rising therefrom—all of these combined to alter whatever prior harmony culture and society could claim [2] "My generation," wrote James H. Tufts, a colleague of John Dewey, "has seen the passing of systems of thought which have reigned since Augustus. . . . Principles and standards which had stood for nearly two thousand years are questioned." The very grounds of philosophy, theology, science, economics, politics and jurisprudence opened to reveal an abyss of doubt and new speculation. Systems of thought were shaken equally with society.

More recently, and more specifically, three important forces have pushed still further toward increasing the already confused character of both society and culture—raising questions which seem all but unanswerable. Since 1945, the most obvious have been (1) the presence of weapons which can obliterate civilization. Within the last five years or so, even the middle range of weaponry, short of nuclear power, has been filled in with great efficiency and ingenuity: rockets, napalm and similar weapons have been developed to accommodate all terrains and intensities of conflict. How will the traditional assumptions of culture, not

[2] The character and relevance of these changes, beginning in the post-Civil War period, are discussed in my *Harvests of Change* (1967).

188

only about the worth of life, but of the diplomacy of war, be adjusted to this new condition? (2) Cybernation, based on the combination of the computer with the automated self-regulating machine, has expanded production while simultaneously eliminating the need for human labor. Its techniques and the kind of work based upon them, as well as conceptions of the worker suitable for them, are already far advanced. How will the American idealization of work and the economic valuation of man fare in the further implementation of these new techniques? Finally, and at the same time that man's individual value seemed diminished by them, these other changes have been accompanied and paralleled by (3) an unmistakable demand for human equality. But what can social equality mean in a culture whose most cherished collective aspirations—for instance, the idealization of wealth and success—all tend to be based on ideals of individual accomplishment? When men desire most to be distinctive, how can they be equal?

That we ask such questions points not so much to answers, but to the immensity of change and to the basis for our uneasinesses about it. Change is accomplished; the questions which it continues to raise provide the contexts in which culture adjusts to altered social conditions. "Once destiny was an honest game of cards which followed certain conventions, with a limited number of cards and values," Paul Valéry has written. "Now the player realizes in amazement that the hand of his future contains cards never seen before and that the rules of the game are modified by each play." As always, our destiny is our culture, and our culture is always our *now*. But what strange tarot is it playing, and what curious faces and suits do the cards show? The deck has been unsealed; the cards click and whir. This is no casual whist, but the sharpest baccarat, with real stakes and risks of all that is.

Certainly there are signs that the adjustment of culture has in part consisted of the abrogation of culture in the sense that we have traditionally known it. In this, technology has been of primary importance. It is a cliché to observe that since the 1850's or 1860's we have been living in an age marked chiefly by technological advance; the effects of the machine on almost every aspect of American life have been abundantly documented. We can calculate in unperplexed statistics, as David Cort has, the rate of invention:

> Up to the year 1620, the total number of true scientific discoveries and inventions was about 150 key items. By the year 1850 the world total had increased to 450. In the next seventy years, up to . . . the end of World War I, a great spurt of ingenuity had tripled this figure to 1,450 key items. . . . But the deluge was only beginning. In the next twenty years, up to 1940, the total passed 10,000. It is still moving at the same rate, standing at roughly 20,000 at mid century. Thus, Man had advanced his technological knowledge and his available tools more than ten times as far in thirty years as in all previously recorded history.

We are well acquainted with the effects of this worldwide acceleration of technological knowledge. That by 1967 farmers had decreased to a scant 7 percent of our population due to the mechanization and consolidation of agriculture; or that from the industrial force as many as forty thousand workers are eliminated weekly, but that production continues to mount—about such statistics we are informed. We can accede with a certain degree of detachment to pronouncements, like the economist Robert Theobald's, that "most of the new factories, the new public works, will employ machines rather than men and that it will be absolutely impossible to give everybody a job." We can even measure the suicidal limits of technology and view calmly the mathematics of the exhaustion of fossil fuels and oils, as certain kinds of economic development consume themselves.

In fact, technology has become something of a bore. One of the chief evidences of the extent of its influence is that it has been made to seem so. While we show a kind of bemused delight over its statistics, we are weary of considering their effects. We shake wise heads over what we regard as outmoded humanistic doubts of the machine, as in Thoreau, Tolstoy, F. R. Leavis or Lewis Mumford. We know much, but are reluctant, it appears, to understand much. Perhaps we have turned our knowledge into a cliché rather than admit that it is relevant to our lives. The success of the machine-process in drawing on human energy and admiration has meant not the loss of standards, but the formulation of new standards, unique ideals, unprecedented rules for behavior. It was doubtless necessary, as Lewis Mumford argues in *Technics and Civilization* (1934), that man should have made his life machinelike in order to make full use of the machine. Man has, in modern America, not infrequently literally given himself up as a sacrifice to the machine—in the nearly fifty thousand automotive fatalities annually, in the daily mutilation of farm and industrial workers. The list is endless and, as one writer has remarked, would allow "some future people to regard ours as one of the most brutal cultures that ever existed." Far more significant than the exterior effects of the machine on our lives, however, are the ways in which technics have been so recommended as emulative principles for human existence that success is judged either by the possession of mastery over a machine or by the specialized ability to create a machine. This shift in the habit-tendencies of social emulation has effected a new style of culture and personality. Writing on "Contemporary American Values" in 1958, Clyde Kluckhohn tentatively concluded: "It is possible that the machine is coming to be taken as the implicit model for human behavior." The evidence accumulated during the last decade has confirmed his suspicion.

Consider the effects of machine-emulation upon the assumptions of culture as revealed in contemporary behavior. Is it not remarkable, for example, that Americans have been able to live so lightly for two decades with the likelihood of total war—with what Jules Henry well calls "The Great Fear"? It is true, as he says, "that war-fear is partly narcotized" by the euphoria of increased consumption and retardation of unemployment; but is it not more deeply true that we take an uncanny and self-perpetuating delight in the engines of terror, a love of their forms, an admiration of their power? In 1945, William L. Laurence, science editor of *The New York Times*, wrote an account of the detonation of the first atomic bomb. The observers at Los Alamos, he said, "clapped their hands as they leaped from the ground," dancing with spontaneous joy. "The sun can't hold a candle to it," one of them declared jubilantly.

We delight no less in our machines of production. Indeed, we make small, if any, distinctions between those designed for war and those for peace; and we test both on ourselves. The principle of temporal regularity necessary for the ordered running of modern urban life means that man must almost entirely yield his personality to transpersonal time systems: to eat, travel, work and make love at regular, punctual and predictable moments. He surrenders, as well, to numerical systems. Like the condemned ones in Kafka's *The Penal Colony,* he is tattooed all over with his sentence: social security, zip code, bank and credit card, postal box, telephone and military service numbers. He tends to ask only questions which his computers can answer. In *Miss Lonelyhearts* (1933), Nathanael West quotes a newspaper clipping: "ADDING MACHINE USED IN RITUAL OF WESTERN SECT . . . *Figures Will Be Used for Prayers.*" Do we pray to the machine? When we hear that a company has air-conditioned its plant only after the purchase of a computer which needs temperature control; when we recognize that many workers develop sudden illnesses and neurotic fears concerning their incapacity for mechanized work and the threat of their personal obsolescence; when workers regard themselves as inherently replaceable parts in a technical serial process—then who can doubt that we have delivered ourselves to the tribunals and inquisitions of the machine? The bargain we made for comfort and convenience has brought, also, self-conquest and control, a constriction of life along with its expansion—what Henry Miller has called the "air-conditioned night-mare" producing "the greatest misery of the greatest number." The logic of this human condition has been strikingly pursued by a student of cybernetics, Donald N. Michael. Like the observers of Los Alamos, he exults over the terrible beauty of the machine. By the 1980's, he predicts, "There will be a small, almost separate, society of people in rapport with the advanced computers. These cyberneticians will have established a relationship with their machines that cannot be shared with the average man. . . . Indeed, many scholars will not have the capacity to share their knowledge or feeling about this new man-machine relationship. Those with the talent for the work probably will have to develop it from childhood and will be trained as intensively as the classical ballerina." Are not these what Nietzsche called the "new barbarians"—"those capable of the greatest harshness against themselves, those who can guarantee the greatest duration of will power" in emulation of the machine? Peace, it seems, as well as war, has its casualties.

Sociologists in the 1950's, in writing of social standardization, vividly and accurately depicted the external aspects of the emulative appeals of the machine. The image of a lonely, gray-suited, status-seeking organization man rises from their writings. More recently, however, we have been learning to see that this man is the creature as much of new ideals in culture as of social dissatisfactions. While certain critics of personality studies have questioned the usefulness of any such concept as "personality," it is clear that like "culture," "personality" is a useful abstraction, calling attention to the norms in "culture" which lie behind individual behavior. Concepts of "culture" and "personality" necessarily overlap, as the individual and society do in fact. Thus changes in "culture" will invariably mean alterations in "personality," and vice versa.[3] New cultural and personal ideals took

[3] This question is critically reviewed by Alex Inkeles and Daniel Levinson, "National Character: The Study of Modal Personality and Sociocultural Systems," in *Handbook of Social Psychology*, ed. Linzey (Cambridge, 1954); Murray Murphey, "Culture, Character, and Personality," in *American Character and*

shape in this century and gained power: they were born in jubilation over technological power and grew in man's humble hopes that he might be made worthy of his machines by learning to imitate them. In the culture of this species, ethics are replaced by technics, values by standards, motives and emotions by mere motion and interpretation by observation.

The essence of the personality created from technological ideals, moreover, is generality and abstraction. Aldous Huxley has proposed the following definition: "Science is the reduction of the bewildering diversity of unique events to manageable uniformity within one of a number of symbol systems, and technology is the art of using these symbol systems so as to control and organize unique events." We have relatively recently perceived the cultural ideal of personality behind the new species of technological man. He has been variously designated as "the authoritarian type of man," "one-dimensional man," "post-historic man," the "New Oligarch" or the "fourth man." Among the earliest to identify this form of human character are Theodor W. Adorno and the other authors of *The Authoritarian Personality* (1950), who describe him as one who "seems to combine the ideas and skills which are typical of a highly industrialized society with irrational or anti-rational beliefs. He is at the same time enlightened and superstitious, proud to be an individual and in constant fear of not being like all the others, jealous of his independence and inclined to submit blindly to power and authority." This kind of personality is the creation of modern culture. Adorno's analysis shares the general outlines of other close students of this new human type. Roderick Seidenberg's *Post-Historic Man* (1950) and Alfred Weber's *Der dritte oder der vierte Mensch* (1953) both prophesy the increasing cultural dominance of the ideal of the depersonalized robot-man, the instrument of a bureaucratic terror machine. The "New Oligarchs" of this species, as Donald Zoll has written, emphasize "dogmatism, conformity and, finally, coercion. Curiously they seem to

---

Culture: Some Twentieth Century Perspectives, ed. Hague (De Land, Fla., 1964); and Victor Barnouw, *Culture and Personality* (Homewood, Ill., 1963).

introspect their own defects, ignorances and intellectual vulner-
abilities, since they increasingly employ greater severity, more
self-protective policies and more cunning to take the place of
wisdom and liberal virtue."

Whatever their specific differences, these analyses all point toward a significant and recently accomplished alteration in modern consciousness, an alteration which began as an accommodation to the industrialization of society, but to which other
assumptions of culture are now beginning to adjust themselves.
These cultural adjustments will allow, in turn, for the acceleration and fruition of the technological process which is causing
the alteration of human consciousness.

There is every indication, moreover, that this new human type
is already proving dominant and able to multiply its kind. Consider that the presence and character of the authoritarian personality was sufficiently developed and remarkable by 1950 to
require, for its analysis, a closely reasoned book of nearly one
thousand pages. The adults of 1950 had been born at a time when
technological multiplication in chain processes was still in its earliest stages; a man who was fifty-five in that year was born at the
same time that the automobile, wireless and X-ray machine had
been invented, before the Wrights made their first flight, when
the fastest means of travel was by rail. He was, in short, born into
a technologically primitive world. But what of the infant born in
1950, who has spent every moment of his life involved with (in
Karl Jaspers' phrase) "the life of technique"? Perhaps we are in
the hands now of this child, who promises to be as rude as the
time which nursed him.[4]

*   *   *

[4] I take some of these observations from David Cort, *The Big Picture* (1953),
pp. 99–100, in complete reversal of his argument. He is complaining about adults
who are "obsolete" (as if they too, in not being "modern" enough, were outdated)
and regretting that the child born (with the atomic bomb) in 1945 would not be
able to begin to "run" society until about 1968. It seems to be turning out, in fact,
that the child living his whole life in the age of technique has taken it more for
granted and has recently been showing signs of impatience with it. More than his
elders, he may be, as one student described himself to me, "absolutely disillusioned
yet absolutely committed." But to *what* he can be committed is the question we
need to ask. What is worthy of his commitment?

It must be clear that since 1950 intolerance and authoritarianism have been increasing in virtually every area of American life. This is in part due to the character of modern work. Accelerating business mergers have meant that by 1960, 40 percent of the several million workers in manufacturing were employed by just 361 firms. Men serving in these vast industrial armies work for the most part at routine tasks which neither demand self-discipline nor link workers to their fellows. William Faulkner told a *Paris Review* interviewer in 1956: "One of the saddest things is that the only thing a man can do eight hours a day, day after day, is work. You can't eat eight hours a day nor drink for eight hours a day nor make love for eight hours—all you can do for eight hours is work." Part of the difficulty of modern culture is that while we have made work unfulfilling, we have found for it no human substitutes. Now, when personal involvement in a job is unlikely and work generates hostility instead of ego-gratification, the self is threatened by profound transformations, and we are seeing realized the fears expressed by Freud in *The Future of an Illusion*: man is failing to find, through his work or through insubstantial personal or communal attachments, satisfactions for the ego; he is more and more seeking to satisfy the instinctual self in sensuality, aggression and brutality. "When men and women find nothing within themselves but emptiness," the authors of a report of The Commission on the Humanities declare, "they turn to trivial and narcotic amusements, and the society of which they are a part becomes socially delinquent and politically unstable."

These characteristics, however, are scarcely confined to those industrial classes with few work satisfactions. Who could fail to see the intolerance which marks all sides in the struggle for human or civil rights, or fail to recognize how narrow in their aims these struggles and their opponents ordinarily are? Poverty programs still normally consider their payments an unearned dole—even to such "unemployables" as families with dependent children, the sick, disabled or aged—and organize their programs on that mechanical principle. Obviously, too, both the government and its critics are marked by their singular one-sidedness; and in general, the political life of the country over which both groups aspire to preside is harshly intolerant. Even the Bill of Rights, as Chester Bowles remarked in *New Principles for a New Age,* "might not be voted today because too few of us understand the need to protect the freedoms of those with whom we disagree." To a considerable extent, democracy at present is exalting as virtues the authoritarian vices which, in other forms, it was inaugurated to correct. "Fear and destructiveness are the major emotional sources of fascism," Professor Adorno and his colleagues wrote, while "*eros* belongs mainly to democracy." But the wise uses of *eros* seem to have been lost.

Even such literary primitivists as Henry Miller, Allen Ginsberg, Norman Mailer and Michael McClure—in idealizing the psychopath, the pervert, the beatnik, the hippie or the criminal as the "forerunners of a new kind of personality"—are often taking over, sometimes inverted, the standards of the authoritarian personality and merely giving them bizarre settings designed to caricature their usual appeals. Is it not true that the dharma-bum, instinctivist and hippie styles are reworked tales for children of golden ages and lotus-eating in "a land where all things always seemed the same"—a frequently will-less surrender to the authoritarianism of drugs or other outward substitutes for truly inward life, and the withdrawal from social change and challenge by those for whom history is no longer a category of the consciousness? Because anti-intellectualism is intolerant of all that society tolerates, one critic writes, "the primitivism which is advertised as a cure for the disease of modern man turns out to be but another form of his sickness."

Intrinsic to our ideals are democratic values; but it is clear that in the present state of our culture, the individual may be losing his self and finding his democracy becoming sinister. We have not, in short, entirely controlled and voided the chief menace to culture: the danger that by worshipping monuments of its own magnificence it will both perpetuate and enlarge its defects. "All that man seeks on earth," Dostoevski's Grand Inquisitor sardonically remarks, "is someone to worship." We have worshipped our machines and given our consciences, too often, into their keeping; and we have withered in the midst of our possessions.

For a brief period after World War II, the visionary hopes of Americans, victorious in the war, were stirred by designs for peace and international cooperation, even while many Europeans—philosophers like Karl Jaspers (in *The Future of Mankind*) or novelists like Charles Galton Darwin (*The Next Million Years*)—were building the dismal science of despair. But in a surprisingly short time, these—and older dystopias like Orwell's or Huxley's—were finding wide acceptance in the American mind. Our own novelists, Ralph Ellison, Joseph Heller and Thomas Pynchon, to much critical praise, made their books visions of apocalypse; and though they may have followed in the tradition of *The Confidence Man* (1856) or *The Day of the Locust* (1939), they won far greater popular audiences than Melville or West dreamed of attracting. Jaspers' belief that calculated "on purely rational grounds" mankind was likely to destroy itself, or Seidenberg's prediction of a time when man will vanish from the scene, "lost in the icy fixity of his final state," now seemed to suit well the deep tensions and fears in the American consciousness. An issue of *Daedalus* magazine appearing in 1965 made explicit what Americans had long been feeling: that their utopian tradition, from the authors of *The Federalist* to Edward Bellamy and the Progressives, no longer possessed the power to dazzle the imagination or fill the heart, even while technology, in bringing material abundance and increasing leisure, had begun to satisfy some past conditions for utopia.[5] Untouched by military

[5] In this tide of woe, even so exuberantly hopeful and unmitigatedly Bellamy-like a book as Morris L. Ernst's *Utopia 1976* (1955) failed to evoke much response in once-optimistic Americans. See Judith Shklar, "The Political Theory of Utopia: From Melancholy to Nostalgia," *Daedalus*, 94 (Spring, 1965), 367 ff.; and also Kenneth Keniston, *The Uncommitted: Alienated Youth in American Society* (N.Y., 1965), Chap. 11, p. 345: "In some corner of themselves most Americans know that 'total' technology is almost as good a setting as total squalor

devastation of their territories, Americans were living, five years after the war, with the terrors of the failure of their hopes for peace.

Dystopias spring from frustration and the power of self-hatred; and from the frustrations of their dreams Americans leaped to imagine the destruction of their collective life. How far this reached even into the fantasies of popular culture is suggested by the appearance of popular dystopic novels like *Fail-Safe, Seven Days in May, Red Alert (Dr. Strangelove)* and a number of other novels about the consequences of a third world war, many of which have been made into successful films. A song like "The Eve of Destruction" could become the most popular in the nation. Americans still spoke rhetorically about the danger of the world being lost, but in their private fancies began to wonder what made it worth saving.

Ironically, this same period witnessed a revival of some forms of the utopian consciousness in other areas of the world. Books with titles like *The Coming Culture* (Thanjavur, India, 1951), *Demain c'est l'An 2000!* (Paris, 1952) and *De Toekomst is Verleden Tijd* (translated: *The Image of the Future,* two volumes, Leyden, 1961) began to appear. "People like myself," wrote Camus, "want not a world in which murder does not exist (we are not so crazy as that!) but rather one in which murder is not legitimate. Here indeed we are utopian." The question of utopia was real for important foreign thinkers, and related in their minds to questions of power, poverty, politics and education. Had not William Beveridge remarked in the early fifties: "The choice is no longer between Utopia and the pleasant ordered world that our fathers knew. It is between Utopia and Hell"? The worldwide outlines of the utopian revival are well suggested by a list of recent prophets of a world community of man: Ar-

---

for total misery. And for most of us, an even more technological society hardly seems an adequate object for human striving. . . . As a result, the pseudo-Utopia of total technology has little deep appeal for most Americans; although for lack of anything better, it comes readily to mind when we are asked about an ideal future."

nold Toynbee, Erich Kahler and F. L. Polak in history; Sir Sarvepalli Radhakrishman and F.S.C. Northrop in philosophy; Pitirim Sorokin in sociology; Albert Camus and Thomas Mann in the humanities; and Sir Julian Huxley and Father Pierre Teilhard de Chardin in biology. The French *Futuribles* project and the British Committee on the Next Thirty Years are signs of the international awakening of the utopian impulse.

In 1957 Erich Kahler, in a chapter called "Possible Utopia," well summarized our anomalous condition: "On the one hand, new 'utopian' prospects of an unprecedented range flare up within alluring reach, on the other the peril of a loss of human control, of an engulfment of mankind in a common disaster has never been so acute as in our day." Yet all of these men, and a few Americans whose work began in the twenties, have elaborated forms of utopian visions. Western civilization, they all insist, has not irrevocably doomed itself to annihilation or savagery and may again create purposeful images of the future which will, as Polak writes, "have the power to tear our civilization loose from the claws of the present."

Taking heart from the prewar traditions of American and the revival of European utopian thought, Americans have begun tentatively in the last few years to attempt to create such purposeful images of the future. At the least, the following very mixed bag of recent books points to some qualified "possible utopias": Francis E. O'Meara, *The New Age* (1962); Warren Wagar, *The City of Man* (1963); Theodore J. Gordon, *The Future* (1965); John Rader Platt, *The Step to Man* (1966); and R. L. Duffus, *Tomorrow's News* (1967). On many levels of argument and opinion these suggest something of both the variety and the extent of the utopian impulse. From the calculations of the respected scientist to the enthusiasms of the vanity-press author, all hint at the way that the future is again becoming real and attractive to us. Daniel Bell has listed some of the evidences that interest in the future is even becoming a fad for our present: "The Columbia Broadcasting System has revamped its documentary program, 'The Twentieth Century,' into 'The Twenty-First Century,' to depict the marvels of the future. *The Wall Street Journal* has been running an intermittent series on expected social and technological changes. *Time* has published a compact essay on 'The Futurists: Looking Toward A.D. 2000.' The theme of the year 2000 now appears repeatedly on lecture circuits and in the feature pages of newspapers." More serious, of course, are several studies attempting to provide procedural guidelines for projections into the future: the Rand Corporation study, "Report on a Long-Range Forecasting Study," by T. J. Gordon and Olaf Helmer; *Resources in America's Future*, by Landsman, Fischman and Fisher; two volumes in the *World Design Science Decade 1965–1975*, by Buckminster Fuller and John McHale; and several of the studies of the National Planning Association. These and other materials are being richly drawn upon by the American Academy's Commission on the Year 2000, of which Professor Bell is chairman and which was created "to indicate now the future consequences of present public policy decisions, to anticipate future problems, and to begin the design of alternate solutions." Taken together, these all indicate the way that we are committed once again to raising utopian questions, even while the mere amelioration of our social problems often seems impossible. Perhaps a good deal of our utopianism, then, is a flight from apparently insoluble problems—a yearning for 1976, which disguises a nostalgia for 1776, or a millennial fixation on the cosmic turning of the historic wheel, unaided by man's will or intelligence, at the fast approaching conclusion of another thousand years. But there are hopeful signs in the way that men have seriously regained the concept—if not the conviction—that a future is available to us and that we can from moment to moment make it what we will.

The nature of culture is always more or less ambiguous. Undoubtedly the main ambiguity today rests chiefly in the tensions between our destructive image of the world and our positive images of the future (which seem to be based more largely upon desire than probability). American culture at the present moment can be defined best by its tensions: intense hopes for change, but an inability or unwillingness to formulate the lines along which useful change might occur; a desire to study culture coolly, but heated partisanship over social issues; plans to raise central questions, but a devotion to the frivolous and the peripheral, a love of the immediate and a scorn of the long-range. These tensions are consolidated in the fundamental difficulty in American culture now: that we can imagine no way of connecting our future with our past or present. We have utopian hopes, but no understanding of how or to what extent they might be realized.

Observing the tentative revival of hopes for the future, however, the historian of culture must not underestimate the power of desire itself to effect alterations in society. Where it exists, the hope for a future is as much a cultural experience as any reasons justifying that hope. The very fact that we are now, in this symposium, asking various writers to give us a picture of America in the present is a sign that we can face the harsh answers which they might give us because we can imagine a future ameliorating them. But obviously the desire itself will not make the desired future.

If there are hopes beyond mere hope, both culture and society must provide contexts for their realizations. We must, then, take the future as problematical and ask what conditions must obtain and what alterations be accomplished before a sense of utopia could be justified. Two essentials for the transformation, I believe, are the dissolution of the authoritarian style of personality and the substitution for it of other ideals in culture. The effective occurrence of either, obviously, is problematical to the highest degree. Nonetheless, if culture is ultimately the deepest experience through which its members go, it is inevitable that we assess the ambiguities involved in its possibilities for a future. The most fruitful areas for transformation in culture and personality, obviously, are science, the arts and education.

*   *   *

It is essential not that technological and industrial advance be retarded, but only that culture develop the possibility of new institutions or ideals for human emulation. Nonetheless, there does appear to be occurring an unanticipated deceleration in technological multiplication. J. R. Platt has persuasively argued for the view "that we are not at the beginning of continually accelerating change, but that we are in the middle of a unique transitional crisis . . . as we make the jump from an underdeveloped scientific and technological society to a fully developed one. . . . The slowing down of growth and the beginnings of our adjustment to it may become one of the major social phenomena of the next 30 years." In several important areas—in travel, communications, weapons and medicine—technological change, while it has hardly reached its limits, still shows what those limits may be, and will not, after all, continue at its present rate. Our senses of space, community, warfare and self, hitherto culturally dissolved by rapid technological change, may soon assume more permanent forms.

For instance, the acceleration of speed, Platt has suggested, "is finished. . . . At around 17,000 miles an hour, we give up air travel because we are in orbit. And this step is already behind us." Between 1868 and 1968, when speed was accelerated from that of the steam engine or the clipper ship to that of the jet or rocket, the acceleration of speed was enormous and rapid. No future ability to travel the same distance in hours or minutes could make so significant a change in human behavior. Change will come in administering and tightening what advances and powers we already possess. The same is more complexly true for the other areas of life which I have named. When the speed of communications passed from that of the pony express to that of the wireless and telephone, and finally to an international computerized consolidation of information, this was qualitatively greater than any we could have again.

We presently possess the secrets of what we call ultimate weapons or final deterrents and have now to calculate their effects in terms of "overkill." By the same token, the successive cures of the major human diseases in this last century increased life expectancy at a rate which is bound to slow down. The increase from a forty to an eighty years' life expectancy is not only mathematically double, but humanly a more significant increase than the addition of another forty years of life could bring. Not only is life expectancy increased and biomedical engineering well begun, but both birth and heredity, including sexual selection and genetic control, are now within our foreseeable control.

We have become so accustomed to think of the multiplication of technological chains as the most important social factor affecting our lives—we have lived so much with change and demanded of our social scientists that they give us explanations of "the normality of change"—that we have tended to ignore the indications that we have already passed the apex of the curve of evolution toward a fully developed technological society. Technical change, though continuing to be of enormous importance, will occur at a decreased rate. Decision making, judgment analysis, information gathering, administration—all still growing in importance—are tending to shift attention away from machine-emulation as a personality ideal and toward a technics of consciousness and intelligence.

This is due not simply to the fact that technology is limited by the environment in which it operates, but also to the fact that the power of technology alone to possess and drive the mind and imagination of men has proved limited. Men, quite simply, are already showing inclinations to locate their enthusiasms elsewhere. The Virgin, in Henry Adams's terms, molded and drew on human energy until about the middle of the thirteenth century, when religious power was replaced by energies released mechanically. But that dream of the Renaissance, a utopia based on the dynamo, made a dystopia for us; and we are reshaping once more our image of the future and thus of our present. We are now sensing that we need to learn how to find not only, as William James proposed, a moral equivalent to war, but also an answer to the problems of cities, international tensions, technology, the machine personality, human suffering and boredom. The important concerns of our future utopias, if we are to have them, will not be over resources but over how to use them.

Science has given us the grounds for the material utopias of which earlier ages, in the tradition of Lactantius and Francis Bacon, dreamed. We should hardly, like the Luddites, want to smash the machine. But we shall not need to imitate it. Now, for the first time, science itself is creating the materials for a reassessment of mind and seems to be stressing the limitations of technology as an emulative ideal. Consider Goedel's demonstration that even in principle, mathematics are necessarily incomplete, since in any finite system there are statements which are true yet not derivable from its axioms; the reemphasis upon the rapid and continuing evolution of man's manipulative and verbal intelligence by such biologists as Julian Huxley, G. G. Simpson and Henry Nissen; the studies by anthropologists of man's creative capacity for culture, along with the studies of Jung and others of the ways man's psyche is both the acme of past cultures and the encloser of those to be; the stress placed by social scientists on the recent growth of a "pan-human conscience." All these have converged in the sixties to culminate in a renewed sense of the subtle and complex, yet still only dimly perceived, inward life of man. To some extent they suggest how far the scientist is himself working toward freedom from the constricting models of technology. He had believed technology to provide the concretization of his discoveries, but he too has learned that it has constricted his truths—in the largest and most human sense, the virtues of accuracy, patient observation and fidelity to perception.[6]

The Russian mystic-philosopher Nikolai Berdyaev was fond of imagining the future achievement of a "New Middle Ages" based on the "Russian Idea" of brotherhood and on Christianity.

[6] *Cf.* Lewis Mumford's query: "Has the time not come, then . . . to release science itself from the humanly impoverished and under-dimensioned mythology of power that Francis Bacon helped to promote?" ("Science as Technology," *Proc. Am. Phil. Soc.*, 105 [Oct., 1961], 511.)

We will hardly have that. But now again, we have a reawakened sense that man holds a significant place in the universe. We sense that he is its most complicated and subtle creature and that his future in it will not lead inevitably to "icy fixity," but, if he is willing to choose it, to an expansion of culture. "Science," as A. Whitney Griswold observed, "once accused of robbing man of his free will, now seems to be giving it back."

These are scarcely grounds at present, however, for self-gratulation. Technology still dazzles, and the one-dimensional personality has hardly been extinguished among us by the tentative revaluations of man by scientists and the reawakening in humanists of visions of a more human future. Our recent concern with the military aspects of technological power hint at the danger that modern Americans may assume an even more anarchical, oligarchical personality. The standard man is still, too often, the man without standards.

For this reason, in our time the arts in general have assumed a special cultural importance. The basis of this is subtly different from past times. Whereas technology necessarily includes the multiplying principle of the chain reaction, the principle of creation and accomplishment in the arts involves uniqueness. Thus, the arts can provide intellectual and imaginative models whereby to measure the rate and nature of technological change. Schools, academies or disciples may grow from the powerful influence of paintings, poems or symphonies; but the works themselves remain nonduplicative achievements, personal and permanent. This explains why, during the age of technique, the arts were regarded as inefficient and why, in the humanistic fields which began their developments during that age, there has been so little attention paid to the sociology of art. In the recent past, interest in the arts, indeed, was a badge of technical incompetence; and there is a well-established tradition in which the artist has attempted to achieve status by making his art accommodate the machine. Thus a good deal of the impetus behind pop art lies in the attempt to popularize it by adapting it to machine techniques —emphasizing surface, imitation, production and salability. This is equally as true of the largely futile efforts to marry, in the tradition of Ruskin and Morris, art to industry.

While the arts have long been regarded as a kind of vitamin, supplied at regular intervals to supplement our machine diet, we are coming to regard them as a primary cultural fuel, hardly tapped, upon which society lives. Moreover, the arts now are becoming—as the Virgin and dynamo have been—the focus of human energies, precisely at the point where economics, society and education converge. John Kenneth Galbraith has made this point in part by insisting that "the American businessman, having accommodated himself to the scientists. . . . must now come to terms with the artist. Artistic perception is as necessary to the modern manufacturer of consumer goods as engineering skill. Indeed, now more so." Today the consumption of the arts is not, as in the past, evidence of "high" culture, but central to the life of culture. For the arts give us, after all the changes society has suffered, and in the midst of change, permanent ways of hinging the mind and judgment to the wide swings of social life.

The formation of the authoritarian personality well illustrates the human issue of technological standards applied to culture. We have lived in a world of fixed quantities and limits; but today the rhythms of society, media, cities and knowledge all press us to acknowledge flux, the lack of fixed boundaries and subjective form. As one of Beckett's characters remarks, "Everything just oozes." Not the multiplication chains of technology, but the variability of art is useful here as a guide to our world. For involvement with the arts is a look in the face of maya—mystery—which brings us to ourselves.

Evidences of the astonishing—and growing—popularity of the arts are everywhere. "The image of the uncultured American," writes economist Arnold Mitchell of the Stanford Research Institute, "has been shattered by a statistical bludgeon," and he has predicted that by 1970, "the trends toward culture will create a total arts market of about $7 billion." The National Art Materials Trade Association estimated in 1960 that there were approximately forty million Sunday painters, a million of whom were actually taking lessons, and both numbers are rapidly increasing. Music provides an even more striking example. In 1950, about 800 symphony orchestras were struggling along in the United States; in 1960, 1250 were thriving on a phenomenal increase in attendance. This is an increase whose rapidity rivals any past technological amplification. In stores, nearly twenty million dollars in sales of classical music are now registered annually. The net profit of 5 percent on sales by a major recording company is significantly higher than the 4.2 percent median profit realized in 1962 by the five hundred largest industrial corporations listed in *Fortune*. At the same time, this was also true for book sales: the nineteen largest publishers listed by *Forbes* in 1963 realized an average profit margin of 5.8 percent, making book publishing one of the half dozen most profitable American industries. The 19,000,000 amateur instrumentalists in 1950 was increased to 35,000,000 by 1963, raising the dollar value of instrument sales by 175 percent. Attendance at art films increased conspicuously during a decade when overall movie attendance dropped by one-third. Though much of this increase is bound to be shallow in its effects, the pattern of interest is unmistakable, and some of its effects must be at least quantitatively good. This expansion of culture consumption and the enthusiasm of youth for unique, anti-authoritarian kinds of experience has led August Heckscher to suggest that "the long dominance of technical over humane values is coming to an end."

There is still wide room for skepticism, however, when the dangers of this expansion are so clear. The chief of these is not that high culture will deteriorate through wider distribution, though doubtless that possibility exists. A far greater danger is that as technology previously divided the relatively classless American society along economic lines, so economic class lines will now be replaced by classes of intelligence, taste and cultural refinement. There is abundant evidence that the consumption of the arts is correlative to economic status—in the high cost of lessons, musical instruments, records and record players, and in opera, drama and symphony tickets. Does not Wall Street's interest in the publishing and culture industries generally during the last decade provide proof that these are becoming areas of profit-interest and also hint at the rates by which their cost will rise? During the decade of the sixties, Secretary of Labor Willard Wirtz announced, of the 26,000,000 new workers entering the labor market, 7,600,000 would be without even high-school diplomas, 2,300,000 having failed to be graduated from grade school. Combine this fact with the estimate that by the early 1980's, technical, professional and managerial workers will constitute one-half of the labor force, and we see that we are in danger of systematically creating a large force of men impossible to employ and so closed off utterly from culture. Class lines fixed on the basis of intelligence, with the arts richly open to some, and all but inaccessible to others, would be the ultimate development in creating a new feudalism of the mind. This would appear even more likely in that, as Aaron Wildavsky has observed, "political elites are far more likely to share the preferences of the aesthetic minority," than those of "the mass of people." Even now, George Gallup reports, a scant 12 percent of the population reads 80 percent of its books, while half of the American people have never read a book at all. The ultimate consequence of such a class division, moreover, far from meaning the preservation at least of high culture for an intellectual elite, would mean that the arts would be transformed by their economic and technological foundations. The artist and his public would imitate technology (They would ask, is it efficient, that is, mass producible?); business (Is it commercial, persuasive?); government (Is it safe? Does it have the "proper image"?); and, in general, the administrative techniques by which it is distributed (Can it attract federal grants, use buildings, be understood and approved by committees?). Were this our progress, the most serious poverty of 1976 would be spiritual.

Not surprisingly, then, American novelists and dramatists are preoccupied today with the extinction of imagination, the dissolution of identity and the abrogation of art; for they work in a society, and through a culture, in which these are powerfully threatened. The effects on our imaginations of their vivid opposition to this possibility may be incalculably useful in preventing it and preserving an intelligible culture. Even here are dangers, however. Anthropologists agree that while heredity maintains our biological development, culture is chiefly preserved through language. "In a society without language," Murdock writes, "each individual would have to begin where his parents began; he could possess only individual . . . not group habits; his behavior . . . would be confined to the organic level." But what happens when the language of the arts becomes absurd in counteracting absurdity, when the images by and through which we see our civilization are as grotesque as the images which threaten its obliteration? What happens, in short, when language, working at its most affective and effective level in literature—or, in a more general sense, through painting, architecture or music—loses its ability to express a wide sense of the principles and continuities of culture by attending to the narrow and disruptive forces which the writer sees threatening him? There are clear signs that the arts will be included in our war on poverty and that federal money may be increasingly used to distribute culture by lowering its private costs. But what heuristic use for man will this culture possess?[7]

* * *

[7] I personally am inclined to believe that in less "popular" arts than the novel and drama—particularly in the striking revivals of poetry and historical, social criticism—wide and humane images of man are fruitfully present. I think of poets like Conrad Aiken, Robert Penn Warren, Robert Lowell and Gary Snyder as united to critics like Van Wyck Brooks, Edmund Wilson, Alfred Kazin, Roy Harvey Pearce in their mutual concerns with the evolution of the whole consciousness and the widening of the sensibilities, on every level of culture and history, of modern man. These all have preserved a heuristic sense that the connection between writers and their audience is in the culture they can share or be made through art to share, and so have remained free from the hatred for civilization and the sense of alienation forced so often upon the novelist and playwright who is compelled, as Nathanael West put it, to "Yell fire and indicate where some of the smoke is coming from without actually dragging the hose to the spot."

Neither science nor art, then, has the power to protect its own integrity in modern culture. The wise uses and the fruits of both depend largely upon our systems of mass education. This means that public education must not only be expanded as rapidly as possible, but also reoriented as to its assumptions, methods and aims. Mass education, which began as an American experiment, will be the necessary future of all cultures in which the life of the spirit begins to rival the life of technique. For without widely distributed education, the life of the spirit threatens to become defined in terms of the life of technique. The public acceleration of education, we well know (for its evidences are everywhere), is as remarkable as that of the arts. The establishment of free schools, Horace Mann declared in his *Annual Report* for 1846, was a measure which "could have been refuted and silenced by a more formidable array of argument and experience than was ever marshalled against any other institution of human origin. But time has ratified its soundness." Only now are its implications fully evident. As in the arts, a glimpse at a few statistics is encouraging. Only one in seven high-school graduates continued to college in 1939; now this has risen to nearly one of every two. Already there are as many Negro students enrolled in American colleges as there are students in higher education in Britain. During the decade between 1964 and 1974 college enrollment will more than double, from four to over eight million. This astonishing increase, perhaps, is not so important as the close ties developing between education, science and the arts. There is hardly a university, even in the most remote places of our country, to which distinguished representatives of the sciences and arts do not come. The college circuit has expanded at such a rate that in many regions, including the South, East and Midwest, schools account for between 50 and 75 percent of the dollar business of major artists' agencies. Important scientists wander freely from their own campuses to others, for conferences, seminars and research. Hardly a college today lacks its own drama group, arts festival or literary magazine. Soon, no college will lack computered connections with other institutions to provide for rapid exchange of information and materials. All of this has been well summed up by Fritz Machlup in *The Production and Distribution of Knowledge in the United States* (1962) as the "knowledge industry," which, he shows, is expanding at a rate of two and a half times that of the national product, and promises a still more rapid increase.

Then, too, education in a democracy is ideally a powerful counteragent to the oligarchical, "post-historic" personality. It is not simply that education, as John Dewey said in 1930, is "the supreme human interest in which . . . other problems, cosmological, moral, logical, come to a head"; or that its problematic character encourages the development of the senses of relationship and judgment upon which democracy relies. More important, universities are centers for a style of human engagement which stands opposite the anti-intellectualism of the authoritarian personality. The suspicion toward academic persons which occasionally crops up in our culture is grounded upon an authoritarian fear of judgment, investigation, skepticism and disinterestedness—qualities which universities attempt to develop. The academic, or intellectual, Richard M. Weaver has written, "is like the savant in society; though in it, he is not wholly of it; he has acquired knowledge and developed habits of thought which enable him to see it in perspective and to gauge it. He has not lost the intuitive understanding which belongs to him as a member, but he has added something to that. . . . He has become sufficiently aware of what is outside [his culture] to see it as a system or an entity. . . . [He] may be a kind of doctor of culture." The life style of education, like that of science and the arts, is one that assumes technology and then proceeds to judgment. And as the university—a centralizing place of knowledge—becomes more central to our culture, its style of mind can come to prevail.

Most commentators on American education hold the ideals I have here been setting forth. Obviously education should be a means whereby the whole populace learns to choose informed and satisfying activities and goals. But many of its critics suggest that American education provides precisely the reverse. The contemporary school, Jules Henry asserts, is "a nightmare," "a place where children are drilled in cultural orientations, and where the subject matter becomes to a considerable extent the instrument for instilling them." Paul Goodman has put the argument against public education even more strongly: "The goal of the school-monks . . . is a progressive regimentation and brainwashing, on scientific principles, directly toward a fascism-of-the-center, 1984," in which "in the tender grades, the schools are a baby-sitting service during a period of collapse of the old type family and during a time of extreme urbanization and urban mobility. In the junior and senior high school grades, they are an arm of the police, providing cops and concentration camps paid for in the budget, under the heading 'Board of Education.' The educational role is, by and large, to provide—at public and parents' expense—apprentice-training for corporations, government and the teaching profession itself. . . ." The schools, he argues, have become a trap, their democracy turned into regimentation, and their values subsumed by commitments to mechanical systems of administration and the belief—on the part of both students and teachers—that life is a matter for rules and routines. Edgar Z. Friedenberg's conclusions in *Coming of Age in America* (1965) are similarly doubtful about the human fruitfulness of education in the United States.

When we read a news item, like ". . . state health official believes some overanxious New Jersey parents are dosing their children with tranquilizers before sending them to school. . . . trying to protect [them] . . . from cracking under pressure for good grades"; when we catch serious educators saying that "it does not make sense to involve a large percentage of our population in the life of our central intellectual institutions"; and when the Dean of Faculties at a major university predicts that the training for technical and professional competence will constitute the central role of the universities—when the schools, in short, emphasize the worst aspects of the technological personality, how can they provide an escape from it? The truth is that we are still too often presented (indeed, present ourselves) with an image and ideal of the good life that *requires* for happiness no further education than simple acquiescence to mechanical ideals; and schools thus teach us what we want—the way to acquiesce. To consume his media and maintain his social group, the citizen does not really have to read or write much; grammar-school arithmetic will suffice for his computations; literature, history, foreign languages, or art—these are areas of knowledge which might make him seem queer to his fellows or odd to himself. He needs only to adjust. But what happens to his spirit in the process, or to the democracy in which he is multiplied millions of times over? Education, as I have said, offers ideally the context for illumination, variety, experiment—a context for unique exercises of the spirit. But too often its results have proved the reverse.

Science, the arts and education seem, at present, to offer the problematic focuses for change in our culture. But, we need to ask, have even these lost their power to offer, unmixed, useful images of the future? In them, certainly, there are many signs of adjustment, but few of fundamental alteration. If not to these, where will we look for paths out of our present?

Our recent utopias, our renewed hopes for a future, surprise us, mixing desires with memories. American culture now is perhaps best characterized as one in which the intertwined contraries of habit and anticipation are dramatically, if ambiguously, before us. Our future is our present recognition of the dangers and possibilities of advance in these contraries. Now again, we need unblinkingly to "celebrate bygones" by accepting our history; but also, to "project the history of the future," and, by projecting, to begin to imagine the ways, however difficult, to make it. For if we cannot attain a measure of harmony in common cultural hopes and ideals, we shall have our communion in mutual ruin and our community in the extinction of culture.

BIBLIOGRAPHICAL NOTE

In addition to the sources indicated in the text, I have quoted from the following, listed in order: Grace King, *Memories of a Southern Woman of Letters* (1932); Cort, *The Big Picture* (New York, 1953), p. 101; Theobald, speaking on a WFMT radio program on the Ad Hoc Committee on the Triple Revolution, quoted in Eric Larrabee, "Time to Kill: Automation, Leisure, and Jobs," in *The State of the Nation*, ed. David Boroff (Englewood Cliffs, N.J., 1965), p. 22; "some future people . . . ," Richard M. Weaver, *Visions of Order* (Baton Rouge, 1964), p. 84; Kluckhohn, *Daedalus*, 87 (Spring, 1958), 105; Henry, *Culture Against Man* (New York, 1963), p. 102; Michael, "Cybernation: The Silent Conquest," A Report to the Center for the Study of Democratic Institutions (Santa Barbara, Calif., 1962), p. 15; Huxley, "Education on the Nonverbal Level," *Daedalus*, 91 (Spring, 1962), 281; Zoll, *The Twentieth Century Mind* (Baton Rouge, 1967), p. 12; "forerunners of a new kind of personality," Norman Mailer, in his essay *The White Negro*; "the primitivism . . . ," Lewis A. Coser, "The Fear of Positive Thinking," in *The State of the Nation*, ed. David Boroff (Englewood Cliffs, N.J., 1965), p. 226; Camus, "Neither Victims Nor Executions," *Combat* (1946), reprinted in *Seeds of Liberation*, ed. Paul Goodman (New York, 1964), p. 28; Beveridge, *Power and Influence* (London, 1953), p. 355; Kahler, *The Tower and the Abyss* (New York, 1957), p. 226; Polak, *The Image of the Future* (New York and Leyden), Vol. II, p. 357; Bell, "The Year 2000—The Trajectory of An Idea," *Daedalus*, 96 (Summer, 1967), 639–40; Platt, *The Step to Man* (New York and London, 1966), pp. 187, 190; "the normality of change," Wilbert S. Moore, *Social Change* (Englewood Cliffs, N.J., 1963), p. 5; Griswold, "Overview," *New Frontiers of Knowledge* (Washington, D.C., 1957), p. 124; Galbraith, *Horizon* (Sept., 1960), 40; statistics on arts consumption are from Alvin Toffler, *The Culture Consumers* (New York, 1964), *passim.*; Heckscher, "The Scholar in a Nowhere World," *Yale Review*, 55 (Oct., 1967), 54; Wirtz, cited in Michael Harrington, *The Accidental Century* (New York, 1965), pp. 250–51; Wildavsky, "Aesthetic Power or the Triumph of the Sensitive Minority Over the Vulgar Mass: A Political Analysis of the New Economics," *Daedalus*, 96 (Fall, 1967), 1124; Gallup, cited in William K. Zinsser, *Pop Goes America* (New York, 1966), p. 74; "In a society without language . . . ," George P. Murdock, *Culture and Society* (Pittsburgh, 1965), p. 76; Dewey, in a personal statement of 1930, quoted in Henry Steele Commager, *Living Ideas in America* (New York, 1964), p. 586; Richard M. Weaver, *Visions of Order* (Baton Rouge, 1964), p. 7; Henry, *Culture Against Man* (New York, 1963), pp. 320–21; Goodman, *Compulsory Mis-Education* (New York, 1964), pp. 13, 22ff., 35; "it does not make sense . . . ," statement by Christopher Wright in "Four Futures," *Daedalus*, 96 (Summer, 1967), 953.

BERNARD ROSENBERG

The Public Taste

"If . . . *Othello* is absolutely better
than *Bonanza*, then the Nielsen ratings
are not so much a justification as an indictment. . . ."

*The subject of culture raises some peculiarly thorny theoretical
problems with respect to the democratic method. Taste, like religion, tends to search for absolute standards. If such standards
are objectively real, not even a majority may dispute them; if
they are not real, mass taste and good taste are indistinguishable.
The consequences of this problem are anything but theoretical,
for they directly affect the kind of television, movies, books,
music and so on that our communications media make available
to us. Bernard Rosenberg vehemently asserts the distinction between "mass-cult" and "high-cult" and has some corrosive
things to say about people who pander to the former and betray
the latter.*

IS MASS CULTURE an abomination, a harmless ano-
dyne, a blessing? These are the real, if too often merely
implicit, questions in an interminable and ferocious debate. No
one yields. (Like travel, disputation very often narrows one—
causing a man to confirm his old biases.) Even now, when most
of us are sick of each other's polemics, the issue will not go away.
And why should it? Could anything matter more than our manhood, and is anything less than that at stake?

Protagonists lambaste antagonists—who clobber neutralists—
in an arena littered with faulty logic, shopworn analogies, dubious data and, over all, the unappetizing remains of a stale argu-

ment. I was once chided by an eminent art critic for sullying myself with this subject matter. He said to me and people of my captious disposition, as though addressing himself to sex censors who privately revel in the pornography they publicly condemn, "If you don't like the goods, stop handling them." (Days after his printed attack, we met by chance at Amos Vogel's Cinema 16 where he and I had gone, for our delectation, to view *Gold Diggers of 1936*.) Of course you can stop handling the stuff, but it won't stop handling you. Or has someone discovered a way not to hear Muzak, not to see billboards, not to be touched by propaganda? We are all deeply and equally implicated in a phenomenon which continues to revolt some of us as much as it pleases others. Many, like Marshall McLuhan and his followers, have managed to swallow the nausea they once felt. At peace in the electric wonderland, they celebrate what used to sicken them. After years of courtship, and growing but unrequited love, McLuhan married the Mechanical Bride whose every gesture used to repel him. He moves and anachronistically writes in a psychedelic delirium comparable only to that of Timothy Leary. (Will they collide and embrace as inner and outer space converge?) Whole pages from that dated medium of Gutenberg's by which they so often go on expressing themselves, could be transposed from one author's work to the other's.

Here then we confront the champions of two debilitating and medically hazardous drugs: TV and LSD. TV, which probably does much to derange the nervous system through constant interruption and certainly hastens the onset of glaucoma, also turns out to be radioactive (and not just from cultural fallout). Color adds to the danger, and color sets multiply like cancer cells. LSD in good solid cubes can induce psychosis. Each is hallucinogenic in its own way. These are the media we are asked to exalt, complete with their appalling "massage" that "works us all over."

To what end? To the end that we should have a transcendental experience hitherto denied the species, to the end that we should explore previously unknown realms—and find God. Can anyone in possession of his senses, a human being who despite Leary's advice has not fully "blown his mind," help squirming and resisting when the Ad Alley physiotherapists lay their hands on him?

So, although I hesitate a split second on account of Harold Rosenberg's admonition (maybe I unconsciously love the thing I profess to hate, but if so, then like Oscar Wilde, I wish to kill that thing), allow me to reenter the fray. Back we go, and damn the opposition. Above all, damn that part of the opposition according to which mass or so-called popular culture does not even constitute a problem. My strongest malediction I therefore reserve for a fellow sociologist, Herbert J. Gans—but solely in his role as culture critic. Gans does excellent community studies, and only now and then, but always disastrously, ventures outside his field.

It is a little thing if in California he lectures Hollywood screenwriters by telling them that they never had it so good. Such talk simply makes his auditors marvel at the staggering naïveté of an apparently sophisticated man. Gans, however, does a bigger and sillier thing when he covers popular culture in prose. His lengthy contribution to a widely disseminated textbook called *Social Problems* bears a subtitle which asks a nearly unintelligible question: "Popular Culture in America: Social Problem in a Mass Society or Social Asset in a Pluralist Society?" Reams of prose follow, all designed to answer that rhetorical question by insisting that his chosen social problem is really not a problem. One can only tell him, "All right, already. If you like the goods so much, go on handling them, but do not trouble your mind with Social Assets. Let the White House compute them. Find Liabilities, possibly a few lying around in some neglected community, uncounted, unweighed. Study them. If not, cease and desist."

Typical of those who attempt to dispose of the problem either by denying it or embracing it is the pose of objectivity. Rational

discourse cannot take place when one group of passionate defenders claims scientific detachment for itself and dismisses
every detractor as hopelessly subjective and emotional. Facts
must be gathered and analyzed, but every one of us is, at bottom,
engaged in a battle over values. Literary intellectuals are licensed
to express their preferences; social scientists, if governed by positivist dogma, must remain disinterested. Whether there are more
television sets than bathtubs in the land (there are) can be statistically determined. Whether this ratio is desirable or not is a
question social science can neither answer nor evade. Moral
judgment comes into play, always and necessarily, and certainly
not as the exclusive concern of sociologists.

Auguste Comte, that brilliant neologist, coined two durable
terms, and unnaturally conjoined one to the other. They are: sociology and positivism. Comte's first publication was *A Program
of Scientific Work Required for the Reorganization of Society.*
The founder of sociology saw a world out of kilter, and quixoti-
cally proposed to set it aright. Here and abroad, Comte's successors have followed in his footsteps. Social scientists, hip-deep in
the values they ritually forswear, a majority of them genuinely
concerned about the malaise of modern man, cannot help being
"problem centered." Given something like race prejudice, over-
population, suicide, international tension or juvenile delin-
quency, they commit themselves to studying the problem in
hand, with a view to ameliorating or abolishing it. Many practi-
tioners apply the pretense of utter detachment to mass communications, but surely, on this topic, everyone is prejudiced.

We had better own up to that simple truth: you tend to be for
mass culture or against it *tout court*. If not, you have mixed feelings, strong or bland, but in neither case are they to be con-
founded with Olympian indifference. Dwight Macdonald, say, or
Ernest van den Haag and I, for rather different reasons, abhor
the whole business. Do evidence and reason support our revulsion? The question is discussable, and it might even be answer-
able. By the same token, when Gilbert Seldes or David Manning

White or Frank Stanton is in the mood to offer qualified, reasoned praise for mass culture, one can come to grips with their case. But apparitions are not so easy to combat. Beware therefore the disguised apologist who hides his ghostly "objective" presence behind a smoke screen of jargon and gibberish. In other words, gentlemen, come on out and fight.

If sham objectivity is inadmissible, so is the contention that critics of mass culture are *ipso facto* critics of "the masses." Some are, and they speak from an aristocratic point of view best elucidated over a century ago by Alexis de Tocqueville. But there are other bases for criticism. I side with that earlier Macdonald who saw the masses (which is to say, everybody) as victims of a merciless technological invasion that threatened to destroy their humanity.

To reject "mass-cult" and "mid-cult" is to espouse high culture—and to do that is to be put down in certain circles as a snob. Very well, there are worse epithets. Shakespeare really does seem to me to be a better playwright than Arthur Miller and a better writer than Mickey Spillane. That they—and Homer and Faith Baldwin—are all popular is as incontrovertible as it is irrelevant. Such enormous qualitative differences separate them that no common frame of reference is broad enough to encompass their works. If to hold such a view is proof of snobbery, so be it.

But there is an attitude far more vicious than snobbery which converts the term "masses" into "slobs." Mad Avenue chefs "know" that finer fare, which they themselves prefer, should not be wasted on ordinary men and women. The communications industry drips with this contempt. Tough executives crudely and brutally assert the complete disdain they feel for their audiences. When a Dr. Frank Stanton or a Dr. Leo Rosten phrases these feelings with elegance, we are only slightly shocked. Intellectuals inside the business world may even deserve a measure of compassion: Mr. Gilbert Seldes of CBS must walk more softly than Professor Gilbert Seldes of the academic world. But it is really distressing that so many philosophers, historians, psychologists and other academics should also be irremediably contemptuous of the people at large. They form a sonorous and gratuitous echo of the noises made for money by manipulators and managers who at least have the goodness to hate themselves for bamboozling the rest of us.

All this talk of culture snobbery and bamboozling brings us at last to that central, unavoidable question that makes the cynical purveyors of and apologists for mass-cult so uneasy. It is a question, incidentally, that also makes Millsian democrats and utilitarians uneasy and probably should make all the rest of us uneasy as well. Quite simply, it is: by what right do we call high culture "high"?

If, as Jeremy Bentham insisted, pushpin (that is, pinball) brings greater happiness to a greater number of people than does poetry, and if there is no other way to compare poetry and pushpin, it follows that the slaves of the Nielsen ratings are home free. Then by any objective standard *The Beverly Hillbillies* are as good as—in fact, demonstrably better than—Mr. Leinsdorf and his Boston Symphony. To prefer Shakespeare to Spillane becomes mere eccentricity, and to publish *Valley of the Dolls* in contravention of one's own better taste becomes a sort of philanthropy—a little self-interested, perhaps, but plainly benign.

If, on the other hand, *Othello* is absolutely better than *Bonanza*, then the Nielsen ratings are not so much a justification as an indictment, and it makes no difference how many people at any given moment think otherwise. In that case there have to be persuasive arguments for describing *The Beverly Hillbillies*— without apology—as cultural garbage and the people who present the *Hillbillies*, as cultural garbagemen.

Does this sound offensively absolutist—a matter of elevating the prejudices of a minority to the level of categorical imperatives? Are cultural standards really exempt from that most cherished American method of extracting decisions from imponderables: majority rule?

Certainly standards of cultural excellence are created by people, and certainly, in the end, they are products of a consensus. But the important thing to remember is that the process has meaning only in a dimension of time. The judgment of one generation is merely a fragment of the consensus of many generations, one vote in the parliament of history. And about some cultural matters, the verdict of history seems reasonably clear. For example, it seems reasonably clear that for human beings everywhere art has always been a fairly serious and central preoccupation and that the most affecting and enduring art has related most closely to what is essential in the human condition. Conrad once summed up the elementary stuff of the novel by saying simply, "Men were born, they suffered, they died." There is more to it than that, of course—men also enjoy, love, wonder about their place in the universe—but Conrad was talking about priorities, and his point was that all these matters are high-priority concerns of art. Presumably he would have felt that showing for the ten-thousandth time what an amiable boob dear old Dad is would rate fairly low in the aesthetic sweepstakes.

Hardly anyone is unaware—at least viscerally—that 99 percent of the material conveyed to us by the mass communications media is aesthetically and intellectually trivial. Why, then, do we put up with it? Worse, why do we vote for it, paying good money for kitsch magazines, elevating worthless books to best-sellerdom and endorsing television imbecilities via the rating polls? It is not—as too many of my colleagues and all mass communicators insist—that the average man is no better than what he votes for. To a truly shocking degree, his vote is the product of communications-induced anesthesia. He is a victim, and his victimized voting tells us nothing about the thing in him on which the future of our culture and, no doubt, our democratic system absolutely depends. I am talking about his *potential*.

I mean to come back to this, for it is the core of my argument. But first I want to say a little more about the ways that mass communications can and do anesthetize us.

Do you doubt that they are capable of anesthetizing us? Competitive, if basically indistinguishable products—like variously packaged and skillfully projected political candidates—are said to be bought on the basis of personal influence. Those who propound this theory, when they are not subverting it (the same distinguished social scientist who acts as prime consultant to the ad racket is capable of writing a book which purports to demonstrate that ads have no appreciable effect whatsoever)—those who propound this theory believe that direct face-to-face confrontation is really decisive: parishioners look to their priests, wives to their husbands, an army of susceptible followers respond to the "influentials" in their midst. Only small children and total amnesiacs could mistake this grotesque picture for reality, but it is not, therefore, a total falsehood.[1]

Let us not overtax our memories. You will recall in the year 1942 Japanese-American citizens and noncitizens were herded into concentration camps, their rights ruthlessly abrogated by an executive order straight from President Franklin D. Roosevelt. Why? Because the only good Jap was a dead one. China was, meanwhile, our noble Far Eastern ally. Now the only good Chinaman (unless resident on the island of Formosa) is a dead one, and Japan is our noble Far Eastern ally. Suppose the year is

---

[1] A friendly critic objects that I have been less than fair in presenting Paul Lazersfeld's famous thesis. But no one protested in 1963 when Joseph Bensman and I put the matter as follows: "The public is unequally exposed to mass communications, and quite often, as the sociologist Paul Lazersfeld has shown, those more exposed influence others who have trouble deciding between candidates and commodities. A personal element is present in what Lazersfeld and Elihu Katz call 'the two-step flow' of mass communications. A heavy consumer of mass culture watches Ben Casey, listens to Chet Huntley, or vibrates via old movies to Clark Gable, and perhaps influences others to smoke Camels, buy EverReady Batteries, prize dimpled masculinity and abandon the undershirt. That messages originating in television, radio and films circulate this way—in a kind of aquatic mazurka, taking two steps instead of one—has mislead some students into believing that personal influence is more powerful than the mass media. Yet, on the evidence so far adduced, opinion leaders who learn what to think from *Time* magazine, from *The Defenders*, from David Brinkley, merely magnify the power of these institutions by incorporating and transmitting their judgments to a still wider circle. I may buy Richard Nixon as my candidate at your suggestion, but if your suggestion comes from the firm of Batten, Barton, Durstine and Osborne, the advertizing agency for the Republican National Committee, *there*, and not in your persuasive skill, lies the locus of power."

1938: Stalin is a butcher, the USSR is a police state, its people are slaves. By 1943, "Uncle Joe" was an amiable autocrat and the USSR was economically democratic and getting to be politically democratic. By 1948 it was okay, or rather, it was mandatory to repeat what had been said in 1938. Later, as President Eisenhower made a move toward rapprochement with Russia soon after settling the Korean War, it looked for a moment as if the infinitely flexible media would be mobilized yet again.

We have learned as well as any people on earth that vice and virtue are interchangeable terms. Pollsters recently discovered that 25 percent of the American public believe Chiang Kai-shek still holds sway over mainland China. Thirty million Americans represent a large reservoir of superfluous goodwill: Red China could as easily be glorified tomorrow as it is reviled today. The trick consists of turning on the faucets of influence, of mobilizing the media.

Tyranny plus technology is the formula for totalitarianism. In this context, technology usually refers to modern mechanical means of production, but it should also refer to modern mechanical means of communication. I do not mean to divagate farther into the relationship between mass communications and political tyranny. Suffice it to say that mass communications have demonstrated such a distressing ability to promote tyranny in the cultural realm that we can only tremble at the implications of their political misuse. Tremble, and fortify ourselves.

How? I think the answer, simply, is to take a more respectful attitude toward our fellow man. My position is that the antidote to mass culture is high culture, that high culture means art and learning and that these goods are potentially accessible to every person not suffering from severe brain damage.

I have never heard the disrespectful attitude more offensively presented than at a conference, some years ago, on mass culture, to which a wide assortment of scholars and artists were invited. A truncated version of what they said may be found in a back issue of the magazine *Daedalus* (Spring, 1960) and in a book called

Culture for the Millions. The conference was rigged in favor of intellectuals who support mass culture. Its centerpiece was a paper by Edward W. Shils who had long contended that "brutal culture" perfectly suited the masses. He repeated his thesis with the utmost gentility, thereafter lapsing into three days of merciful silence. Others took up the cudgels; but as a peripheral participant, I had no opportunity to deal with Shils' peculiar system of classifying his opponents. As an anti-anti-mass-culturalist, Shils had some while before explained that writers upset about mass culture are mostly disillusioned Marxists, angry at the masses they foolishly idealized in the thirties. Now I realize there are many more ex-Trotskyites than there ever were Trotskyites; but as a case in point, I, who beginning with my first "scholarly" article in 1948 have consistently found fault with Karl Marx's thought, really did not then, or ever, belong to a school of German sociologists into which Mr. Shils squeezed me. Anyhow, my target—like that of most anti-mass-cultists—was not the masses, but those who gull and dehumanize them.

To the fore of the conference stepped Arthur Schlesinger, Jr. He pointed out—with no mention of their notorious inadequacies—that IQ tests show an unequal distribution of intelligence in the population. Additionally, he suggested the existence of an AQ, or aesthetic quotient. Some few people are naturally responsive to art; the masses are not; everyone gets exactly what he is capable of absorbing. Neat, equitable, democratic—provided only that most people are natural inhabitants of Slobbovia. Are they? I would suggest several lines of evidence which indicate that they are not.

Almost all introductions to sociology contain a brief list of "universals," or institutions found everywhere. Religion and the family nearly exhaust the list. Anthropologists are likely to add art. From Frazer to Kroeber and beyond, anthropologists have been fascinated with primitive art. Few sociologists are expert in primitive art, and even fewer display interest in its civilized manifestation. Nevertheless, art is universal. No human society, however oppressive its circumstances, is devoid of art. This singular datum merits some sociological consideration. At present, it receives hardly any.

Since art is universal, the aesthetic impulse may be an integral part of human nature. I have argued elsewhere that it is. The individual needs food and shelter simply to survive; I would contend that he needs art about as much as he needs sex. Either drive can be extinguished, and he will go on living, but not without paying a heavy price in the diminution of his being. Small children in the United States spontaneously express themselves with whatever art materials they find. Youngsters react to pictures and to music with a measure of authenticity rarely attainable later on in their lives. What happens? It is like what happens to American taste buds. Frozen and packaged foods, above all bread (the staff of life—that compost of air and glue), those oats which only horses ate until Mr. Kellogg sold them as dry cereal: a diet like this from infancy onward can deaden anybody's palate. With gruel today and gruel tomorrow, who can savor gourmet meals? Similarly, extended pseudosexual behavior produces fixation at that level, virtually barring "the real thing," true sexual fulfillment. In precisely the same way, kitsch and instant education, if ingested for long enough, lead to cultural and intellectual dyspepsia or anesthesia.

In *The Theater of the Absurd,* Martin Esslin describes an unusual presentation of *Waiting for Godot,* a play that flopped on Broadway after the daily reviewers declared it to be excessively obscure. The production mentioned by Esslin took place in a maximum-security prison before a truly captive audience—which was enthralled by a play it found perfectly intelligible. The Freedom Southern Theater does vanguard drama successfully before rural Negroes who dig the message that a meaningful contemporary play somehow cannot convey to jaded middle-class theatergoers seeking expensive entertainment. The Théâtre Nationale Populaire performs in tents outside Paris; proletarian theatrical enterprises have been revived in England; Shakespeare clicks in the park or on the street. What does this enthusiasm signify if not the capacity of common men to surmount the trash that is heaped upon them? They too are able to have aesthetic experiences. One percent of the public views living drama with any regularity on the stages of North America. An ambitious, and no doubt unrealizable, goal is to double that number, all the way to 2 percent. Those who go are homogeneous: overwhelmingly upper middle class, professional, disproportionately Jewish. Blue-collar workers shun theaters and bookstores all over the Western world—which does not prove that they are constitutionally unresponsive to the drama or incapable of reading good books. Workers in Buenos Aires buy Argentine classics (deliberately priced low on an experimental basis) at kiosks instead of bookstores, which they would never dream of entering. A change of locus—for instance, theater in union halls and not in ever more lavish "cultural centers"—is frequently all that we need to reanimate the aesthetic impulse which lies dormant in every man.

Dedicated artists and teachers realize all this. The custodians of mass culture and their academic satraps do not. By their gross underestimation of human potentialities, they drug us beyond any hope of redemption. We must continue to do battle with them or become willing accomplices in the creation of "joyous serfdom." For, to withdraw from that battle out of fatigue, boredom or despair, is in large measure to be morally accountable for losing it.

If Godard can do three or four low-budget films a year and make money producing art, albeit not necessarily great art; if Pacifica can operate a network of FM stations, broadcasting views that may be politically repugnant, but are usually dissident and provocative, and all this on a shoestring; if even Hollywood, after destroying much of its best talent (Welles and Huston in our time, Griffith, Von Stroheim and Keaton long ago), can offer directors enough leeway to be creative without forcing them into exile or into obsequious submission, and Warsaw or Budapest can do the same; if little magazines with limited circulation can survive; and if subscription TV finally emerges as something less than a disaster—then, the direction in which we must try to move is clear.

Art does not have to be swamped by machines—provided the machines are used to foster pluralism, diversity and decentralization. However Sisyphean a job it may be, the present process which involves depersonalization, concentration and deracination must be reversed, and as rapidly as possible. For, just as only the young can effortlessly learn a second language, so there is a chronological point after which generations bred on TV cannot assimilate the best that has been written and said. Sub-art systematically unfits a person for art, and vice versa. They really are incompatible. Not mere dabbling, but *heavy consumption* of one eventually obviates the other. You cannot have a lot of both.

If art is long, sub-art is longer and life remains incredibly short. I would rather miss a flower in the jungle of mass culture (possibly the Beatles are such a flower) than lose myself in that jungle. "Liberalized" totalitarianism isn't good enough for most of us who still reject any oppressive system. Similarly, a thaw in the arts, here or elsewhere, does not produce that rich and wonderfully varied garden we have every right to demand.

The artist is basically an anarchist who should have as much solitude and tranquillity and as much withdrawal from commercial or political clamor as society can provide. He and we desperately need his creations. The human spirit will perish without them. As things stand, I can only agree with Herbert Read that Shelley chose his epithet well in calling poets *unacknowledged* legislators of the world. Read goes on, "The catalyst is unchanged, unabsorbed; its activity therefore not acknowledged. It is peculiarly difficult for the artist in society to accept this thankless task: to stand apart, and yet to mediate, to communicate something to society as essential as bread and water, and yet to be able to do so from a position of insulation, of disaffection. Society will never understand or love the artist because it will never appreciate his indifference, his so-called objectivity. But the artist must learn to love and understand the society that renounces him. He must accept the contrary experience, and drink, with Socrates, the deadly cup." Perhaps not forever. Surely now.

OTIS L. GUERNSEY, JR.

The Arts Versus Most of the People All of the Time

"... The majority is always obsolete."

Otis Guernsey, Jr., like Bernard Rosenberg, is concerned with the question of aesthetic standards versus the taste of the majority. Yet Mr. Guernsey's reasoning is based on the premise that "absolute standards" are an illusion in the sense that none so far produced in human history has proven unbreakable. Does this mean, then, that art is rooted in chaos and that its products are a succession of meaningless ephemera? No, says Mr. Guernsey, it does not; and he explains why.

ONE OF THE qualities I admire most in my friend Miles Van Valzah Hayes is his mathematical virtuosity (he has devised and published a new unified-field theory which goes like this: "The universe consists of a complex quaternionic field which is a function of space-time such that its rate of change is proportional to the square of its magnitude"). Another is his ability to keep his cool in raillery without resorting to donnish humor or other academic dry-cackle. Badger him, and he digs in; roar at him at your peril. Recently I observed him under attack by a quarrelsome press of numbers all talking at once; like Douglas Fairbanks opposing a stairful of swordsmen, still he held the ground with: "You may be a majority, but according to the theory of evolution and the survival of the fittest, the majority is always obsolete."

This was meant as a *joke*, of course, fired in self-defense. Its feather was meant to tickle. If it happened to be attached to an arrow, well, that's the way it goes sometimes. I remember being tickled twice by this remark, once when my friend Hayes flung it around himself like the invisible shield in the toothpaste ads, and once more just before turning out the light that night. It wasn't until 3:20 or maybe 3:30 A.M. that I was awakened, suddenly, by an echo like the sound of a shot: it's true, the majority always *is* obsolete according to the theory of evolution! Even as the many plump, soft-footed, dappled herds graze buttock-to-buttock on the grassy plain, the few fittest, hard-hooved mutations are scrabbling on the rocky hillside, preparing to survive and inherit the earth. Does this mean by extension that democracy is a fallacy? Is popularity a sign of decay? Are standards, even aesthetic standards, evidence of cessation of growth? Is the majority always wrong, *by definition*? Must we rethink all the concepts upon which America and Western civilization (and communism; especially communism) are founded? At 3:30 in the morning?

Then came a wave of relief: no, the majority isn't obsolete at any time of speaking. It's only *obsolescent*. Well, then. It's only a joke after all, an exaggeration for effect like the punch line of a good limerick. The majority is the perfect expression of the present, it *is* the present and it owns the present. In any future projection the majority may indeed be obsolescent, but until drought or flood or ice or whatever, the present belongs to the plump, soft-footed valley herds. Right! So (for example) in politics, the majority rules. All men in the present are Created Equal in their basic needs for food, warmth, shelter, love and so on, and are Endowed with Certain Unalienable Rights to grow and enjoy without interference. Of *course* our political democracy is the best system because, ideally, it makes the present as safe and comfortable for the majority as possible, while protecting the minority on its tangential journey into the unknowable future. What is

231

good for the majority is good for the present; and it is not necessarily bad for the future, *provided that the rights of minorities
and eccentric individuals are protected.* God bless America!

But wait. God bless political America, sure, even economic
and social America (and, in time, mend our Every Flaw). Our
organizational concepts, it seems (by 4 A.M.), are compatible
with the theory of evolution and the survival of the fittest. But
how about creative America—science, engineering, the arts? Can
our democratic concept of majority rule (or, for that matter, Karl
Marx's of the dictatorship of the proletariat) be applied to these
activities? Has the Western momentum toward democratiza-
tion, beginning with the Renaissance and peaking in the surge of
Jeffersonian democracy, carried us too far? Should majority (and
therefore, by evolutionary definition, obsolescent) convictions
dominate America's creative personality as they dominate her
political and social conscience?

The questions are rhetorical—and the answers, even By the
Dawn's Early Light, are No, Yes, No. God forbid that any consensus of goals and tastes should dictate in science ("Why
should we spend all that money trying to get to the moon, and I
can't even find a taxi to Bonwit's") and the arts. Yes, our hearts
and minds are so deeply dedicated to the ideals of political democracy, it seems, that we cannot help applying these ideals to everything, indiscriminately, like trying to measure lima beans by the
yard. No, majority ideas should *not* dominate the creative side of
life; quite the contrary. Activity here must be unfettered from
the present (and thus the majority); progressive; inventive; *forward*-looking toward a future calculated to render the uses and
tastes of the present obsolete, not so much by contravention as
by expansion.

We recognize this need in science and shape our attitudes accordingly. We live with the knowledge that everything we inhabit
and own is obsolete the moment it leaves the drawing board. It is
a point of national pride that our cities, highways, vehicles, communications devices, home appliances, medical techniques, etc.,

are the best in the business, but nowhere near as good as the ones in development. Nixon could lord it over Khrushchev in that Moscow display kitchen, not only with the miracle of the capitalist present but also with the only article of faith which outranks "E Pluribus Unum" in the American dogma: "You ain't seen nothin' yet!" That's what the design and scientific community is *for*, to render the present obsolete. Any suggestion that its thinking should be confined to the present needs of the soft-footed herds would be laughed down straightaway.

Our arts too are evolving, boiling with imagination and change. Playscripts at the Café La Mama and elsewhere "off-off-Broadway"; new architectural shapes such as Frank Lloyd Wright's Guggenheim Museum; underground movies; mechanical sound experiments; Andy Warhol's and others' explorations into multimedia, even "environments" and exploding sculpture are all departures from convention, innovations in form or concept, changes. None has yet been assimilated by the majority taste, but without them the 1960's would be a less interesting decade. Some of these art mutations will turn out to be growth and some merely waste (as in natural evolution), but our democratic reflexes are of little use to us in trying to judge which is which. The survival value of a work of art cannot be rated by a vote of the present majority. It's a good bet, though, that future fitness will grow out of innovation rather than imitation. The inexorable current of the millennia favors the happy exception—or, to put it another way, time is on the side of the way-out ones. It's likely that some of the above-mentioned exploratory works will survive the majority tastes of the late 1960's and render them obsolete.

The principles which structure society can't be extended into the arts, because the inner logic is different. Society can be regarded as a uniform density of interconnected individuals, like the cells of the body—one cell, one presence, one vote. I imagine that the arts, on the contrary, must be a greatly varying density of activity around an inner core. This center of the dynamo tends to

233

be inert with numerical superiority; dense with majority opinion; heavy with popularity; thick with the absolute standards of the moment (only a contradiction in terms will suffice to introduce the word "standards" into a reverie about the arts). Out on the perimeter, in a thin support environment, is where the action is, the creativity, the experimentation, the *raison d'être*. Every so often a strong force out on the edges begins to pull attention from the center and perhaps, after sufficient passage of time, shift that center of majority taste—that "absolute standard of the moment"—this way or that. Thus, a Pablo Picasso's lifetime of creative energy and brilliance may somehow influence the fair tenant of a Junior Four in the East Seventies to display a cubist work instead of a Lautrec over the Knoll sofa. (This is not to disparage Lautrec; he made it the hard way, too. Besides, the cubist work matches the drapes.)

An "absolute standard of the moment" is a form of wish-fulfillment arising from our need to believe that everything is known and categorized for all time, as in a fourteenth-century map of the world, or a *Reader's Digest* article. I feel that taste is a real function of the human being, but, like any of man's selec-tivity functions, it is geared to the changing and evolving disposi-tion of the individual and to the changing and evolving disposi-tion of his time (consider the recent taste for "camp" in which "bad" taste becomes "good" taste by virtue of its "badness"). I know that our experience includes not only artistic ephemera but also the occasional real miracle of art which is instantly recogniz-able and universally and enduringly popular (the Parthenon, Winged Victory, *Alice in Wonderland*). The mating of popular taste with one of these miracles creates the comforting illusion that all is not chaos; that absolute aesthetic standards really exist and may be determined by measuring this outstanding work, analyzing it, certifying it "great" and locating it as a handy checkpoint in the maze of creation. Reassuring as this illusion of "absolute standards" may momentarily be, I question its reality. In the short span of human history, no aesthetic standard has

234

proven consistently effective or unbreakable. In the practice of the centuries the arts have continued to develop in defiance of fixed points of aesthetic definition; otherwise they would be stunted, stagnant. What makes a work of art "great" and enduring may not be any objective aesthetic characteristics, but its appeal to an element of the human personality that is particularly slow-evolving rather than to one which is capable of easy change. In any case, I know of no absolutes which have survived the process of evolution for any significant length of time. Consider, for example, the space-time function in drama. The ancient Greek playwrights were convinced that the best way to achieve a revelation of reality in their works was to follow absolutely the space-time dimensions of reality itself. Accordingly, they wrote their plays with the action taking place continuously, in one place, at one time. Their good taste—acting upon their experience of Aeschylus, Sophocles and Euripides—confirmed this belief for them and made an absolute standard out of dramatic unity. But their absolute, like all others, proved to be just another dinosaur drowning in time. In the twinkling of an eye, a couple of millennia later, the drama had thrown off this convention like Houdini shedding a straitjacket. It expanded beyond reality to fit the space-time dimensions of man's thoughts, as per the go-anywhere, do-anything theater of Shakespeare's *Henry V*, with its direct appeal to the audience to create a whole spectacle in imagination:

> Piece out our imperfections with your thoughts:
> Into a thousand parts divide one man,
> And make imaginary puissance;
> Think when we talk of horses that you see them
> Printing their proud hoofs in the receiving earth;
> For 'tis your thoughts which now must deck our kings,
> Carry them here and there, jumping o'er times,
> Turning the accomplishments of many years
> Into an hour-glass . . .

It has been said more times than anyone can remember (mostly, I think, by Nunnally Johnson) that if Shakespeare were writing today, he would be writing for the screen. A few centuries after his time, the movies have expanded the space-time function beyond the dimensions of the imagination until, at their best, they can employ this function for mind-*expanding*. In their arrangement of images the movies cannot only depict any combination, direction and rate of times, places and actions, *they also heighten the audience's ability to perceive*. No longer is it necessary for King Harry to brandish his sword to convey an image of physical power. A close-up of the sword's hilt, at rest in the scabbard, would communicate the same image, and *King Harry can be doing something else at the same time*. Now, almost any function of space-time in drama is possible—including a script like that of Alfred Hitchcock's *Rope*, which conforms to the absolute standard of the Greek unities. We might suppose that this cinematic manipulation of space-time was a purely mechanical rather than aesthetic accomplishment, except that we find it taking place in live drama on our contemporary stage as well. Jean-Claude van Itallie's *America Hurrah* is one of the most imaginative recent works of the New York theater. Consider the space-time function in this exerpt from its script:[1]

> *The actors play various aspects of a party in slow motion and muted tones. They completely ignore a Girl at the Party who goes from person to person as if she were in a garden of living statues.*

> GIRL AT THE PARTY: And then after the ambulance took off I went up in the elevator and into the party. Did you see the accident, I asked, and they said they did, and what did he look like, and I said he wore a brown coat and straight brown hair. He stepped off the curb right in front of me. We had been walking up the same block, he a few feet

ahead of me, this block right here, I said, but she wasn't listening. Hi, my name is Jill, I said to somebody sitting down and they looked at me and smiled so I said his arm was torn out of its socket and his face was on the pavement gasping but I didn't touch him and she smiled and walked away and I said after her, you aren't supposed to touch someone before—I *wanted* to help, I said, but she wasn't listening. When a man came up and said, was it someone you knew and I said, yes, it was someone I knew slightly, someone I knew, yes, and he offered me a drink and I said no thanks, I didn't want one, and he said well how well did I know him, and I said I knew him well, yes, I knew him very well. You were coming together to the party, he said. Yes, I said, excuse me. Hi, my name is Jill, did you hear a siren, and they said, oh you're the one who saw it, was he killed?

She has been speaking rapidly and excitedly, but now she begins to resign to the fact that no one is listening.

And I said, yes I was, excuse me, and went back across the room but couldn't find another face to talk to until I deliberately bumped into somebody because I had to tell them one of us couldn't come because of the accident. It was Jill. Jill couldn't come. I'm awfully sorry, I said, because of the accident. She had straight brown hair, I said, and was wearing a brown coat, and two or three people looked at me strangely and moved off. I'm sorry I said to a man, and I laughed and moved off. I'm dead I said to several people and started to push them over, I'm dead, thank you, I said, thank you, please, I said, I'm dead, until two or three of them got hold of my arms and hustled me out. I'm sorry, I said, I couldn't come because of the accident. I'm sorry. Excuse me.

The Girl at the Party is lowered to the floor by two of the men then all fall down except the actor who remains seated as the Psychiatrist. The Third Applicant, on the floor, props his head up on his elbow and speaks to the audience:

THIRD APPLICANT: Can you help me, Doctor, I asked him.

This scene exemplifies the American theater influenced by the movies, in mutation, evolving fast. The Girl at the Party is both witness and victim, and embarrassed guest as well. The time is all moments after, before and during the accident and before, after and during death. The Girl at the Party is speaking to the audience, to herself, and to the other guests, who can't hear her because they choose not to and because she is dead. She is grieving and dying and apologizing for being dead—and then, abruptly the time and place and action is none of these. If *America Hurrah* obeys any aesthetic absolutes of space-time, it is setting them as it goes along.

Yet a doubt persists: something lasts, some absolute endures and does *not* become obsolete. The Eohippus and the Percheron are not *entirely* different. *Electra* is a creature of the same species as *Bonnie and Clyde*. What is it that lasts—a definable aesthetic shape, an absolute standard? I doubt it. It seems to me that in order to discover artistic "absolutes" we must look, not at the art itself, but at the human beings for which and by which it was created (just as it is nature that shapes the evolving creature, not vice versa). It may be that the *only* aesthetic absolute is the human body and spirit, the whole human being. What we call "art" has one characteristic in common in all manifestions in all ages: it relates in some way to human life. And it has one effect in common: it is perceptible by a human being.

By perceptible, I don't mean understandable or likable to a present majority or even minority. I mean simply, physically perceptible. The importance of this is obvious, say, in music, which can produce pitches out of reach of the human ear and therefore meaningless, art-less (unless recorded and slowed down so that we can hear them). Another example of the tyranny of the human physique in art is to be found in the subtitling of motion-picture dialogue. The human eye can absorb subtitle words only at 6.6 words in ten seconds, on the average, while the human ear can absorb the *spoken* word in dialogue more than twice as fast. Translation of movie dialogue printed on the screen must be tyrannously short in comparison to the spoken dialogue, but this is an absolute aesthetic of the form. Longer titles *cannot* be absorbed by the human eye within the time it takes to speak them, and they become gibberish; imperceptible; their relationship with the human being severed; no longer art.

What *Electra* and *Bonnie and Clyde* have in common, of course, is not an aesthetic standard, but their humanity. They are perceptible representations of people. In both cases we perceive that the characters on the stage are up-tight, and we recognize the humanity of that. When they kill (Sophocles offstage, Arthur Penn on), we perceive it and feel horror. If human beings were to mutate radically in the future; if, for example, we breed all compassion and even squeamishness out of our natures, we may evolve beyond perception of *both* of these works. They would then become meaningless gibberish, as obsolete as the type of human beings to whose attention they were directed.

How about the United States's arts concept? (Let's not leave that viscous word c–lt–r– lying around, someone might come along and step in it.) Are we and have we been evolving toward new inspiration, or are we being evolved into obsolescence? In my early-morning opinion, America's arts concept is beautiful, if not perfectly beautiful. The United States has provided one of history's outstanding environments of freedom for artists to grow in all directions, in all disciplines—and if you can't say that, you need not speak further. Within my lifetime America has exerted the major influence in the performing arts, leading the way in the development of the cinema and the stage musical comedy/play. Our country has produced the most gifted poets writing in our language (Gertrude Stein and T. S. Eliot) and the most gifted writer of prose (Ernest Hemingway). From Dixieland to Benny Goodman to rock 'n' roll, we have set the beat for the new music which in turn evolved into the Beatles' *Sgt. Pepper's Lonely Hearts Club Band,* with continuing American encouragement. America has generated the most exciting new choreographic concepts (George Balanchine's) and provided an enthusiastic audience for dance artists from all over the world. In architecture we have realized the great dream of the skyscraper. I cannot evaluate America's fine-arts contributions (except to note that we have made a fine art of the comic strip in *Pogo, Peanuts,* Jules Feiffer and even *Dick Tracy*), but I can point with pride to Thomas Benton, Andrew Wyeth, Richard Lippold, Jackson Pollock, Alexander Calder and maybe even some of the pop-op contingent.

Meanwhile, the American economic system has supplied the fertilizer necessary for artistic growth, supporting the training, functioning and appreciation of art handsomely—sometimes even too much so. (I cite the multi-million-dollar arts centers mushrooming by means of foundation grants, federal benevolence and civic benefactors in every overgrown cow town west of the Pennsylvania Turnpike. By no stretch of our imagination can we fill these aluminum and travertine palaces with either stimulating programs *or* enthusiastic audiences. It takes longer to write a play than to build a theater, and you cannot drive people into writing plays or music, or acting, or playing the violin, merely by building more and more auditoriums in defiance of current trends of supply and demand—of creative inspiration and the evolution of taste.) Even as they worship success in all forms of endeavor, Americans have grudgingly accepted the fairy-tale-like fact that today's ugly artistic duckling may some day win recognition as a swan—probably after the artist's death. In this respect the American majority really *does* comprehend that its tastes are habitually obsolescent, and that the future probably belongs to the suspicious eccentrics we find in our midst. Americans will give any derelict the benefit of almost any doubt, if there is the slightest chance that the derelict may be a poet. The hard-hoofed mutation is relatively safe on the American hillside (more have

240

migrated here than have run away), and relatively free to pursue his destiny. America calls its mutations a lot of names ("egg-head," "sissy," "beatnik," "bum," "queer," "kook," "hippie"), but in practice it handles them with a care not enjoyed in most national environments.

Well, there must be *some* imperfection in America's artistic rationale, or that sun would be rising on an aesthetic utopia. But no, that cannot be, because there in the first red rays I see the outline of the Pan Am Building. No, we have here no utopia, partly because we have taken one of our proudest politico-socio-economic concepts and applied it, wrongly, to the arts. I am thinking of popularity—and, by extension, our almost religious faith in the holy cause of profit. Time was when profit was merely a mathematical concept—only money. Today, the idea of profit has political significance (capitalism versus communism), social significance (an antidote to disorder and depression), emotional attraction (The Hand That Feeds You), personal value (as a symbol of success)—all of which is fine, except that it spills over into the arts, too, and exerts a disproportionately strong influence on aesthetics. We tend to excuse any artistic venture that is a money-maker, and suspect any one that isn't. We have let the sneaking feeling creep over us that popularity plus profit equals *both* plenty *and* good.

Applying the popularity-profit concept to evaluate or motivate the arts could, in time, grow into a tragic flaw, like Macbeth's ambition or Othello's jealousy. Popularity is a fine thing in the soft-drink business, but it is to be mistrusted in the arts because it very often signifies that the product has gone flat. That which is most popular and titillates majority taste is almost always as obsolete as a four-toed gazelle. (I use the word "almost" as a hedge against the magnificent exception, the Picasso or Stravinsky.) Conforming our arts to some kind of popularity-profit concept leads to all the obvious fallacies signaled by the old, familiar phrase, "bigger and better." It leads us toward the Pan Am Building and away from the waste-space beauty of Lever House and the Seagram Building. It drains our Broadway theater of some of its originality by encouraging a succession of musicals with built-in popularity, based on tried-and-true novels and plays instead of on new material created especially by and for this time. It froze the American movie community into outmoded attitudes and caused the dispersal of its most creative personalities. I don't know what it is like to be a young painter or sculptor growing up in the present environment, but I imagine that the scramble for instant popularity must be creating some confusion among young people, particularly as reported by the slick magazines in headlong, week-to-week, four-color competition to blast out with the latest and most sensational pop-camp put-on. I am sure that this popularity-profit concept is inhibiting the art of literary revelation by reserving its strongest support for those writers who have learned to spell "fuck" but have very little understanding of what the word means.

Our devotion to popularity and profit has led us into the error of delivering over our precious airwaves *twice*—during the development of both radio and TV—to the rating concept, the fanatical conviction that the majority is always right, that the most popular show makes the most money and is therefore the best and worth the most attention. Our finest democratic instinct of respect for the majority has, I think, played us false here. We have accepted the idiot reasoning that what is popular and therefore most profitable for the spider webs is good for all of the country all of the time. We have forgotten, or pushed somewhere into the back of our minds, that *the first responsibility of a majority is to protect the rights of the minority*; otherwise there can be no progress, no mutation and evolution toward an ever-richer art form. Our network TV programs are stagnant with obsolete material catering to what is conceived to be the majority taste at the moment, with no effective protection or cultivation of minority tastes. It isn't enough to book a few "think" programs on Sunday afternoon, when everybody wants to be outdoors anyhow, and expect in exchange to go hog-wild in prime time all the rest of the week. Who cares about "think" programs, anyhow? The *entertainment* is squeezing closer and closer to zero. We discard programs like *Danger Man* and *The Man from U.N.C.L.E.*, both of which had at least a style, a flair, and retain the teeth-aching tastelessness of *Hogan's Heroes*. Here, in American television, we permitted the nipping off of the budding promise of the early "live" TV dramatists: Paddy Chayefsky, Gore Vidal, Tad Mosel, Arnold Shulman, Sumner Locke Elliott and others. Instead, we settled for *The Ed Sullivan Show* and *The Red Skelton Hour*, because (it said in the ratings) that was what most of us wanted to see all of the time; never mind what a few paltry million wanted to see some of the time.

If there is any lingering suspicion that maybe the majority taste of the moment tends to be right instead of obsolescent, think back if you will upon the golden years of that other popular American entertainment medium, the motion picture. In the perspective of time, the catalyst of evolution, do the movies which looked biggest *then* cast the longest shadows *now?* Of course not. For example, here's a list of motion pictures: *Cimarron, The Great Ziegfeld, The Life of Emile Zola, You Can't Take It With You, How Green Was My Valley, Mrs. Miniver, The Best Years of Our Lives, Gentleman's Agreement, An American in Paris, The Greatest Show on Earth, From Here to Eternity, Ben-Hur.* Some of these were pretty good, but this is scarcely a roll call of Hollywood at its dynamic or fanciful best, as we see it today. Yet it is a partial list of Academy Award winners between 1930 and 1960—films which the artists themselves, *by majority vote*, designated as the best. I have off-loaded this list of winners to make my point. I have left out such films as *All Quiet on the Western Front, It Happened One Night, Gone with the Wind* and *On the Waterfront*, which *did* win the award in their years and *do* seem to be surviving as part of the screen's fittest. But no Chaplin film ever won an Academy Award; no Marx Brothers or W. C. Fields movie. Such genuine mutations of the cinema art as John Ford's *The Informer,* Orson Welles' *Citizen*

Kane, John Huston's *The Treasure of the Sierra Madre* or Fred Zinnemann's *High Noon* were defeated in the voting.

Finally, with a new morning sun in my eyes, I am brought to the conclusion that, indeed, the experience and taste of the majority *are* perilously unreliable as guides to evolutionary survival in the arts. Popularity *is* a sign of decay, and the appearance of aesthetic standards *is* prima facie evidence of cessation of growth. In our approach to the arts here in democratic America, we must bear in mind the principles of evolution as well as those of the Declaration of Independence, because both are essential to continued healthy development. The majority, so gloriously achieving in all other pursuits of national and individual happiness, is apt to be wrong in present judgments of the arts, *by definition.*

Exceptions to these conclusions are admitted without prejudice. Not all instantly popular works of art are obsolescent. Not all struggling innovators are geniuses. There are glaring exceptions to every assertion I have made in this frenetic dawn (for example, *The Beverly Hillbillies* is extremely popular, and profitmaking almost to the point of exaggeration, and, I think, a highly evolved work of TV satire); and none of the opposites to these assertions is necessarily true. Even (I must confess grudgingly) my friend Miles Van Valzah Hayes does not win them all.

But—"According to the theory of evolution and the survival of the fittest, the majority is always obsolete"—pow! A gasser.

ERIC M. MANN

Students and
Their Universities

". . . Most students would leave the
university within a year if they were
guaranteed their diploma whenever
they chose to leave."

*As Professor Martin has pointed out, the role of the university
in the cultural life of society is crucial. It is preeminently the
medium through which one generation transmits what it believes to be the matters of greatest importance to the succeed-
ing generation. And never in American history has the form and
content of university education been subjected to such widespread criticism as at present. Much of this criticism originates
among the students. The youthful author of the essay that follows is a national officer of the Students for a Democratic Society, and his comments on American higher education may be
taken as representative of the radical student critique.*

UNTIL QUITE recently I considered myself a liberal.
I attended an Ivy League college where I was vice-
president of the Inter-Fraternity Council. While I was critical of
certain aspects of American life, I liked our country and thought
that its faults could be corrected with a little hard work. I can
remember having fantasies of starting an organization called
Idealism Incorporated. Its staff, over which I presided, dressed in
three-piece suits, worked in luxurious offices and used Madison
Avenue and Wall Street methods to solve great domestic and
foreign problems.

245

I now consider myself a radical. Three major developments contributed to that change. To begin with, my idea of Idealism Incorporated was stolen by the Kennedys. That was just as well, for, in the event, it led to the risking of nuclear war because the Soviet Union wanted to put missiles in Cuba, precisely as we had done in Turkey. It led to the appointment of an Attorney General who was so busy violating the Constitutional rights of a corrupt union leader that he didn't have time to investigate the desperate telegrams of Mississippi civil rights workers. Then there was the war in Vietnam, which exposed the dishonest nature of an electoral system in which a people that overwhelmingly voted for peace were obliged to stand by while a policy of genocide was inflicted upon the Vietnamese in their name. Finally, there was the growth of radical student organizations, such as Students for a Democratic Society, which focused my attention on many of the abuses of the American university system. Until the development of this movement, students such as myself attributed their painful and unproductive university careers to their own inadequacy and inability to fit in.

The spectacle of the President of the richest country in the world unable to speak at any major university in his own country without fear of a massive student demonstration symbolizes the failure of American society, and the university system that serves it, to win the loyalty of many critical and sensitive young people. An examination of contemporary university life gives ample explanation for this growing movement of student resistance.

Although a university education is a prerequisite for most of the prestigious and high-paying jobs in our country, the university does not actually prepare most of its graduates to carry out specific, job-oriented functions. The university does not train the majority of its graduates in employment skills because most of the lucrative jobs in our society don't require many formal skills, and those skills that are necessary can best be learned on the job.

The primary function of the university is not to develop competent people. It is to develop malleable people. The university plays an essential role in our society by turning out large numbers of individuals who can fit in as interchangeable parts in the large corporate and government bureaucracies that dominate American society. The finished product of the university is the corporate man. The essence of corporate manhood is a willingness to accept other people's rules for how the game is to be played. The university is the game in microcosm: a four-year process that doesn't train one for a job, but is virtually compulsory for the socially ambitious because one can't get a good job without "that slip of paper."

The training in game-playing doesn't begin at the university. It begins early in the student's life. He is dropped into a public school system in which things aren't logical—they just are. Boys line up according to size on the right side of the room. Girls line up according to size on the left side of the room. The next year boys line up in alphabetical order on the left side of the room and girls line up in alphabetical order on the right. It really doesn't make any sense, but it wasn't designed to make sense to the student. They are rules for the teacher's convenience in "managing" the class. Students who wish to succeed will learn not to ask too many questions, but to help the teacher get order—the paramount virtue in the public schools. Even the most liberal, middle-class schools impose rules on students that are only duplicated in our prisons and our army.

The rules are only part of the game. Good scholarship is the other. Work is usually boring, but instead of instituting an exciting curriculum to stimulate students, school managers develop an elaborate system of rewards designed to make the student forget his boredom. Students are encouraged to accept uncritically the curriculum that is offered to them, and to strive for stars on the wall next to their name, for being elected to class office, for being appointed monitor, for making the honor roll, for having their work hung up on the wall and, perhaps most important, for avoiding having bad reports sent home to their parents. Students who play the game best are usually despised by their classmates, but they are also envied by those same students and held up as models by the adults in the community.

The process moves into high gear by one's junior year in high school: the year the first College Board examinations are given. Students and parents get involved in a stylized conversational pattern that often leads to outbursts like, "My son got a 672 in Math, 701 in English. He's applying to Princeton, Haverford and Berkeley. Hobart's his insurance school. My husband wants him to go to Princeton but Berkeley's got a better physics department, but it's so far away and anyway it's his decision . . ."

The key to success on the College Boards is to learn how to answer other people's questions well. The key to answering other people's questions well is to give them the answers they want. The key to not doing well on the College Boards is to ask questions of one's own. Possibly the most dangerous question is: "Why should I take this test?"

The College Boards are frightening because they reflect a society in which people are asked to participate in a process and accept a set of values which they had no influence in determining. In middle-class America the College Boards are compulsory. Of course one doesn't *have* to take them, but the price of rejecting "The Test" is being ineligible to attend most of the colleges in the country.

I remember getting my College Board scores in my senior year in high school. My parents had spent money to send me to a weekend course to prepare me for the Boards. I went down to the guidance office and was given a piece of paper with six numbers on it. The numbers were 567 in English, 609 in math. I didn't want to tell my friends. I was generally well-liked and considered to be rather intelligent. But that was before the curse of the six numbers. I was afraid that my scores might prompt someone to comment, "Hmmm. I thought he was smarter than that. Funny how you misjudge people. It's probably because he's such a good talker. You know, come to think of it, just the other day he made a really stupid remark . . ." My fears of such an evaluation were based on my declining self-image, produced by the test scores, and by my knowledge that my judgments of others had changed after I learned how they had done.

Students who consider rejecting the whole process get little encouragement from their parents. The College Boards are not an accidental phenomenon; they are an institution buttressed by a hidden but powerful coercive authority: the college admissions offices. The parent often agrees that the whole process is degrading, but usually ends up telling his child to "go along with the system." "Wait until you have a college degree. Then you can rebel all you want." Such advice is both a confession of powerlessness and a less-than-honest promise of better times to come.

The university system is a continuation and intensification of the game. The university shapes almost every significant aspect of the student's life, while allowing him to make large numbers of decisions that are in no way central to his educational experience.

To begin with, the American university is based on the dubious assumption that education is primarily a process of reading and writing. University catalogs proclaim the diversity of courses available to the students. They can read about medieval history, problems in American society, contemporary literature, trends in psychology or advanced physics. But what if they don't like reading? What if they would like to start a tutorial program in a poor neighborhood or work on an underground newspaper? What if they would like to paint, sculpt or write poetry—not in quantities and in time limits prescribed by the faculty, but at their own pace and in their own way? What if they would like to work in Appalachia organizing poor whites or in our urban ghettos organizing poor blacks? What if they would like to work as a longshoreman, make their own movies or work in a nursery school? Sorry. The university does not consider this education, even though these are the things the university is supposedly training students for. But ask people who are presently doing these things, and who have gone to college. Ask them what relevance their college degrees have to their competence in their work. How relevant would your own college experience be?

It may seem somewhat absurd for a university system in a highly pragmatic and materialistic society to continue to maintain such an academic approach to education when it is clear that university scholarship is irrelevant to most of the vocations its graduates will pursue. Some university administrators advance the argument that university education, especially in the liberal arts, is designed to encourage students to enjoy knowledge for its own sake. It sounds good, but it flatly contradicts the otherwise consistent value judgments of the university system. ROTC isn't for its own sake, grades and class rank aren't for their own sake, curfews for girls and social codes that declare love-making grounds for expulsion aren't for their own sake, university defense contracts aren't for their own sake, and neither is the red-carpet treatment afforded to recruiters from the large corporations. A university education isn't academic because university trustees are committed to the pursuit of knowledge for its own sake. It is academic because if it were not academic it would no longer be a university education.

American university leaders realize that the university structure is irrelevant to the needs and interests of its students. But they also realize they have nothing with which to replace it. Courses can be made more interesting, lectures can be made smaller, new subjects can be introduced and old requirements can be dropped. But the central fact remains that most students would leave the university within a year if they were guaranteed their diploma whenever they chose to leave.

The modern university is valuable to students who receive specific technical training and students who enjoy scholarship. But that is analyzing the university from the point of view of the student's needs. The university can best be understood from the point of view of the needs of the large corporations. In that context the university is a useful institution that keeps students out of the job market for four years and turns out graduates who are anxious to join the corporate team. A student who doesn't particularly like to read, but has been willing to read over eighty books a year for four years, is just the type of man our corporations want. They aren't interested in what he has read; they are impressed that he was willing to succeed in a process that didn't make sense to him and which he didn't find enjoyable.

A solution for the alienation that most students feel about their university education is to limit the university to students who need specific training in job skills, students who are interested in serious scholarship or students who just want to take some time off to study an area of particular interest. College degrees should not be required for most jobs—especially B.A. degrees—and the university should become a less powerful institution in our society.

Such recommendations will never seriously be considered in the type of society that presently exists in America. The university is the recruiting and training arm of the large corporations and government bureaucracies. Until people in this country control those institutions instead of being controlled by them, we should not expect any significant changes.

Although the university will continue to grow in importance and power, so will a student movement to reshape the content of American university life. In the past few years it has become clear that the trustees and administrators of the major universities have more tolerance for corporations that manufacture napalm, government agencies of international espionage and an army that is practicing genocide in Vietnam than they do for students who commit misdemeanors while trying to oppose the presence of those institutions on campus. It has also become apparent that university presidents are willing to let local police forces use tear gas and billy clubs to disperse crowds of demonstrators who refuse to leave. This brutality is usually justified by university administrators because the demonstrators were interfering with the civil liberties of the recruiters for the CIA or the

United States Army or companies like Dow Chemical that manufacture napalm. In this case the free speech issue is a spurious one. For if, as the demonstrators believe and abundant evidence confirms, the United States is involved in a deliberate war of aggression against the Vietnamese people, then it is the duty of citizens to resist that policy with every means at their disposal. The free speech of the recruiters must be weighed against the fact that the institutions these people represent are committing mass murder, including a conscious policy of killing civilian populations, in order to suppress a popular Communist revolution in Vietnam.

At first, it seems truly astounding that despite the widespread opposition to the war among university students and faculty, not one major university president has taken an outspoken position of opposition to the war. This development is less surprising, however, if we perceived the university as an integral component of the military-industrial elite that controls our country. Many university presidents are products of the large corporations, the government bureaucracies or corporate law firms. Those who did not attain their position through this route must still contend with the fiscal reality of the American university, which is primarily financed by large corporations, government grants and large contributions from alumni who have made their money in the corporate world.

The growing movement of resistance against university complicity in the war in Vietnam has given many students a new perspective on the role of the university. When students become aware, usually through the research and protests of radical student groups, that major American universities are involved in government-sponsored germ-warfare experiments and clandestine training programs to develop more efficient police-state methods for unpopular governments such as the Diem regime in Vietnam, they often come to realize that their disagreements with the university administration are more than a "generational problem." They reflect a conflict between people who reject the role of the large corporations in shaping their lives, and university administrators who are institutionally and ideologically tied to the corporate establishment.

Student groups that actively challenge the present direction of the university often discover that the administration will respond with a variety of coercive measures ranging from suspension of radical student leaders to using local police to assault demonstrators. But the university establishment is not limiting its retribution to dissenting students. It is consciously weeding out young faculty members who refuse to play the professorial game. Superficial observation of a particular college faculty may give the impression that there are many genuinely radical professors who have attained secure positions. But faculty members who can be generally described as being "on the Left" usually fall into one of two major stereotypes. The best-known type is the campus socialist. He is a well-respected member of the faculty community, is often a member of the faculty social élite and often boasts about his ability to get along with even the most conservative members of the faculty and administration. Politically, he is very critical of American society, "responsibly" critical of the particular university at which he is employed and downright conservative about his own courses. He is a stickler about grades, much prefers to lecture than to listen to the views of his students and is most critical of radical suggestions that question the political relationships within the university—for example, demands for greater student power or programs that challenge the rights of faculty to give grades that will be used by draft boards to determine a student's military status. He openly calls himself a socialist and writes and speaks about the need for a new social order, but he disagrees with almost every action initiated by radical student groups because "it will alienate people."

A more prevalent, but less successful, type is the young faculty member whose primary allegiance is to his students. He puts little stock in grades, and is willing to give all his students A's to protest the use of grades to determine whether or not students can keep their draft deferments. He experiments with new methods to involve his students in the planning and day-to-day direction of the courses he teaches. He is often called by his first name; he spends considerable time with his students after class; and when a decision is made to sit in at the administration building, if he supports it, he supports it by sitting. A few years ago, faculty members like this were often dismissed behind the smoke screen of the "publish or perish" issue. It is now becoming quite clear that teachers of this sort can publish all they want and still have a good chance of perishing. The dismissal of young faculty members who often provided for their students the only positive contacts with the university has been another important educational experience that has swelled the ranks of the radical student movement.

Once the university begins to lose its legitimacy in the eyes of its students, a liberated student body armed with new insights begins to discover abuses almost faster than they can oppose them. This is explained away by university spokesmen and the mass media as youthful irresponsibility and protest for its own sake. Actually, it is more a matter of students having come to understand and challenge the rules of the college game. College doesn't really make much sense, but it is internally consistent. Almost every aspect of university life has been rationalized to serve the vision of corporate America. Once a student decides not to share that vision, he finds himself examining his daily life with a new perspective. His protest is marked by the embarrassment, pain and anger of a person who has just realized that he has been swindled.

Many students are frightened and depressed about the lack of jobs that provide integrity and service. The spectacle of Peace Corps volunteers in the Dominican Republic watching their own government invade the island to come to the aid of a right-wing military junta, or of Peace Corpsmen in Ecuador protesting their involvement in programs that are clearly designed to "buy off" a social revolution, reflects the dilemma that young people face in our country. More and more engineers are looking up from their books to wonder if the only use this country has for their skills is to design better rifles for our National Guardsmen to use against black people in the ghetto or better missile systems for a military establishment that never runs short of enemies of the people. The self-admitted failure of the Poverty Program after a few short years of throwing crumbs to the poor—not because the poor didn't want to help themselves but because the big-city mayors didn't want the poor causing so much trouble—indicates that there will be few meaningful jobs in government service as long as our government continues to be controlled by and serve the interests of a powerful corporate élite. Student radicals will be increasing their demands upon the university to do more than just turn out people for the slots that have been created for them. The university should be in the forefront of a movement that demands jobs with integrity and social value for people and for the type of society in which such jobs can be expected to exist.

The radical student movement has given focus to the widespread attempts of young people to develop a personally satisfying approach to sex. Most college students today are not as liberated as they would like to be. They know their parents' ideas are stifling and unrealistic, but they don't feel completely comfortable with their own. Advocates of more conventional sexual behavior point to the great anxiety that most young people have about more permissive norms to prove that traditional mores are grounded in a more realistic assessment of "human nature." Actually, all that this anxiety indicates is that when people exercise genuine freedom in an area that is permeated with social myths and taboos, they will have many problems working out their own attitudes on how to relate physically and emotionally to others.

The process of developing a healthy attitude toward sex is difficult. The American university makes students' efforts in that direction even more difficult. Students who feel alienated, insecure and powerless will find it hard to have healthy sexual relationships. Students who experience little meaning in their role as students and look forward to even less in the roles that are available to them as adults cannot help but feel powerless; and this sense of impotence inevitably causes many students to feel threatened by the manifest power of sex.

Alienated men can't deal with women who don't want to be molded, and alienated women are often afraid to resist the molding process when they realize that their needs for security can best be met by playing the role that is expected of them. Too often, the result is that sexual encounters between students become games that are both ritualized and fantasized.

These games are bad, not just because they are dishonest, but because they don't accomplish their purpose: making people happy. Many young people are presently trying to reject these games, and are trying to develop honest and healthy relationships to replace them. The radical student movement has helped to create a more friendly environment in which to work out these problems by challenging the moral authority of the university, positing new sexual mores through rhetoric and example and reinforcing its members by creating a counter-community that openly rejects traditional norms.

These sources of student dissatisfaction existed before our government became militarily involved in the war in Vietnam. But the war has been the cutting edge, the issue that has cut through the web of liberal rhetoric that has kept the student population pacified for years. The Vietnamese revolution has been instrumental in the development of a humane and critical student movement by exposing the dishonesty and immorality of those who run our country and by showing American students that the power of the American military-corporate élite can be resisted. Radical students now realize that it is easier to protest corporate domination than to build a mass democratic movement able to end that domination. Fortunately their efforts will not end with graduation. They will not "adjust" to middle-class life. Many will move into cities, take jobs and continue to try to organize others into a mass movement that can begin the long job of breaking the corporate stranglehold.

WILLIAM JOVANOVICH

America Revisited:
Radicalism
and Alienation

> "What has changed during my own
> lifetime . . . is the nature of intellec-
> tual dissent by students . . . [from] in-
> tellectualism as content . . . [to] in-
> tellectualism as style."

*In the preceding essay, Eric Mann argued that because univer-
sities are primarily recruiting instruments for "the large corporate and government bureaucracies that dominate American
society," their reform was intimately connected with the need
for restructuring American society as a whole. William Jovanovich takes a different, more complex view. Universities, he says,
are coming to represent a new type of dominant institution,
tending to supplant rather than reinforce the old-style corporations as wielders of power. Thus, in effect, the universities are
effecting a restructuring of society; and, Mr. Jovanovich implies,
a student dissent based on alienation may therefore become less
and less relevant.*

I N E V E R Y educational drill there is a familiar irony: in
order to instruct the young about the ways of society, we
separate them from it. Yet the isolation of students is not finally
the educator's will, nor is it done entirely for his own accommo-

dation. It used to be fashionable, and maybe it still is, to deride the amount of time that professional educators spend on the logistics of moving children in and out of buses, classrooms, cafeterias and playing fields. The fact is that these logistics are unavoidable so long as the schools are expected to undertake an enormous task of incarceration each day, which is to occupy about a third of the population so that, presumably, the other two-thirds can get on with the work of the world. As a result, institutional education undertakes, however reluctantly, two pragmatical functions: it renders children docile and it gets them out of the way.

Viewed in this way, certain social attitudes may be seen to result from the means by which society daily disposes of its children. In his autobiography *Words*, Jean-Paul Sartre suggests that the traditional conservatism of peasants is perpetuated by a simple circumstance: whilst their fathers work in the fields, the young boys are left at home with their grandfathers and from them learn the homilies of the past. On the other end of the social scale, the British upper classes send their children away from home at an obscenely early age to be segregated both by age and by sex. This is not done wholly without sensibility, however, for the British are quick to deplore their own practice. There is hardly a single autobiography by an English writer—Stephen Spender, Evelyn Waugh and C. S. Lewis come to mind—that does not dwell at length on the beastliness of life at an English public school. Yet, the very father who recalls the public school as being near intolerable will still send his son to it, presumably because he believes that to endure such schooling is to undergo a process of natural social selection.

As for how Americans marshal their young children through the day, I am not sure what social inferences can be drawn from it. Probably not too much should be read into our practice of leaving children almost entirely to the care of women, that is, at home with their mothers and at elementary school with female teachers. This practice is inevitable in an industrial society where there is typically an overemployment of educated men; and it is not, for example, any more the evidence of "Momism" in the United States than it is in Japan, where the same practice occurs. If indeed it is useful to observe the effects of isolating youth by the process of formal education, then I think the decisive period in the American experience occurs at university age. In colleges and universities the declared aim is, of course, not to incarcerate youth but to liberate them, yet paradoxically we regard the student's experiences as being restrictively special and unrepresentative.

Surely the isolating of many millions of young people in universities—a substantial part of the American population between the ages of eighteen and twenty-five—helps to account for a relatively new development in American social criticism, which is to conceive of "The Young" as a bloc, almost as a social class in themselves. The basis for such identification is not really chronological age. According to certain "pop" social critics, "The Young" are people whose ideas and attitudes devolve from a state of life, rather than a stage of life. Their modes of thinking cannot be dismissed, as in former times, as merely a usual phase in the evolution of a generation; rather, their attitudes are said to relate to their particular position, which is a state of social suspension. "The Young" become, in this sense, those persons who are not assimilated into established society for one reason or another, whether because they are still in school or because they are voluntarily jobless or because they are on the road as adventurers, delinquents or eccentrics. By this definition, too, "The Young" are a social phenomenon that can even be said to contradict the process of aging: new recruits enter the stage of social suspension to take the place of former members who pass over into the workaday world. Then again, some of the old members refuse to pass over, and so become non-students.

Now, it is rather modish to speak of "The Young" as comprising quality of personality that is explainable only in its own terms. "Alienation" as a key term in contemporary psychology

259

and sociology has passed from scholarship into cliché almost overnight. *Time* recently gave lengthy attention to a description of the youth of America as a special class and was obviously intrigued by the notion of alienation, variously describing it as a new disease and a new philosophy. For some years, a number of intellectuals have tried to test the validity of certain social and political ideas according to their acceptance by students. Paul Goodman was one of the first to posit that, because students are outside the established society, one ought to be as concerned with learning from them as with teaching them. Even to complain that Goodman and others are "bootlickers of the young" is to recognize the force of this new mode of identification. When Stanley Kauffmann, in *The New Republic*, attacks the notion that "what is Young is good, true, pure, and hopeful; what is Non-Young is tainted, false, impure, and hopeless," he is himself confirming the distinction.

It seems to me that to regard youth as a bloc, to ascribe to them particular prejudices and recognizable patterns of intellection, reveals an increased awareness that education is a powerful social determinant. This contemporary view reveals something else: it reflects a *changed* experience. What has changed during my own lifetime, between the 1930's and the 1960's, is the nature of intellectual dissent by students. The difference can be characterized, I think, as one between intellectualism as content and intellectualism as style. To restate the difference in terms of active dissent from conventional society, one can say that one form of intellectualism leads typically to radicalism, the other to alienation. To illustrate this distinction, recollection may serve my purpose, though nostalgia may also obscure it. When I was a young man I felt keenly that my mission was to discover America. Today, I often feel that my mission is to preserve it. Every man is a tourist from another time.

When I entered college during the late 1930's, the graduation from high school was momentous in creating a class difference in American society. For the eighteen-year-old who went on to college, the rites of passage were beginning; for the one who went right to work, they had ended. Going to college opened a gap between the student and the worker, for if the student could believe that he was continuing his youth, the worker was convinced that he had all but abandoned it. George Orwell describes, in the context of the 1930's, how a man's view of aging is related to his economic opportunity. In his essay on the "camp" comic postcards of the English artist Donald McGill, he speculates: "One of the few authentic class differences, as opposed to class distinctions, still existing in England is that the working classes age very much earlier. . . . The working classes reach middle age earlier because they accept it earlier. . . . And this reflects, on a comic level, the working-class outlook that youth and adventure—indeed, individual life—end with marriage." Orwell concludes that "It is this ancient wisdom that McGill and his colleagues are reflecting, no doubt unconsciously, when they allow for no transition stage between the honeymoon couples and those glamourless figures, Mum and Dad." This observation is clearly more pertinent to English society than to American, where the preponderance of the middle class has always created an *ambiance* of ambition and hopefulness; yet it was in part relevant to the United States a quarter of a century ago. By the time they had reached the age of thirty, there were actual physical differences between those Americans who attended college and those who did not. One sees these differences amongst the middle-aged of today.

The college student of the 1930's had reason to believe that higher education could ensure his youthfulness. The popular models of the "collegian" in magazine fiction and the movies supported the belief. There was, moreover, a certain romance about the executive life in corporations, most of which were still new. Given an important job and preferred position, the college graduate hoped to acquire the objects and affect the styles that would lend adventure and eventfulness, no less than comfort, to his later life. In the meanwhile he could have Fun, like Ginger

Rogers and Ray Milland at the Big Game. That the college student was more often than not frustrated in his hope, we all know. The fiction of F. Scott Fitzgerald, John Marquand and Robert Penn Warren depicts the disappointment following upon the broken promises of affluence. (None of these writers, however, tried to make of the end of youth an historical event, as Vance Bourjaily does, so absurdly, in *The Man Who Knew Kennedy*.) However much it meant giving hostage to illusion, the fact is that attending college during the 1930's was generally regarded as a privileged passage *into* society, not a means of confirming one's alienation from it, or of persisting outside it.

What may be hard to comprehend about that attitude, today, is that society during the 1930's was a most difficult place to pass into, even for those who declared allegiance to its tenets of establishment. The Great Depression almost completely dominated not only social thinking but individual consciousness; and while a minority of students spoke of reforming the social order, practically everyone spoke of getting a job. That the social order was in an appalling mess was generally conceded, but the young did not consider themselves its special victims. Even the college radicals did not identify themselves strictly by their generation. For them the current slogan "Don't trust anyone over thirty" would have seemed ridiculous, not only because it is a self-liquidating policy, but also because most of the radicals in the country were in fact middle-aged. Indeed, the only age-group that maintained a conscious identity during the 1930's was the elderly. Charles Townsend and Upton Sinclair organized old people to demand that they be compensated because of their age —as the survivors of an economic disaster.

There were, of course, many college students engaged in an articulate, and activist, dissent from the contemporary social order. Their dissent largely took the form of political doctrine and party politics, and for this reason most of the campus radicals I knew were Socialists, Trotskyites, Communists and far-Left New Dealers. Significantly, these radicals had only a tenuous and uneasy connection with young workers. For one thing, the campus radicals were not themselves working—their aging process was already set to a different clock—and for another, many of them were of middle-class origin. I myself recall having a distaste for the Marxist campus radicals because they presumed to speak for workers but were, so many of them, without experience in the ways of poverty, the laboring life and unionism. I was born to an immigrant family in a company-owned mining town. My father carried a rifle against the scabs in the Colorado coal strike of 1913–1914. When I was eleven I watched strikers, with bullet holes in their coats and caps, visit my father one night after having been fired upon by the National Guard. At sixteen I drove a Montenegrin through the coal towns of northern Colorado so that he could recruit Slavs to fight against the fascist Nationalists in Spain; within a year he was killed in the Republican retreat from Aragon. Yet, even with this background, I found little in common with the intellectual radicals I met at the University of Colorado and at Harvard. They seemed to me to be at the same time sentimental and doctrinaire, which is possibly the worst combination in the human personality.

But my own disagreement with the campus radicals was not, ultimately, based on questions of personality or style. It was, rather, a disagreement over politics and systems of social philosophy; the two were largely equated at that time. Most radicals in the 1930's were consciously intellectual in the European sense of the term, which is to say that they readily accepted historical explanations and ideological interpretations of the social order; they saw the events and circumstances of their own time through the prism of positivist ideas. Their intellectualism, in short, was based on *content* and it therefore had limited but fairly constant referents. Dissent had a social purpose for this kind of intellectual, who believed that he could forecast the course of the social evolution. The typical dissenter among university students of the thirties was an historicist. Economic and political phenomena proceeded from historically determinable sources; these phenomena should be judged, therefore, by systems of reasoning and not by personal or absolute values. Nor was historicism limited to Marxists, who of course owned a convenient dialectic; it was a familiar approach for even those intellectuals who were radical without following a party.

Now, the content of radicalism and dissent was rather formidable—one needed to read widely to argue it well—but it was also inflexible. A familiar condition of radicalism during the 1930's was the intellectuals' irritation that the political evolution of American social order did not proceed as expected. Roosevelt and his New Dealers borrowed programs and measures and tried them out expediently, with little regard for ideological consistency, and seemed quite satisfied with short-range plans, so long as they produced perceptible results. More significantly, the American working classes did not behave as expected, which means mainly that they did not follow European models and form parties. Yet it is significant to note, in comparing the nature of dissent during the 1930's with that of the 1960's, that none of us who were the campus intellectuals in the aftermath of the Great Depression was inclined to despise our own time. We did not, however much we disagreed on political rationale, complain that the modern age was in itself a bad thing. Specifically, we did not look upon the emerging developments of technology, of mass education, of increasing urbanization as being part of an other-directed social process that was victimizing us personally— that was depreciating us as individuals. Few of us then would have assumed that there had been past periods in American society when life was more humane. Of course, some of the radicals of the thirties, who at that time wanted to overturn society, have come to middle age with a desire to escape it. I liked them better in their youth, even when they were puritanically doctrinaire, for now many of them strike me as merely sentimental. One sees them abroad, the very ones who are refreshed by the simple, colorful life of Sicily and who are charmed by Luigi Barzini's prescription that the Italians can teach the rest of us the arts of

humane life, but who seem not to have read the works of Danilo
Dolci or to have seen the sickened faces of children in western
Sicilian towns that represent two thousand years of humane civi-
lization.

My recollection is, naturally, tempered by the content of my
own life. I do not mean to reveal a footless pride in my poor
upbringing, and I take caution from what T. S. Eliot once told
me about an English writer: Eliot said that he referred too often
to his illiterate grandfather and ought to stop congratulating
himself on the old man. Still, autobiography may serve my purpose here just once more. My elder son, a 1966 graduate of Harvard, wrote me recently as follows:

I was in Cambridge yesterday, being young. It was an
excursion. There is a mood of nastiness in student life:
the issues are magnificent but the ideas are brutal, like
the slogans: "Make Love Not War" and "The War is
Good for the Economy, Invest Your Son." The only
heroes are the people who sell you what you want. Ful-
bright and Kennedy are well-liked, as Willy Loman
was. . . . I remember during my second and third years
at Harvard the tremendous energy we put into civil
rights demonstrations and projects. There were meetings but also there were collections of clothing and
money. But all that has died. Not because of the white
backlash or Stokely Carmichael, but because helping
the Negro takes consistent energy and organization.
After the sit-ins and the marches came the more difficult problems of voter registration and open housing.
That required work, not protest, and few people are
able to commit themselves so fully. We were not passionate enough to be patient and disciplined: you know,
Hobbes complained that men are evil not from the
strength but from the weakness of their passions. . . .
So it is now less civil rights than Vietnam that is the

blunder of the old and the crisis of the young. But no one seems to understand the situation in Vietnam because it is new, historically new. The issue of pacifism is tawdry except for the real pacifists; for most of us it is rhetorical. Marines don't really want to kill babies and maim old women. South Vietnam is a question of politics, not morality. It is the only big question since Cuba, and like Cuba, it brings out the fears and prejudices of liberals and conservatives, and it makes parents remember to be old and stodgy and the children remember to be young and wild. . . . Why is it that intellectuals, in your generation and now, it seems, in mine, are so violent themselves. Alger Hiss was impressed by Stalin because he played for keeps. Orwell knew the fascination of violence in politics for intellectuals who knew murder only as a word. Everyone is hot for confrontations and neither generation listens—even to itself. Stanley Kauffmann complained about the "Salingeresque mystique"—what horrible usage; it belongs in an editorial in *TV Guide*—but Holden Caulfield had no reverence for generations. His problem was communicating with people his own age. As I remember, the only people he likes are his mother and young sister and the mother of one of the boys at Pencey Prep whom he meets on the train—he feels sorry for her because her son is such a crud.

Whether my son is any more representative of his generation than I am of mine is perhaps not at issue. It seems to me that his observations reflect a relevant difference between my former preoccupations in university life and his own. It is again, I think, the difference between intellectualism as content, a mode of thinking based on historical referents and systematic meaning, and intellectualism as style, based on individual sensibility. Dissent can be viewed as having abandoned radicalism and doctrine and invested itself in alienation and solipsism. Although my son questions whether Vietnam is mainly a question of morality, not politics, he is nonetheless concerned with his own values in judging a public crisis. Moreover, what relates public policies one to another is not their supposed objective connection, but, rather, his own moral responses to them. He readily personifies public issues. He is obviously distressed by the problem of personal communication, not alone between generations but also within his own generation. He has discovered, somewhat uncomfortably, I think, that student dissenters today are quick to be outraged but quick to forget. In another context, he once told me that the classic question of whether the ends can ever justify the means—a big question in my day, when radicals so often answered one way for the Communists and another way for the Nazis—was really a "sniveling conundrum," because means and ends are indistinguishable. It seems to me that the difference between us lies right there. As a young intellectual I sought to acquire an epistemology; I sought evidences to confirm what were the true and good ends of American society; that is, *I wanted to know the right things.* My son, twenty-five years later, would seem to be concerned with finding supportable personal values, with embracing a tolerable life style, a sensibility; he seeks the means to respond honestly and truly to the acts of American society; *he wants to feel the right ways.*

While I do not look upon my son's preoccupations as typifying an alienation from society, they could be so regarded superficially, that is, by *Time* magazine. Alienation, which can be defined in various socio-psychological terms, seems generally to reject systems of ideas that have a present or prospective social consequence. Indeed, in its extreme form, alienation is a rejection of *all* systems of logical thinking, and therefore of all political structures and parties, whether these support or contradict the prevailing establishment. Kenneth Keniston, in *The Uncommitted,* says that alienation amongst contemporary youth is "the explicit rejection of traditional American culture," but I am less persuaded by this definition than by his insight—a brilliant one, I think—that the alienated youth of today feels that an earlier culture was ideal. He suggests that alienation is in part a form of nostalgia. "In practice," he says, " 'alienation' has become an increasingly rhetorical and at times entirely emotive concept, often synonymous merely with the feeling that 'something is wrong somewhere,' and that 'we have lost something important.' Most usages of 'alienation' share the assumption that some relationship or connection that once existed, that is 'natural,' desirable or good, has been lost." In short, the alienated person feels in some way cheated: society had a chance to make things good and it blew it; specifically, the old folks blew it. Surely, this is an aspect of alienation that makes it hard to credit that young people around the world are undergoing a universal experience in being "uncommitted" to the society in which they live. For this kind of nostalgia is peculiarly American. It is difficult for a Chinese or a European to feel that someone has stolen his birthright and dissipated his inheritance. Possibly only an American can support the romantic notion that his own country was once a *tabula rasa*, feasible, free and uncorrupted. This notion is deep-dyed in our literature. As I have pointed out in another context, again and again the American writer has displayed a sense of aggrievement that something was lost on this continent, lost pointlessly and needlessly: one of his characteristic moods, to be found in Herman Melville no less than in Saul Bellow, is a haunting, brooding sense of disappointment.

There is, in these two qualities of intellectual dissent, political radicalism on the one hand and personal alienation on the other, an opposite approach to the concept of an ideal society. The young radical of the 1930's was disposed to believe that an ideal society could be achieved by political action that followed, and sometimes hastened, the process of historical inevitability. The alienated youth of the 1960's would seem to believe that the ideal society has been lost, and is not recoverable by conventional political means; therefore, his only recourse is to protest any action by any authority that strikes him personally, and absolutely, as inhumane, self-serving and insincere. What results is the oppositeness between a reliance on the content of intellection and a reliance on a style of intellection.

This kind of distinction, admittedly overgeneralized in these terms, is obviously more familiar to survivors of the "Old Left" than it is to present members of the "New Left." Irving Howe, in his collection of essays, *Steady Work*, doubts that many of the present-day campus intellectuals could qualify as radicals in the old sense of the term.

> Their radicalism [he says] is vague and nonideological; it places a heavy stress upon individual integrity, perhaps more than upon collective action; it seldom follows from any coherent theory of modern society. The campus radicals respond most strongly to immediate and morally unambiguous issues, such as Negro rights, free speech, etc., yet they also feel strongly that they are "alienated" from the prevalent norms and values of the society. . . . they cast about for a mode of sociocultural revulsion from the outrages, deceits, and vulgarities of our society. . . . In contrast, the radicalism of an earlier generation, despite numerous faults, had at least this advantage: it did not have to start *as if* from scratch; there were available movements, parties, agencies, and patterns of thought through which one could act. The radicals of the thirties certainly had their share of Bohemianism, but their politics were not nearly so interwoven with and dependent upon tokens of style as is today's radicalism.

This is, in essence, the contrast that I perceive from my own revisit to America.

It is not difficult, as you can see, to damn the old radicals as sentimental and doctrinaire and the new "uncommitted" as romantic and absolutist, and so to suggest, rather too comfortably, that the more things change the more they are the same. This is not, in the event, my purpose finally, which is to examine not only the changed quality of student dissent but also the relation of education to intellectualism. The number of students today quantifies, rather than qualifies, the attitudes of young people. At least one-half of our population will be able, within a generation, to say that they spent time in an institution of higher learning. Hence, going to college does not presently create an immediate or a lasting class difference in American society. For this reason and others, the difference between workers and students —except for most Negroes and severely dispossessed whites—is not as great as it once was. It has been lessened by the accessibility of common experiences, notably as these are generated by a general affluence as well as by pervasive popular media. Even the young worker now has the chance to persist in a stage of youthfulness, that is, to enjoy the illusion of unexpectedness and eventfulness in his life. He can with good wages acquire the objects, and with the new media affect the styles, that help him to delay the end of youth. It is commonplace that nowadays it is harder and harder to distinguish between the student and the worker, between the very young, the near-young and the middle-aged, and indeed between men and women, at least superficially. And one can only rejoice in this. That is, rejoice unless you *must* despise everything contemporary and see in this phenomenon the proof that the "mass-cult" has triumphed finally in America. This kind of despair should not be humored, I think, if for no other reason than that it makes one a sadist to be kind to masochists.

Still, despite their vastly enlarged enrollments, the university, college and junior college systems cannot ignore the question of whether they serve still to isolate, or in some way restrict, the view of students from the working, income-producing run of society. Given the student population that will reach possibly twenty-five millions by the end of the century, it is too late to question whether it makes sense to conduct higher education on

270

campuses. It is too late not because the education argument in favor of campuses is irrefutable but because the financial commitment in them is irreversible. Could we propose the dissolution of the universities as property-holders—in the manner of, say, Henry the Eighth and the monasteries—then some issues might emerge that are now somewhat obscured because they are held to be impractical. We might, for example, challenge the medieval terminology that is used to explain the locus of the modern university. We continue to assume that it is a sanctuary for scholars, but of course scholarship can be readily accommodated now in a number of places, wherever information is available and serious people can be intermittently invited. Or we contend that the university keeps teachers, like priests, unimpeached by the temporal will of the government, yet the modern university is patently a part of the government establishment in the United States. The very terminology impresses the conviction that students are held, so to speak, outside society for their own good, so that they may glimpse the ideal before they descend into reality, so that they may be blessed before they are profaned.

It seems to me that much of the argument over the purposes of the modern university, whether in the works of John Gardner or Clark Kerr, is distressed by the recurring notion that the university is a surrogate for society, that is, either a substitute for society or a simulation of it. It is, in fact, neither. College and university systems are texturally enmeshed in the whole organization of the American social order. Local and state and federal budgets are preponderantly committed to education, including its higher institutions; teaching is a common profession; seven million students constitute a tremendous social force by sheer number. One can be a humanist and still recognize that the modern university is a large component in the service industry in America, which increasingly typifies our economy rather than the industry of construction and production. Colleges as a group are tending to supplant the large corporation as the rising new institution that wields power because of its size and oligarchic nature.

Despite John Galbraith, whose evidences can be questioned, the corporation is not growing as an economic force. America has become, as Victor Fuchs says, "the first service economy" in the world's history. More than half of the employed in the United States are engaged in handling services, and more than one-third of all services are performed by nonprofit organizations. Students and teachers alike are involved in services; they are both processors of information, as Marshall McLuhan and Jacques Ellul maintain. When we finally come to credit this idea, we will perhaps pay young people direct incomes for the work they perform as students. Maybe then the notion of the university as surrogate for society will be dissipated, and it will be seen that education is the real business of America and not merely its beneficence. Maybe then we can discard, too, the notion of university life as isolating, unrepresentative and restrictive in effect, a notion that remains traditional but is, I observe on revisiting America, less and less actual.

If the colleges and universities are a major institution in contemporary life, and a part of its major industry, then the nature of intellectualism on the campus is not a singular or parochial issue, but rather a universal and representative one for society as a whole. Indeed, alienation is not really the privilege of the college student or "The Young": it is not unknown amongst university instructors, corporation executives, writers, bureaucrats and others who, in handling the stuff of information, find themselves asking whom it is they speak to and for what end. Hannah Arendt, in commenting on the disaffection of older liberal intellectuals, suggests that there are getting to be too many intellectuals. If alienation persists as a socio-psychological condition, it perhaps has a new future. The alienated person of the 1970's and 1980's will not be disaffected because of the broken promises of affluence—nobody believes in affluence any more—but because of the broken promises of intellectualism.

For intellectualism as a style of life, not less than materialism, can disappoint, especially if it is not tested critically. Intellectualism that depends mainly on sensibility, which I take to be the typical orientation of the new radical whether or not one calls him "uncommitted" or "alienated," has distinct limitations. It is highly susceptible to shoddy thinking and to rhetorical jargon; it slips easily into the manqué. Its test critically is quite different from that of the old-style radicalism. The student dissenter in the late 1930's was quick to vouch for the content of his thinking, for its sources and its rationale, but he was less inclined to examine his own moral stance and to declare whether he would, in defense of his social objectives, violate human beings with lies and other expediences. But the student dissenter of the late 1960's should, I think, submit to a different test. When he asks, "What is tolerable for human beings?" he has left out half of the question: the other half is, "What is possible for human beings?" It is the particular need of universities today to pose the whole question, "What is tolerable and what is possible?" and to provide students with the means to answer it, however incompletely and uncertainly at the time. Too many instructors are satisfied to exercise their right, which is to think freely, without exercising their power, which is to challenge the thinking of others.

The issue is certainly not that simple. Daniel Bell, in *The Reforming of General Education*, says that the contemporary university is caught in a crisis between "the two major orientations toward the future that divide the intelligentsia today—the technocratic and the apocalyptic." By "technocratic" he means mainly scientific discipline, which is devoted to rational problem-solving and which leads to professionalism in vocation. By "apocalyptic" he means devotion to sensibility and personal experience, as opposed to reason or tradition, as measures of the truth. If this is truly a crisis arising from opposite positions, then I think the university is the best place to resolve it. Most of the harsh distinctions we make between the work of society and its expressions are self-indulgent, I think. The university is precisely the place where one need not declare between being a professional or a pilgrim, between science and art, between problem-solving and problem-posing. To oppose these is to misread the nature of humanism, which is to see in man's creations the wholeness of his genius and the incompletion of his vision. Given his rights and using his power, the university instructor should find it possible to respect the potentiality of learning without depreciating the contemporary way of life, and to honor the past without necessarily despising the present. And accepting the concept of a democratic society, he should find it hard to participate professionally in the education of the *total* population while disdaining the inconstant quality of their culture. When Daniel Bell says that some older humanists are "contemptuous of mass culture because it is produced only to be consumed," he exposes their unreformed suspicion of universal education. Education for the millions is produced for consumption—for various use and reuse by individuals who only together make up the social order —and it seems to me that it is not really profound to ask, rather rigidly, whether such education serves utility and function more than art and sophistication. Rather, let us ask whether such education will make life more tolerable for more people, and will therefore serve not only their desire for the good life but also serve to refine their definition of it.

Ultimately, the question of distinguishing between familiar modes of intellectualism, of contrasting and comparing the old radicalism with the new alienation, may not be relevant. For what I perceive, as much from observation as from hope, is the emergence of a new kind of intellectualism which will reconcile and inform content with style, social purpose with personal sensibility. It is an intellectualism that perceives the practices of universal education as being at once its source and its aim. It arises from a growing awareness that education is involvement without indenture; it is the means by which one can increase oneself by serving another, by which to commit each to each. A humanistic education is the most reasonable and least violent way to confront individual prerogative with social demand. We have perhaps forgotten that the American declaration that it is possible and necessary to educate the whole population is a very radical idea. It is radical precisely because it makes society vulnerable to itself, open to change, subject to dissent, liable to disbelief. Universal education becomes, ultimately, a way to distinguish people one from another, not by their possession of knowledge but by their expression of it.

If a new intellectualism, a new synthesis, is arising, with education as its determinant, then I think it will create new forms of dissent—dissent over the values that should inform both teaching and learning; and more, dissent over the exercises of power by popular education as an institution and, indeed, as an industry of social services. Such dissent will, possibly, avoid the excesses of the old radicalism and the new alienation without necessarily limiting their permissiveness. One would hope, particularly, that it will be less doctrinaire and brutal. Intolerance is traditionally the pride of the propertied elite; today it is also the sophistication of the dissenter who so often conventionally despises the present, who is nostalgic about the unexamined past and untraveled distance, who uncritically suspects the popular culture and who personifies national issues so that we may conveniently deal with personages rather than with complex meanings. A certain tolerance ought to be possible among more or less educated people. It ought to be respectable for an old dissenter like me to ask a new dissenter like my son to describe his purposes, and it ought to be respectable for him, in turn, to ask me to admit my motives. In fact, it is possible. Revisiting America, I know that practically every tolerable thing is possible; we have not, after all, blown our chance, lost our option, closed the society. Someone once asked Mahatma Gandhi what he thought of Western civilization. "I think it would be a good idea," he said.

V

American Society and the Individual

ASSUMPTIONS: SOCIETY

The organization of American society is compatible with its free political institutions. It has been largely successful in attaining its difficult goal: a proper blending of the principles of social equality, individual freedom and majority rule. Classlessness and guaranteed universal minimal standards of welfare and of equal educational, social and economic opportunity promote equality in American society. Individual freedom is protected by a wide spectrum of inviolable individual rights. Majority rule is preserved both by law and by a willingness of dissenting minorities to abide by the law until such time as their views may be shared by the majority.

ASSUMPTIONS: THE INDIVIDUAL

Enhancing the dignity of the individual citizen, developing his capabilities for self-fulfillment, is a prime concern of the Ameri-

can government. This concern derives both from basic religious and ethical beliefs and from a rational assumption that functioning democracy depends on an increasingly informed, satisfied and responsible electorate.

The environments which help to shape the character of the individual—his home life, education, religious training, occupation, etc.—are therefore, in varying degrees, also matters of public concern. The object of this concern is to develop typical traits of character—independence of spirit, respect for the rights of others, cooperativeness, sense of civic responsibility and others —which will make the individual a better, more constructive citizen. America has been more successful than most countries in developing these socially and politically desirable traits in its citizens.

RICHARD H. ROVERE

Alienation and the Future of Democracy

"If in the end we prove unable to make a go of democracy, there is a fair presumption that no one else will be able to do so either."

Perhaps the most fundamental of all American assumptions is that which asserts the prime value of the individual. Our social system, and the political and economic systems derived from it, are supposedly constructed in such a way as to maximize the free expression of this value. Yet, paradoxically, any social system— simply because it is a system—necessarily limits individual freedom and therefore can never fully resolve the permanent tension that exists between the claims of the individual and the claims of society. A succession of rough compromises that are temporarily acceptable to the majority and to most minorities is the best that can be achieved. But what happens when compromise is impossible or when the system itself is challenged? This is the crucial topic about which Mr. Richard H. Rovere writes.

I NDIVIDUALITY is the aim of political liberty," James Fenimore Cooper wrote in 1838, in *The American Democrat*; and a decade later, in his *Civil Disobedience*, Henry David Thoreau insisted that "there will never be a really free and enlightened state until the state comes to recognize the individual as a higher and independent power, from which all its power and authority are derived, and treats him accordingly."

How wrong—how mistaken in prophecy—our American moralists have been! Had Cooper and Thoreau been right, the Great Society would be all around us, its every member happy and fulfilled. There would be no civil disorder, and of course no war in Vietnam. "Alienation" might be a legal and pathological term— but not a widespread social phenomenon and a fundamental "issue" in the Presidential campaign of one aspirant, Senator Eugene McCarthy. Civility would prevail and, the state having long since accommodated itself to the examined consciences of "individuals," there would be no point to the kind of civil disobedience to which Thoreau felt driven by the Mexican war. Thoreau was an eloquent man, a noble spirit in a mean time, but his logic was often flawed, and it was his proposition—one wonders if he could actually have believed it—that if the state liberated the individual, the individual would liberate the state and everything would be just fine. Jefferson and Tocqueville knew better, but they had known more of the world than Concord and did not think that all truth was contained in "the mind and heart of me." It seems not to have dawned on Thoreau that the social whole might be something greater than—or at least something quite different from—the sum of its parts. With his view of man and of the state, he would have had a hard time understanding what has happened in this republic in the century since his death, which is that the state has come to behave toward the individual pretty much as he thought it should, but that it is still, alas, given to folly and wickedness, still very much in need of "enlightenment."

I am assuming that the individual *qua* individual (as distinct, be it clearly noted, from the individual as a member of the whole society or of any minority within it) has rather little to complain about in the United States at the present time. Though a day may come—and before very long—when this will not be true, it seems to me clear beyond serious dispute that the liberties specified in the Bill of Rights are honored and in general vigorously upheld by the state. The government that Cooper distrusted and Thoreau despised imposes no effective limitations on speech or any other form of individual expression. I may say what I choose and disseminate it in any way I find possible, no matter how much offense I may give society in general or any of the groups that constitute it. In matters political, moral and religious, my rights as an individual take precedence over any and every consensus of public opinion. I am seldom held to any test of factuality or damage. Indeed, the more powerful my adversary happens to be, the more unrestrained may I be in smiting him, for the courts have ruled that the bigger they are, the harder they may be hit. If I wish to proclaim my hatred and defiance of authority, constituted or otherwise, I can expect opposition but not, as a rule, interference; should interference be attempted or proposed, I can demand and get the state's protection.

It may be objected that what I describe as rights and liberties are in fact privileges and immunities that are largely dependent on status—and, even at that, honored only in certain jurisdictions. Were I a black Mississippian not exercising but merely asking for my "rights," I might be speaking my last words on earth. As a white New Yorker denouncing authority in Mississippi, I might meet the same fate. Status is important in this society—in fact in any society—and if I threaten that of another man in certain circumstances, I may lose my right to live. But if I lost it in such circumstances, I would have lost it to another individual, not to the state, even if the individual happened to be an agent of some provincial government. For the individual, equal protection is assured by the state that exercises national sovereignty. In England, in November 1967, a Black Muslim named Michael Abdul Malik was given a year's imprisonment for what the sentencing judge called "attempting to raise hostility" against white people —an offense under the Race Relations Act of 1965. A couple of weeks later, the London Sunday *Times* was fined twelve thousand dollars and court costs for having printed an unflattering but accurate description of the same Malik in a picture caption. But in the United States, Stokely Carmichael and H. Rap Brown, though they may encounter difficulties over passport regulations and statutes dealing with the possession of firearms, are as free as any benighted honky to preach hatred and incite others to civil disorder, and a journalist is free to use any language he chooses in describing them.

Is the individual free to *do* what he wants as well as to *say* what he wants? Of course not. No society can protect anyone's rights without a criminal code. However, my freedom of action is probably greater than any that has ever before existed in an organized society. I can adopt any style of living that does not interfere with the right of others to do the same. There are no limits to my freedom of association except the possible reluctance of others to associate with me. There are almost no remaining constraints on sexual activity between consenting adults. In recent years, there has been established a right unnamed and unclaimed seventy-five years ago—the right to privacy. The right to withhold support from and participation in certain undertakings of the state—such as war—no doubt falls short of what Thoreau wished, but it is vastly broader than it was in his day. Conscientious objection to military service is respected under a steadily broadening definition of "conscience," and it is conceivable that the courts will one day extend a similar respect to the kind of tax-withholding for which Thoreau spent a night in a Concord jail. In ways too numerous to cite, the state has yielded to Thoreau's smug assertion that "any man more right than his neighbors constitutes a majority of one already."

The political order may accord to the individual liberties which the social or economic order may be said to nullify or to diminish in value. As the Marxists used to say, what good is freedom of the press to anyone who does not own a press? A man has to have a home before he can call it his castle. But, to repeat, the early libertarians regarded the state—the central, sovereign state —as their antagonist and did not distinguish it from the social and economic orders. Their conflict was with government, and by all the measures most of them employed, the victory is already theirs. Furthermore, when the conflict has been with oppressive social and economic power, the state has as often as not been the ally of the abused individual. Thoreau's conditions for a "free and enlightened state" have been achieved.

Yet never in our history has the individual seemed as wretched and despairing as he is today—and seldom have free men anywhere felt so thwarted and powerless in their relation to the government they have democratically chosen. I speak particularly, but by no means exclusively, of those who have sought and in some measure achieved "individuality." The conformists seem hardly less in revolt than the nonconformists. Never have disaffection, alienation and frustration been more widespread. And —what is the most alarming thing of all—never has the kind of liberty the libertarians valued so greatly been held in such low esteem than by those who possess and use it. Thoreau's hope for the redemption of the state was, of course, absurd. Liberty does not create enlightenment; it merely brings it within the realm of the possible. But at least one might suppose that liberty would be valued for its own sake and be seen by the individual as one means for building a society that would be somewhat closer to his heart's desire. It is clear in 1968 that one can suppose no such thing. There now seems to be something new under the American sun—a disenchantment not only with the society in which individual liberty thrives as it seldom has in the past but with the idea of liberty itself. In a survey of attitudes among liberal and radical college students and teachers late in 1967, Nan Robertson, of *The New York Times*, found that those who have the most grandiose and in some ways the most humane visions of a different, better America place little value on their Constitutional rights. "The most radical among them displayed total scorn for individual liberties," Miss Robertson reported. Nor, evidently, is this contempt limited to the very young who—lacking much acquaintance with, to say nothing of respect for, history— take freedom very much for granted. Mary McCarthy, a writer with a richly informed sense of the past and an honorable record of libertarian activity, has lately described "freedom in the

United States . . . simply as the right to self-expression, as in the dance, psychodrama, be-ins, kinky sex, and baking ceramics."

The disillusionment of the radical students and of such of their elders as Miss McCarthy has its origins—as what does not in this country today—in the war in Vietnam. What they have all discovered, though it is hard to believe that Miss McCarthy did not know it all along, is that the war cannot be stopped by the individual's exercise of liberty. Miss McCarthy was quite explicit about this: "The uselessness of free institutions, pleasurable in themselves, to interpose any check on a war of this character, opposed, though not enough, by most so-called thinking persons, suggests that freedom . . . is no longer a political value." By "value," she means, I am sure, "weapon" or, better perhaps, "force." Certainly this is what Dwight Macdonald means when he explains that he took up "resistance" in the summer of 1967, when "it became evident to me that two years of writing, speaking, and demonstrating against the war had not got through to our President." (Macdonald is a man of awesome ingenuousness. He has been writing, speaking and demonstrating for thirty-five years, through five Presidencies, without, so far as is known, "getting through" to a Deputy Assistant Secretary of Anything. He must have rated Johnson as an especially quick study.) The bitter truth is that we cannot use our liberty or our individuality to make the President cease and desist in Vietnam. Indeed, when we try, he insists on telling us that he is doing it all so that we can hold on to our right to dissent. Under the circumstances, the most we can do is vote against his policies when the proper time comes and in the meanwhile try to persuade others to do the same. This kind of activity, however, we undertake not really as individuals—as right-minded majorities of one—but as fragments of society.

I have suggested that there is something new to American experience in this disenchantment with individual liberty. I think it is without precedent. But I also think I detect a common element in the attitudes of Thoreau and Mary McCarthy. Neither is willing to accept liberty as an end in itself. The classic libertarian position, one has always supposed, is that the whole point of the struggle is to get the state off one's back—to achieve individuality, as Cooper said, and to achieve it for exactly the purpose Miss McCarthy scorns, "self-expression." Kinky sex and ceramics could be part of it—as well as a man's right to hold and proclaim his own vision of God or of beauty. The idea was not to control the state but to avoid being controlled by it, so that the individual, as Cooper put it, "is left to pursue his means of happiness in his own manner." But Cooper was a conservative, a right-winger of sorts, while Thoreau and Mary McCarthy represent another tradition—that of "social conscience" and political reform. They ask the state not to leave them alone but to give them power, to let them be part of the life of the state and share in what nowadays is called "decision making"—so that, as Thoreau professed to hope, that state would be made "free and enlightened" and, as Miss McCarthy would have it, freedom could be used to "interpose a check" on the war in Vietnam.

It is easy enough to say that they are mistaken as to the nature and value of individual liberty and have even turned inside out the classic defenses of it. But one is then compelled to ask if these arguments were ever themselves reasonable and honest. Has the desire for freedom ever been only a desire for self-expression or self-fulfillment? The great appeals for liberty have often stated the case in these terms—"Give *me* liberty or give *me* death"—but while there have been some valorous and lonely battles waged by individuals, the great crusades for liberty were collective undertakings (not for "me" but for "us") in which the aim was a collective liberation. Not many of those who have fought for liberty, if only in some bloodless demonstration against oppressive authority, have themselves had much to gain from destroying censorship or establishing the right to free scientific inquiry. No doubt there are in every society a few people who have faith, justified or otherwise, in their individual ability to create something of value or to uncover some hidden truth about the

285

world and ask nothing of their fellow man but noninterference. But, as the cases of Henry Thoreau and Mary McCarthy so amply demonstrate, even among the most gifted there can be so powerful a yen to change the world that a devaluation of freedom seems called for when it develops that free speech and free thinking and free love are not particularly effective instruments of change. And among the less gifted, those who are incapable of using liberty in a solitary pursuit of truth or beauty, disillusionment is bound to be commensurately greater. Eric Hoffer long ago pointed out that mass movements are built and staffed by "uncreative men of words."

And so it may be idle, even stuffy and pedantic, to point out that some Americans have misconstrued the nature of liberty and that they ask far more than can reasonably be expected of it. If this is a species of irrationality, it is only one of several that are to be found in this country today. To confront one's contemporaries with the ideals of the founders and early ideologues may be as irrelevant as attributing to the founders the present maladies of the nation they established. The fact is that the society in which we live is not the one the founders intended it to be or the one the ideologues hoped it would some day become. In it, the individual has a wide range of liberties and, thanks mainly to its affluence, a wide range of opportunities for self-fulfillment. But, as John Kenneth Galbraith has written, "the presumption of this society is no longer individualist but collectivist." He might have added that this is no recent development. Ours is a mass society in which ideas get lost or diluted or distorted in consensus—and this is not a word that Lyndon Johnson invented or gave currency to, but one that Theodore Roosevelt selected as descriptive of the way it is in our political system. Universal education, perhaps the most distinctive of our institutions, created not a nation of individualists, but a literate mass that formed itself into a market for mass culture and consensus politics.

It was doubtless inevitable—that is to say, predictable—that there would be extraordinary tensions between the free individual and the free but generally unresponsive society. For freedom and individuality are not sweet but galling when they cannot be put to good use, which for most men means some power to control events. This side of the New Jerusalem, there will always be a reformer of sorts dwelling in every sentient being. Each of us wishes that the mass would adopt at least some of his values, and some of us want a good deal more than reform. "Quite simply, I want a new civilization," said Ezra Pound, who went mad from wanting. A classic instance of how galling a powerless freedom can be is to be found in the memoirs of George Kennan, perhaps the most brilliant diplomat of the century. Kennan entered the Foreign Service of the United States in 1925, and the government paid for an education that put him on the road to becoming our leading authority on Soviet affairs and about as well-informed as anyone else on Germany and Eastern Europe. From the late twenties down to the end of the forties, he provided Washington with interpretations of men and events that can, in hindsight, be seen to have been almost spectacularly accurate. What use did his government make of the talent it had so wisely developed and of the analyses that might have saved it so much grief? Not until the very end of his career did his superiors —the ambassadors and Secretaries of State and Presidents he had served—trouble to listen to him. In his memoirs are dozens of memoranda drawn from his and the department's files; though some were written more than thirty years ago, they make compelling reading today. Had they been read upon receipt by those to whom they were addressed, this essay might bear happier tidings than it does. But many of them, in all probability, were never read by anyone before they were published by Kennan himself and, ironically, given mass distribution by the Book-of-the-Month Club. Though he is by temperament anything but a whiner, Kennan, as an autobiographer, is an aggrieved chronicler of rejection and of a frustration so deep that, having "no reason to believe that my views would be interesting or welcome in official Washington," toward the end he almost gave up trying; and in the end, even after a brief period of belated recognition, he got out, hoping that he would have more impact on events by writing of history than by writing policy recommendations that policy-makers never read. Out of public life, he has contributed much to enlightenment but discouragingly little to public policy.

George Kennan was not ignored because his views were radical —they were anything but that; he wanted no new civilization— or because he was held in low esteem. It would be closer to the truth to say that he was ignored because his views were complex and—despite the exemplary lucidity of the prose in which they were couched—not easily grasped. The views that Kennan advanced were those of an *individual*, an Emersonian Man Thinking—thinking as hard as he possibly could, thinking his way through illusions to what he perceived as reality. His views could seldom be reduced to slogans; indeed, they often ran counter to the slogans currently in vogue and obscuring hard truth. The consensus could not accommodate them.

We are, as I see it, in this fix: ours is probably the only kind of society which can liberate the individual, and it is at the same time a society in which he is less likely to find fulfillment than he might under certain kinds of authoritarian rule. Dissent is tolerated and at times encouraged, but unless and until it is organized on a mass scale—developing in the process a new orthodoxy and, inevitably, a new dissent—it is not more likely to influence events than it would be in the Soviet Union. Like the rich man with his money, the free individual learns that freedom cannot buy happiness. He suffers anxieties of a kind he would not know in a totalitarian country, where the notion that a few scattered voices might change national policy could no more take hold than the notion that a local astronomy club could send a rocket to Venus. The anxieties may be endurable when he differs with the society over matters that he regards as being at least debatable and subject to compromise; they become unendurable when he persuades himself that because of his powerlessness men and women in large numbers are dying in hideous ways each hour of every day.

When the failure to prevail through freedom becomes thus unendurable, it is only, one supposes, a short step to a renunciation of freedom itself. This would be particularly the case in a country in which not even the oldest citizens can recall a time when the individual *qua* individual was subject to the more severe forms of repression. In our time, the civil-rights movement and the labor movement have had their martyrs, but even when Joseph R. McCarthy flourished, no one lost his life as a fighter for the freedom of the individual. (Some may say there were losses no less grave, and this may be true, but the sufferers who live in memory are those who have died or at least bled for a cause.) A right that has long been secured is less prized, and more easily despised, than a right won in our own or our father's time.

It is not, then, difficult to see how, in this worst of American times, some of the young and some of the not so young can, as Miss Robertson put it, display "total scorn for individual liberties." But to understand is not to pardon. If individual liberties are held in contempt simply because they produce no quick political results, liberty of all kinds will be in jeopardy. Of course Dwight Macdonald cannot talk or write the President of the United States out of the war in two years. Nor can Stokely Carmichael create Black Power by extolling it before a thousand crowds. The test of liberty can never be narrowly pragmatic. Freedom of expression does not assure greatness; it may, on the contrary, smother it in outpourings of mediocrity. But if for this or any other reason it is to be held in low esteem by those who wish to change society, they will soon enough find that the likeliest kind of change their attitude will promote is in the direction of reaction and regression.

We appear to have reached a point at which there can be no communication between the alienated and those who have, as I do, a continuing commitment not only to the professed ideals of this society, many of which are dishonored every day, but to its political and legal institutions. Alienation is not, I suppose, a point of view that can be dealt with in discourse of any kind. Still, it seems to me that those who are coming to perceive the limitations of liberty owe it to themselves to confront not only the disagreeable facts about those limitations, but the facts, many of them no less disagreeable, about the nature of this society and its place in history and in the world. Such a confrontation can be dispiriting indeed, for it can produce despair not only about American possibilities but about human possibilities in general. It must begin, I think, with an acknowledgment of the fact that the United States was born in a revolution led by men of uncommon intelligence and integrity, men whose ideals were of an elevation rare in the history of revolutions. They provided us with model charters of freedom and with a governmental structure that, whatever its defects, has been workable enough to endure for almost two centuries. They achieved a political unity that was in time, though not without strife, to become continental. The continent we claimed was enormously rich and fertile, and this made easier the maintenance of the liberties for which the charters provided. In the first century and a quarter of our national existence, we attracted from a Europe unable to achieve much in the way of either liberty or unity millions of settlers eager to share the opportunities our continent offered and, for the most part, eager to share our ideals. We enjoyed, in short, good fortune of a kind unknown in the past and unlikely to be known in the future. It is not, I think, chauvinistic to say that if in the end we prove unable to make a go of democracy, there is a fair presumption that no one else will be able to do so either.

The alienated feel that the evidence is already in, that we have compromised ourselves fatally, and that the role of the individual is either to destroy the society or drop out of it. In that case, if I am right, they must concede the futility of the very idea of human community and the fatuousness not only of change but of criticism. For myself, though I have not known a time of greater anguish over our possibilities, I want this society to be preserved, and I hope for the strength to maintain my only commitment to it. Despite the horror of Vietnam, despite the squalor and hopelessness to which we have condemned generation after generation of Negro Americans, despite the vulgarity of much of our culture, we have, I think, done much to keep hope alive in this world. Until the Negro is fully franchised and represented, we cannot rebut those who are cynical about our democratic professions. Nevertheless, our history has been one of a steady extension and strengthening of democratic procedures, and this extension continues in this period. The rule of law has likewise been extended and strengthened—more in the last decade than in any period in the past. Though our economy can fairly be described as exploitative, we have, by the exercise of democracy on behalf of equality and of compassion, compelled it to distribute the product of our agriculture and technology more equitably than it is distributed in many countries which claim to have institutionalized economic egalitarianism.

As for our failures, they seem to me—to use a phrase expressive of some of our shabbier values—about par for the course. The war in Vietnam is a monstrous miscarriage of a foreign policy that may very well have been ill-conceived to begin with; but I do not think it morally more odious than similar undertakings on the part of other great powers—most notably and most recently, the French in Indochina and Algeria—who now censure us. Among the alienated, it is terribly fashionable now to say that ours is a "racist" society. Of course it is. I should like to know of an organized society anywhere of which this cannot be said. I have yet to visit a country in which the dominant majority, even where it is physically indistinguishable from any of its minorities, is not persuaded of its own innate superiority. I think it far less remarkable that we can be accurately described as racist than that we can be described as a people who have shown some eagerness to be free of this condition and have elected leaders and representatives committed to this form of liberation.

Though I have been writing here of "this society" as if it were an entity that the individual can sensibly be "for" or "against," this way of approaching the problem has never made much sense to me. There are too many loose and loosely connected phenomena here, too many currents and crosscurrents, too many forces in tension and contention, to speak of the whole thing as a machine in operation. There is plenty to be despised and rejected. There is much that stands in need of radical change or of destruction. There is at the same time much to be defended and preserved, the liberty of the individual being to my mind the first of these because it is the most needed for the realization of any possibilities. The work of any sentient individual, of anyone interested in appraising the utility or inutility of freedom, would seem to me to be to cast a discriminating eye on the nation—not to determine whether it is good or bad but to associate these qualities with the specific values and institutions that come within his field of vision. His judgment will not be reflected in Presidential cease-and-desist orders or rewarded by vast transformations of the economic order. But the exercise of liberty will be a defense of liberty, while its disparagement will surely lead to its atrophy and disappearance and to the end of any talk about human possibilities.

JAMES W. CAREY

Generations and
American Society

". . . The radical Left and the hippies
are competitors to name and give semblance to this generation."

*The conflict between the individual and society is not expressed
solely in terms of active dissent by relatively disprivileged minorities. Alienation may also be largely passive and unfocused. Perhaps the most disturbing example of this is the apparently deepening tension between people of different age groups. William
Jovanovich has already discussed alienation as an intellectual
style among young campus radicals. Here Professor James W.
Carey describes it more broadly as an attitude characteristic of
a whole generation.*

S OME TIME AGO I publicly argued ("Harold Adams
Innis and Marshall McLuhan," *Antioch Review*, Spring
1967) that the industrial revolution and the rise of the middle
class have had the cumulative effect of increasing the importance
of generations as basic social units. I suggested that the technology of print and electronic communication, the media used by
the middle class to construct and extend their hegemony, isolated youth from tradition and drove out of existence forms of
communication which promote intergenerational solidarity. I
also implied that unless we act to counter the effects of our technology we could look forward to a steady worsening of relations
between generations—increasing instances of political conflict

293

drawn along age lines and an increased tendency for social relations to take place separately, within homogeneous age groups.

Although I still think that argument is substantially correct, it is rather too sanitary. Most of us face the so-called generation gap in direct and immediate terms: the cultural spectacle of the hippies (or whatever group has replaced them by the time this is published); the political agony of the New Left; and, most important, the struggle to maintain contact, understanding and community with our children and students.

Lacking historical consciousness, we fail to realize that nineteenth-century youth groups anticipated in almost every way the spectacle of modern youth. While the emergence of rebellious, independent youth groups is a concomitant of industrialization, the particular focus of youthful rebellion has always been against the embourgeoisment of society with all that implies intellectually and culturally. The epithet "it's bourgeois" is not a modern invention, and it signals a revulsion from those forms of industry and culture which we identify with the middle class: abstemiousness, strict separation of work and play, sexual rigidity, philistinism in the arts, rationalism—particularly quantitative rationalism—in scholarship and industry.[1]

While some commentators apparently believe that it is only the modern student who has formulated a counter-idea of knowledge and culture, we are instead witnessing the old conflict between romanticism and rationalism—between the Bohemian and the bourgeoisie—in modern dress. In their desire to defeat and discredit the middle class, contemporary youth have adopted the same strategies innovated by their nineteenth-century counterparts: the promotion of a counteridea of knowledge based on the primacy of passion, subjectivity and openness, thereby condemning the disembodied, objective, rationalistic knowledge of

---

[1] A remarkable, elegantly written and mysteriously under-utilized book on nineteenth-century youth and culture is Cesar Grana's *Bohemian versus Bourgeoisie* (New York, Basic Books, 1964). I am heavily indebted to this book for clarifying some of the historical dimensions of the problem of generations. This work has been reissued in paperback under the title *Modernity and Its Discontents* (New York, Harper & Row).

the middle class. Like contemporary youth, many of the children of the nineteenth century also railed against the powerhouse society of the middle class, with its emphasis on power, wealth, productivity and a certain style of success. Instead they substituted their own more idealized visions of the past and future. Such youth also erected new, anti-bourgeois standards in art and literary life and condemned bourgeois images of democracy.

Rebellious youth groups have always paraded their alienation as a carnival which displays not only their romantic and hedonistic passions but also their contempt for middle-class life. They have adopted, in Professor Grana's apt phrase, "voluntary stigmata" as identifying badges of social contempt. Consequently, their dress, manner and social style—be they modeled on some displaced aristocracy or on the poor and the *lumpenproletariat*—must explicitly convey not only their revulsion from middle-class life but also their determination to experiment with two of the fetishes or "hang-ups" of the middle-class mind: drugs and sex. Finally, we ought to remember that such youth groups have traditionally drawn their membership not from the aristocracy or the poor but from the middle class itself. Such groups are created by apostasy; the contempt they exude is typical of the apostate, ashamed of his past and unsure of his future.

As Professor Grana warns, one must not attribute the rebelliousness of contemporary youth to the cold war, totalitarianism, or for that matter, Vietnam and the racial crisis. Our problems go deeper than that. The exodus of contemporary youth from middle-class society in one sense reenacts the traditional disenchantment of young people who cannot find breathing space for their imaginations within middle-class society. It is probably off the point to say that contemporary youth are rebelling against "the nothingness breeding in the suburbs," as the psychologist Benjamin Wolman has recently argued. What is wrong with the suburbs is that that is where the middle class currently lives. It is not so much that middle-class parents are *necessarily* leading hollow, empty, shallow lives, but that a certain tradition of intellectual protest has always identified middle-class life with hollowness, emptiness and shallowness.

In short, while youth groups come into existence with industrialization and the rise of the middle class, they organize themselves specifically to oppose the bourgeois spirit and the powerhouse society. One part of most youth movements normally opposes the spirit and culture of the middle class, as do the hippies today; another part—currently the New Left—opposes the industrial state. Collectively, however, both the youth movements and the bourgeoisie represent different styles of intellectual response to the onset and growth of industrialization. One joins, glorifies and gives impetus to the expansionist powerhouse society; the other yearns for the mythic bliss of Eden—for peace and harmony—and thus poses its will against the powerhouse.

There is something typically American about our contemporary youth. In style and rhetoric they return to certain cultural themes that are characteristic of other protest movements in our nation's past. Prominent among these themes is the American desire to find a sort of spiritual "passage to India," a union with the East, that will allow us to escape the unfortunate legacies of Western industrialization. It is a passage to nirvana. As in past generations, the vehicle of passage, or perhaps transcendence, is to be the very technology which, in another guise, is so thoroughly despised. In an age when the passage was literal as well as spiritual, it was to occur over roads and bridges, thus romanticizing the technology of communication and transportation.[2] The technology of contemporary travel is, of course, drugs; and the "trip" to nirvana occurs not by expansion of consciousness through contact with nature but through contact with the netherworld of hallucination. As in other ages, the object of the trip,

[2] The theme continues today in the person of Marshall McLuhan who promises youth they are bearing a new, Edenic world created out of the revolutionary and restorative powers of electrical communication. McLuhan contrasts nicely with another best-selling author, Maxwell Maltz, who in *Psycho-Cybernetics* (New York, Prentice-Hall, 1960) attempts to appropriate the new electronic technology to shore up the flagging optimism and confidence of the traditional middle classes. Maltz may be thought of as an electrical Norman Vincent Peale.

whether on foot or LSD, is to achieve "communication"—to re-create the root meanings of that word: community and communion.

American youth, in concert with our history, are still on the road, still defining freedom as the ability to move, still looking for salvation in a trip, still entranced by the idea that the road west leads to nirvana, still searching out a garden in the midst of an industrialized world.

On the darker side, one finds in contemporary youth movements many of the same old realities which the powerhouse has traditionally imposed upon the American dream. Close to the surface of youth movements one finds the same ethos of violence, the same capacity for duplicity and propaganda, the same lust for success that has always dominated American culture. Indeed, to be a radical or hippie today is for many of the participants just another way of being a social success.

In discussing youth movements we are dealing with a broad, evolutionary social development in which almost every modern phenomenon can be matched against a nineteenth-century counterpart in Europe and the United States. What then is distinctive about the contemporary "problem of generations?"

First, and perhaps most important, there has been since World War II an extraordinary acceleration of the scale and visibility of youth movements. We are now much more conscious of the cataclysmic effects of our technology and social organization, even though these effects were implicit in industrialization from the beginning. In somewhat overwrought prose, the Irish writer Max Caulfield puts the matter directly:

> Young people, more self-concerned than ever, have cut themselves off from the wisdom of the ages; detached themselves in a new way from the values that have been laboriously built up. Not only have the cobwebs been swept away, all the furniture has been smashed to smithereens. There are Red Guards everywhere.

297

But is it entirely true that "young people have cut themselves off from tradition"? Haven't they, rather, been detached from ethnic, regional and religious traditions by the process of embourgeoisment and by the expansion of technology into the family, the school system and other areas of life previously closed to it? For that matter, in the United States the larger traditions of culture and scholarship to which Caulfield refers have never really existed. There are very few "classic" traditions from which youth *can* be detached. Ours has always been a culture of rootlessness and restlessness, devoted above all to change. Our only tradition has been the pragmatic, which carves life into finite episodes to be managed by the most practical of means. In many aspects of the current youth movement one observes young people attempting to create instant tradition and ritual that will have more than episodic significance, that will have enduring, even transcendent, meaning. That such efforts are made reflects the time and energy available to the young and, more important, a generally higher level of education that allows the young to sense, albeit indistinctly, what we are missing. Unfortunately, as Alfred Kazin has pointed out, "intellectually and spiritually our students do not know that the wheel has been invented and try to do it themselves. This is how deprived they are—and how clever."

We are now witnessing a spiritual exodus from the middle class on a scale far more extensive than ever before because of the almost total embourgeoisment of society. Quite simply, there are now many more candidates for apostasy. Moreover, with the rapid international expansion of industrialization, we are able to witness the growth of youth movements on a world scale.

Not only has the scale of youth movements increased, but also their density. It is now awesomely in the power of television to dramatize the alienation and hedonism of youth, to take it out of an invisible corner of the city and move it to the center of the social scene. And since television finds the merchandising of agony one of its principal commodities, this cultural spectacle is thrust upon everyone, including those who would prefer to avoid it. Television gives youth groups a powerful weapon with which they can intrude upon and embarrass middle-class life, a weapon they have long needed to make their demands at least symbolically effective.

There is a strange corollary to this. The willingness of the middle class to gaze at its own condemnation—indeed to take guided tours through it—strongly suggests how much of the thrust and confidence have gone out of the middle class and thus out of this middle-class nation. Perhaps it is true that the culture of a dominant group decays before its power; perhaps it decays because of its power. Remember that youth groups who proclaimed their rejection of middle-class culture in previous ages were confronting a middle class that had a popular culture as well as an ideology to support its claims. In the nineteenth century the middle class was capable of producing a style of life in which it had confidence and which was projected as a standard of achievement, behavior and morality for society as a whole. All this was reflected in a popular culture which proclaimed the worth of middle-class values and glorified the optimistic future which opened to those who pursued those values.

In our own time popular culture has largely been captured by an anti-bourgeois spirit. The official culture of this middle-class nation daily proclaims the absurdity of the life we are all—artist and businessman alike—so busily pursuing. The great audience for the literature and culture which excoriates the bourgeois life is the middle class itself. Thus the middle class has few protections against the thrust and revolt of youth. No matter how much individual members of the middle class protest against the inchoate world view of youth, they are in the absurd position of not possessing an ideological defense, and in many cases are secretly in agreement with their children.[3]

[3] Of all the casualties and tragedies in the contemporary world, none are more deserving of sympathy and understanding than those middle-class parents who have only recently climbed out of the working class. They normally paid for the trip up at great psychic cost and much reorganization of their own instincts. I

The direction and effectiveness of the contemporary youth revolt are thus determined by the exhaustion of middle-class faith in progress and by the death of the doctrine of natural rights—particularly the natural moral authority of property. The argument needs little elaboration. Rationalism, the intellectual doctrine of the eighteenth-century liberal middle-class revolt, destroyed the intellectual authority of religion and substituted natural values. When the contradictions of rationalistic faith intruded on consciousness, the authoritative basis for natural rights and natural moral values was shifted to the concept of utility. Standards and priorities of social utility were to be established by science.

Thus the first principles of science became the last absolutes; science became the new source of authority and value and the justification of middle-class enterprise, institutions and social policy. The upshot of the shift was to enthrone the scientist and to encourage the penetration of science and technology to all corners of social life. The powerhouse society was reconstructed on a new and more extensive basis: the marriage of all intellect to science and technology and to the corporate state, a move which, as someone has said, threatens "to create a whole new system of living in which the world becomes a laboratory and the people in it become objects for experiment and control."

Contemporary youth rail not merely against the bourgeois spirit, but against the reconstruction of that spirit on a new basis that has borrowed the culture, mentality and ideology of the technocrat. Self-conscious and articulate youth are protesting against the almost total statisticalization of mind and society,

---

suspect they frequently doubted that the trip was worth the price but were assured by the dominant culture that it was. And now that they have made the climb not only do their own children tell them they bought a vacuous wish but the dominant culture now provides them with images that can only be used to dissect the idiocy of their own behavior. The recriminatory tendencies in such situations are reinforced by our belief, the product of the dominant psychology, that the proximate environment of a child has more to do with how he turns out than the general culture. As a first step in dealing with generational problems we might purge from the common language that often heard phrase, "What have we done wrong?"

against a new monopoly of knowledge with no ultimate moral justification and perhaps with little practical justification. They do so at a time when not only the romantic but the rational mind begins, as Nietzsche predicted, to doubt the authority and efficacy of science as a source of values or even culture. But if not science as a source of authority, what else?

Indeed what else? What models exist as sources of imagery out of which youth might construct models of personal behavior? Where can they find authentication for an effective ideological protest against the corporate state? When nineteenth-century youth inveighed against the bourgeois spirit and the powerhouse state, they frequently chose cultural models in the form of an indigenous, though increasingly powerless, aristocracy. At the very least they had some contact with pre-industrial intellectual traditions. But as Tocqueville and virtually every other commentator on the American scene has argued, the particular characteristic of this country is a driving egalitarianism and the absence of a traditional aristocracy. Youth movements in this country have, as a result, often romanticized the voiceless people of this society —workers, Negroes, the rural poor—and have attempted to incorporate their styles into protest. The paradigmatic experience of such youth groups is to be rejected by the very people they emulate; for the voiceless, the first luxury is that of joining the middle class.

When youth turns from real groups as models to the universities or to intellectual traditions generally, they find little out of which they might construct either a viable selfhood or an effective ideology. The classic tradition of wisdom philosophy and political philosophy was one of the first casualties of the drive to technicalize the entire mental world. When students turn to the social sciences, they often discover not articulate images of man and the social stage, but the dissolution of even the notion of self and society in the acid of such metaphors as "system" and "process." The same situation is found in the arts, where the rise of modernism leads, in George Lukacs' phrase, to both the disintegration of personality and the attenuation of reality. The person, the self, in modern literature becomes a container containing nothing but shreds of his own reality; the objective scene or society in which life is lived disappears into the flux. As Joseph Wood Krutch has recently argued, our society has been prejudiced in favor of every scientific and aesthetic image which reduces the status and visibility of man and the reality of the concrete social world.

What, then, are the cultural sources out of which one might construct a self or a viable vision of politics? It is precisely this conundrum that binds together the hippie, the New Left and the majority of middle-class youth. This is not the first generation of young people to feel insecure about their identity or to feel a vague and indistinct sense of selfhood. Youth is a natural period of uprootedness, and problems of self-identification always rest heavily on the young. Yet traditional though these concerns may be, they are enormously exacerbated by our modern preoccupation with the Socratic injunction, "Know thyself"—a command that looms larger in the consciousness even as the notion of self fades. The truth is that we are exceedingly poor in the materials with which to do the job. The problem is not, as with Kierkegaard, the fear of losing a self through inattention. It is not related to John Stuart Mill's concern that persons who do not follow their own nature may end up with no nature at all. Rather, the difficulty is that we have so organized our life and educational system that most persons have no self to lose, no nature to follow. It is not a question of whether to be like Jay Gatsby who rejects a former self and puts on an artificial personality with which to pursue what seems to him higher virtues. Most modern youngsters are more like that character in one of Montaigne's essays who, when asked what he knew, announced that he couldn't answer unless he could point to a paragraph in a book.

I am suggesting that the ever earlier exposure of children to the mass media, to the school system and to impersonal agencies of socialization, means that no emotionally charged core of attitudes, values and knowledge is ever likely to be acquired, that persons simply tend to become the total of the social debris collected around them. And in adolescence they discover that under the shifting façade of their social appearances there is not really an "I."

For these reasons the radical Left and the hippies are competitors to name and give semblance to this generation. Both groups appear to have dealt with the problem of "self" by a total commitment to a culture and politics, no matter how indistinct. This commitment absorbs the self, makes available attitudes and a vague ideology, and promises to give some coherence to life. But it is not authentic culture or politics, in the sense we have normally used those terms, because for most adherents it is principally a form of therapy rather than creation. The commitment of these groups is more admired than followed. Yet many young people who do not formally belong to groups nevertheless work out these same sentiments, with a few intimate friends, at sessions with the school psychiatrist, in endless discussions about communication, openness, honesty and "being oneself." Among many, if not most, middle-class youth one finds the sentiment expressed in the almost universal desire for a moratorium: a vacation from the anticipated oppressiveness of the middle-class life that will follow college. It may only be a sojourn in the Peace Corps, a period in a job that requires little involvement or commitment, a year of hiking through Europe, a short stay in a hippie community. Anything will do that might allow time to find and put on a personality as one might a prosthesis.

Finally I must mention the commercial exploitation of generational differences which has driven a wedge even further into the natural gaps dividing people of varying ages. I am thinking, for example, of the age-grading of the population into housing groups—from age-segregated suburbs and apartment houses to dormitories and old-age homes—which severely reduces intergenerational contact. I am thinking also of the age-grading of markets (such as the "nubies") because they provide an easier handle for selling goods. And of course I am thinking of the parasitic use of youth culture as a source of fads and entertainment, a use that threatens to turn the New Left into traveling minstrels and hip culture into the latest middle-class appurtenance. But most of all, I am thinking of the deliberate attempt to sell individuality through marginal differentiations in consumption styles, with the result that consumers become, in John Quirk's admirable phrase, "a class that oppress themselves." The related and perhaps even more objectionable strategy is to turn youth— the most anarchic and rootless period of life—into a universal cultural model. Either way, the point is to exploit intergenerational differences. These strategies are splendid contributions to the chaos of our society, for while they guarantee the rapid obsolescence of commodities in all domains, they also severely exacerbate all the potent instabilities of our culture, divide us from tradition and traditional styles of life and unnecessarily deepen divisions between generations.

When all of this is said one quickly realizes that, to paraphrase Whitehead, everything of importance about American society has been said before by someone who didn't invent it. One also realizes that Camus's conviction about Europe applies even more forcefully to this country: the disease of America is to know everything and believe nothing. The problem of this country has always been to find legitimate room within it for those styles of life and imagination that are fundamentally at variance with those of the dominant class. Right now, the problem is to find reasonable room for all those who recognize the human impulses the powerhouse society denies: the poetic, magical, romantic, religious and ethical aspects of thought and behavior. The problem is vastly more acute now, for there has been a loss of insulating space and there is thus less room for existence outside of the institutions of the corporate state.

Properly motivated and interpreted, the hippies and New Left could force us once again to face what is the eternal dilemma of the American imagination: the incompatibility between our desires for wealth, power, productivity and success on the one hand and for value, peace, harmony and sufficiency on the other. We are heirs to the Enlightenment which, by way of arguing that man could be God, induced us to believe that we could have our cake and eat it too. For all our protestations about the good life, the national imagination has always found power more interesting than peace, wealth more desirable than sufficiency and, like Milton, the devil more interesting than God. The chance to choose in any sense between these models may simply be behind us, back in that "vast obscurity . . . where the dark fields of the republic roll on under the night."

Some among modern youth would like to force this choice on us again, with full realization of the historical origins of our problems. For most, however, there is only false consciousness and a failure to realize either the roots of our dilemmas or the historical origins of the mentality we turn upon them. Such youth unnecessarily and vindictively turn upon those with whom they share an impulse but lack a common age and a common language. Perhaps there is simply too much talk about generations, on their part and mine, for it unfortunately beclouds the fact that, in William Styron's words, "we're all in this together and we're in for a pretty rough time."

FLOYD B. McKISSICK

Society, U.S.A.

". . . This culture, this society founded
on evil and oppression, will not survive."

*The problems of the American Negro have, in one way or an-
other, crept into nearly every essay in this book; and the reason
probably has even less to do with the immediacy and violence of
the challenge than with the moral and theoretical dilemmas it
poses. The American system, in addition to the minimum legal,
political, economic and social guarantees it gives to all individuals, provides a specific methodology by which minorities may
attempt to make good their claims. But what if the guarantees
are inadequate and the methodology fails? As Professor Masters
earlier pointed out, the historic American answer has very often
been to resort to individual law-breaking and violence. Is this
the only recourse open to the Negro now? Floyd McKissick of
CORE does not quite say so, but there is no doubt about the
militance with which he says that if the system is incapable of
meeting Negro demands for individual rights, the system must
go.*

W HAT MAKES society? What factors combine to create that phantom which is so widely revered and so
rarely understood?

What is society? The sociologist defines it; the theologian
muses; the teacher speculates; and the politician guesses. And
everybody has a different answer. Webster defines society as:
"Companionship or association with one's fellows; usually friendly

or intimate intercourse. The social order or system restricting the individual . . ." Other definitions are given. Yet no popularly accepted definition begins to define "society" in terms relevant to the black man, and as a black man, that is what interests me most. For, in America, "society" is never used so consistently or effectively as a weapon against any other group—ethnic, religious or racial—either today or in our country's shameful past. For this phantom is really no more than the sum total of all the customs, beliefs, values and institutions of a given culture; and in America it adds up to, in the words of one fairly typical black Harlem resident, "A crock of shit."

Such a judgment may seem harsh, crude and a bit unrealistic to the average white American who is enjoying the fruits of his "affluent society," or even to his somewhat less fortunate white brother who still has a chance of becoming part of that society. But to the majority of black people living amid poverty—and even to many of those who have reached the black middle class —it is something of an understatement.

In preparation for this article, I conducted a five-hour, one-man survey of Harlem bars and restaurants. The answers to the question, "What do you think of American society?" were not surprising to one who has spent his whole life as a black man in America—particularly to one who has spent a great deal of time in the North, as well as the South. The answers from black businessmen in Frank's Restaurant on 125th Street differed little from those of men who frequent Small's, the Big Apple, Wells', Jock's and other popular Harlem bars. Almost all expressed contempt for American society—contempt and disillusionment, disillusionment with the dishonesty and corruption of an entire structure.

For America works hard to create the illusion of justice and equality. The time and talents of some of the best minds in white America are spent in perpetuation of this myth of the "affluent society"—"the just society"—"the free society."

We are a nation of slogans. Madison Avenue executives are

paid millions annually for coining phrases to lull America into a sense of well-being. They are paid billions to maintain a society created in the image of white America. Periodicals and magazines as well as books are dedicated to the sale of the American Dream. But the tag on that dream may as well read "only whites need apply," for acceptance into the majority society is something black people can never really hope to achieve under the present system.

The American Dream is still a dream of lovely plantations with contented darkies catering to and serving their white masters. *Gone with the Wind* has broken box-office records for decades because it offers an escape to a mythical plantation about which white America persistently dreams. Even in today's industrialized society, black people are still relegated to the functions of menials and servants. In the public mind, black people are the unemployables, the uneducables; and white America holds fast to its dream.

There is no tag that warns the black child: "Beware Society." He is constantly told—at school, at church and by the public media—that he has a responsibility to society, a debt to be paid. He is taught that society must be served and that all threats to society must be eliminated for the greater good.

In spite of these massive efforts to force black people to "Think White," most black people simply do not see American society as do whites. I imagine that white Americans feel great pride in their ownership of property, power, wealth and international influence. Even poor white Americans can identify with the white power mongers and vicariously enjoy a sense of importance. This is not so for a majority of black people.

Black Americans can afford no such luxury. Any black man who identifies with the American power élite is blessed with an extraordinary imagination, for black people are consistently the victims of the gilded few. And although it is the gilded few who control the black masses and their white counterparts, it is the white middle class and even the white lower class who protect this evil system by relishing the advantages guaranteed by whiteness. It is often the lowest economic sector of the white community which is most vicious in its racism, for to the poor white, the racist fantasy is psychologically necessary for survival. At least, they reason, they are better than "the niggers."

The more affluent and sophisticated Americans—the stockholders, the controllers—need not spew forth their racism publicly; they can afford to be gracious and liberal—to dine with "educated Negroes," while living off the residue of slavery. Yet every single millionaire—every single well-to-do white man whose fortune was "Made in America"—has blood money in his pockets—profits extorted from black men and women. Every single white man has profited from the slavery of the black man, and, understandably, he has a guilt complex—a complex which is justified by history.

The inheritors of tainted money—money gained during slavery and in the days of economic oppression immediately following the Civil War—compound the evil by reinvesting in the racist structure from which their wealth was originally gained. It is money that makes money in this society. The original wealth has been reinvested by the slave traders and plantation owners to form the base of the American economy—an economy based on blood and death.

As a lawyer in the South, I saw many, many times what was done by the courts in the name of "society," what was done by the white racists who control the entire power complex. It is unlikely that any major changes have occurred during the three years of my absence. The structure was far too well established to have been altered much in so short a time.

One case which comes vividly to mind is that of a young man whom I shall call Ben Jones—a black man who shot a white man in self-defense. That man had been carrying a loaded rifle and had gone, with clear intent, to use it on Jones.

I remember standing in the small Southern courtroom, surrounded by the white bailiff, the white sheriff, the white judge, even the white court clerk. (These men, according to our legal traditions, represented Ben Jones's peers.) The white judge mounted the bench and the court was tense and silent: "Ben Jones. You have been found guilty of a crime against society. You are sentenced to imprisonment in the State Penitentiary for the rest of your natural life . . . Every man owes a debt to society and every man must pay his debt to society when he has wronged that society."

A scream from the back of the courtroom. Jones's pregnant wife. I felt myself reel. Sweat beaded on my brow. My stomach churned as I looked helplessly at my client. I repeated over and over to myself: "Keep yourself together. Don't blow a fuse. Don't make it hard on your client." As I watched them lead that young man away, I vowed to fight that monster "society" until I died. I vowed that, even if given the chance, I would never willingly be a part of that which was extracting this terrible debt from Ben Jones.

Ironically, society has never paid its debt to Ben Jones or to any of the poor black Americans who have spent their lives in poverty and suppression—to the millions of descendants of slaves. Society has never made payment on the lives of millions of black slaves who have made it possible for that white society to be built. Society owed Ben Jones a debt even before he was born; society owes a debt to all children born without chance, born in oppression.

The general American concept of society and man's relation to his society is particularly warped and cruel when applied to black people. It would not be unreasonable to demand payment of dues to a society which protected rather than exploited its inhabitants—which provided them with livelihood, dignity and freedom. To extract dues—whether in the form of taxes from the poor or lives on distant battlefields—from society's stepchildren can only be viewed as a cynical continuation of feudalism in an industrialized society.

American dogma is particularly hypocritical, especially con-

310

fused, regarding that which we call "society." For, when convenient, "society" is a benevolent phenomenon to which we all owe
allegiance. In this context, "society" is invoked, by all from the
President of the United States to the local schoolmarm, as that
for which we must fight and, if necessary, die to preserve. (Understandably, the black man has difficulty accepting this thesis.
After all, his share of society is sufficiently less than the average
white man's to insure that if he is black he will live approximately ten fewer years than if he were white.)

When convenient, however, "society" can also be described as
an all-encompassing evil—unassailable by virtue of its hugeness
and power. We are told that society is responsible for poverty,
ignorance, disease and discrimination. We are rarely told that
the real responsibility lies with the white people who control the
goods, services, money and racist attitudes which daily create
more poverty, more ignorance, more disease and more discrimination—all of which, in fact, comprise society.

We are told that teachers cannot be held accountable for the
racism in our school systems; that reporters and editors are not
personally responsible for slanted, anti-black press coverage; that
the cops can't eliminate the racism in law-enforcement; that
judges can't cure the racism of the judiciary; and that the laity
and clergy have no control over the racism which pervades American churches. The individual is supposed to be powerless against
this society. It is said that society is too all-encompassing, too
firmly established to be changed or destroyed by only a few.

Such reasoning does not account for the fact that American
society is what white people in America say it is; for after all, they
are the decision-makers. They alone control the economic
wealth, the political power and, above all, the power of the press
—that "free" press which is used to control the thought processes of all other groups in this country. White America, through
its institutions, its moral and intellectual establishment, expresses what white people want to believe about themselves and
what they want to believe about black people. When a decision

is made by the economic-political establishment, that decision is transmitted into reality through the instruments of NBC, CBS, ABC, *The New York Times* and the Luce publications, to mention a few—for, in America, people believe in what they read. In America, people believe in the "free press."

Of course dissent of a kind is tolerated. One paper supports Nixon, another Rockefeller, another McCarthy. One editor leans to the Republicans, another to the Democrats. But real dissent—strong disagreement with either the capitalist structure or its racist policies—is stifled. Real dissenters are arrested and held on miscellaneous charges, from "possessing firearms" to "inciting to riot." Those who would defy the draft are carted off to jail, and even those who would peacefully march in opposition to a cruel and immoral war in Vietnam are barred from public parks.

And following the Bay of Pigs fiasco, even President Kennedy implied that if the press would not censor itself, the government would do it for them. Is this freedom of the press? Is self-censorship, undertaken for fear of official restriction, any less degrading than censorship enforced by an oppressive government?

Perhaps the most effective instrument for thought control in America is the church. Few Americans dare to question or attack motherhood, the flag or religion. Yet the church is one of America's most racist institutions, and one of the most dangerous. The church holds out hope to the black child. Black children become convinced that there is hope, only to have that hope trampled and to be trampled themselves for daring to dream.

Apparently this is the appointed role of the church and of society in general, for the majority of white people do not rebel against injustice to blacks. The only sympathy they allow themselves is of a paternalistic variety: they will rally to the aid of a deprived black family whose home has been burned down (occasionally), but no care is given to those thousands of black families who are forced to dwell in firetraps.

Daily, men who speak for the Christian Church find Scriptures to justify every moral wrong, every evil, in this society.

They do this today and they did it in the time of slavery. The economic welfare of the church seems uppermost in the concerns of the clergy and the church (The Lord Loves a Cheerful Giver) and the church is supported by the same men who control the schools, the press and the industry.

Priests and preachers (white and black) join in defense of this economic structure, frequently equating capitalist exploitation with Divine Will (The Meek Shall Inherit the Earth). America, they preach, is the savior of the world, the great civilizer. America, they say, can do no harm, has done no harm, will do no harm. Slavery, although wrong, brought Christianity to the heathen; and if the pagan suffered, it was the will of the Lord. Any benefits to white society, apparently, are incidental and not intentional, for white America is charitable. Did they not give their slaves their religion?

But religion, a part of the system itself, did its dirty work in making slavery possible, in keeping slaves under control and in supporting the institution. (Jesus the Lamb was the image of Christ most often emphasized in preaching to the slaves; Jesus the fighter, the militant, was reserved for the white folks.) One must also remember that churches, as well as America's Founding Fathers, owned slaves. In America, memories are pitifully short and consciences pitifully weak.

Those few courageous clergymen who campaign for justice do so in defiance of a formidable tradition. We cannot hope to change America without changing its most hallowed traditions and beliefs, and black people must force themselves to reevaluate their devotion to religious institutions dominated by racism.

Black people must consistently battle every aspect of a society designed to perpetuate their misery. The white man often fails to realize that his security and happiness depends upon the misery of the black masses. Therefore, black people cannot afford to restrict their vision to any one aspect of this society, believing that if only that one institution or custom or belief were changed, this racist structure would fall. It will not fall. It will not change until

313

it comes under constant and deliberate attack by all black Americans and all white Americans of decency.

Thus, it falls to the victims, the nonparticipants, the black people, to change society into a force for good and justice. If the change is not made—soon—this culture, this society founded on evil and oppression, will not survive.

T GEORGE HARRIS

From
Rugged-Individualism to
Helpless-Individualism

> "The awe-arousing character of con-
> temporary decisions, no less than the
> incredible size of business and govern-
> ment organizations, often drives the
> lonely crowd into the politics of panic."

*T George Harris, like several other authors in this book, sees the
Negro problem as part of a larger phenomenon in American
life: the growing helplessness of the individual in his peren-
nial contest with society. Even the most humane society, no
matter how scrupulously it cherishes the ideal of individual
rights, can grow to such size and complexity that it will tram-
ple on those rights. But, says Mr. Harris, alienation and violent
protest are not the only recourses open to an individual. He can
still participate in the creation of politically effective sub-units
of the great society.*

I F YOU VISIT a Kansas City country club, you do not improve your popularity by praising the club's contribution to
the theory of village communism. Nor does the owner of a Park
Avenue cooperative apartment generally welcome the thought
that he dwells, on federal subsidy (tax deductions), in a luxurious
kibbutz. And, come to think of it, very few Southern Baptist
leaders announce the building of yet another big church, with
community kitchen and recreation facilities, as testimony to the

economic principles of the commune. The higher people live above the poverty line, the more they are apt to use cooperative devices—and the less they admit, or even notice, the consequences of this fact.

Below the poverty line, an extreme form of individualism tends to be the rule. Casual observers of this phenomenon preach that the U.S. fosters "socialism for the rich and private enterprise for the poor." This cliché is misleading, but it points to a useful line of questions. Poor people, especially urban Negroes, do not suffer from excessive involvement with the nongovernmental economy, a rich mix of individualism and "groupism." That is what most black people are systematically denied. Instead, the poor are deeply dependent upon a public, that is, governmental, economy that has become increasingly digital in its newer programs, sentencing each victim to solitary confinement under a case number. This recent trend, as examples below may suggest, is a direct reversal of the New Deal's main thrust under the cooperative power of unionism and farm organizations. By one of history's political ironies, the welfare state has adopted the fallacies of rugged-individualism and expanded them into a general theory of helpless-individualism.

Since the helplessness theory influences policy as well as the way people act, it tends to be self-confirming. Government action, being consciously legislated and then administered by bureaucracy, must be somewhat logical. Therefore, it reflects the more popular doctrines of the moment. Other impulses and habits, perhaps unacceptable in current theory, have greater effect upon institutions outside of government. It is tempting, then, to look suspiciously into present social thought for the conceptual sources of despair. Ritualized pessimism, like ritualized optimism, is a poor substitute for honest analysis. Norman Vincent Peale's positive thinking is not validated by being stood upon its head.

Conventional wisdom, codified by Harvard's John Kenneth Galbraith, now divides all of life into two parts: (1) the public sector, best exemplified by federal government and (2) the private sector, characterized by the giant profit-making corporation of the industrial state. Galbraith's public sector generally wears the threadbare toga of virtue while his private sector sneaks around in the dirty underwear of sinful desire. Taking this cue, others have created a formidable body of literature on the evils of automobile tail fins, television commercials and teen-age cosmetics. The semantic prejudice built into the public-private division is itself provocative. Perhaps the middle-aged generation of social critics, frightened in youth by Freud's insight, shares a total distrust for objects associated with the inner self, especially for tail-fin sins. The post-affluent college generation is less bugged by this latter-day brand of puritanism. It has turned toward affirmation of the private self, often in protest and in a psychedelic passion that gets desperate enough, in some hippie cases, to be self-killing.

The private-public notion, though convenient, offers a rather crude way of dividing up pluralism. On the private side, men and women are cut down to cogs in profit machines. On the public side, the person is reduced to one of 75,000,000 units in the quadrennial voting statistics. Under this simplistic model, personal conviction cannot lead to direct action that, by itself, has any meaning. To act on a humane motive is to subvert the commercial system, or to undercut the monopoly on virtue assigned to public agencies. Therefore, the only way to implement belief is in politics, narrowly defined as influencing policy or votes, not deeply understood in the Greek sense of the responsible *polis*.

This view of society is, of course, very reassuring to news reporters, economists, sociologists and others who make a social specialty of articulating issues for the edification of the passive masses. Political campaigns can thus be judged by the values of the lecture hall. The education of the voters, ever in doubt, can be measured by periodic pop-quizzes in which public opinion samplers do the proctoring. When the polls reveal perverse opinions, reporters are forced into somewhat cynical duty as theater critics. They explain sub-rational conduct in terms of "images" and the platform style of politicians. The residual function of the ballot, especially in Presidential primaries, is but to keep the pollsters honest.

From Left to Right, the political consequences of two-sector theory have been widely if not happily accepted. Partisan groups compete mainly in the invention of symbolic teaching aids vivid enough to win headlines or TV time. The struggle has escalated the idea of demonstration, brought poetry to picket placards and encouraged the adoption of causes, like the Filthy Speech Movement, novel enough to hit the news. William F. Buckley, the Right's method actor, has made a career out of his belief that politics (in his case conservatism) is less a matter of what is done or not done in government and more a matter of what is now being said. The pseudo-event, as Daniel Boorstin argues, has become the stuff of political action. Out in the broader culture, the individual is left with a Hobson's choice. He can go the existential route with the late Albert Camus, and in blind courage declare his engagement with a life that is, and must be, absurd. Or, he can cop out with the escapists who are only half kidding about the campy doings of Batman, Napoleon Solo, Marshal Dillon, Travis McGee and several equally unreal James Bonds. The super-hero is an elaborate spoof of human dignity.

The purpose here is not to belabor Mr. Galbraith's two-piece horse, but to show one way in which a set of popular concepts interlock to produce what may be called helpless-individualism. These unmanning ideas happen to be in vogue at a moment when the individual is expected to show superhuman gifts of skill and wisdom.The necessity comes in many forms. As Negro migrants out of the South have discovered to their rage, the present stage of industrial development requires universal literacy, if only to take in the information needed to jump from job to job in a volatile economy. The pressure on college students has been well reported. One computer expert in the educational-industrial complex puts the point with precision: "The second industrial revolution, like the first, just squeezes another ounce out of a man." In spite of the now-dated fad about the "glut of leisure" and the "triple revolution," an on-the-road reporter has to admit the evidence of his eyes, plus sketchy data from "human capital" research: if you count the time most people spend today preparing for work by educating themselves, they labor longer hours and at a more frantic pace than they did through two centuries of mule culture.

To give the screw one more turn, there is an ominous quality in the decisions that men are—more and more—forced to make. With the political acceptance of Keynesian thought, plus the statistical base of the New Economics, a democratic government must accept responsibility for controlling economic forces once thought to be safely out of human reach. The decisions, moreover, are inescapable. For a policy maker to refuse to use fiscal and monetary tools—to fall back on the economic laws once thought immutable—is as much a decision, albeit a negative one, as to opt for overuse. The international currency strain requires central bankers to make up in paper for nature's parsimony in gold.

The same necessity to play God confronts men in almost every discipline. Though only English doctors have got into public trouble about it, the right-to-die crisis bugs the white coats in each hospital. Do you have the right to torture a human vegetable by keeping synthetic life in it? For how long? Control of nature has brought many unpleasant options. Mountains and rivers have shrunk as barriers, but a man-made superhighway is an impassable moat. With the sudden rush into the atomic-power generation, men will, in five years, be choosing between adequate lights and hot rivers. Cheap atomic generators suck in floods of cooling water, then pour it back seventeen degrees hotter. This is called "thermal pollution." Then there is Dr. Strangelove's well-known problem about whether to end civilization. To refuse, as men have done thus far, is to aspire to an achievement outside earthly tradition: to live with national hostilities, rather than settle them by a roll of the dice called total war.

Even religion has finked out from the comforting role it played for the first era of individualists. In the spirit of the times, leading theologians argue, as Harvey Cox does in *The Secular City*, that God now requires man to operate without the assumption of divine help and coaching. We're co-creators.

The awe-arousing character of contemporary decisions, no less than the incredible size of business and government organizations, often drives the lonely crowd into the politics of panic. The results are untidy. In the first national exposé of the Black Muslims, and later of the John Birch Society, I found the kind of pathology that rises where men and women become aware of their inability to affect the forces that impinge upon their lives. If present pressures drive a larger and larger proportion of the population into such groups, then it is foolish to expect sensible conduct of the electoral process. Dr. Murray Levin of Boston University, having polled voters in the Boston election and researched returns in Cleveland and Gary, believes that the country congratulated itself prematurely. "A regressive and nativistic Populism," he insists, "is possessing both white and Negro voters on the lower-income levels."

Perhaps so. The symptoms are too substantial to ignore. However, a more promising possibility, somewhat traditional, has begun to take shape in the area of greatest difficulty, the ghetto. The new direction contradicts both liberal and conservative orthodoxy and has already been unsettling to middle-class intellectuals. Several years before the civil-rights movement burned itself out, rumblings of discontent turned "white liberal" into a black cuss word. Few liberals realized that they tended to treat Negroes, like Rousseau's noble savage, as substitutes for their own lost innocence. John Killens, bitter prophet of racial suicide (*And Then We Heard The Thunder*), enlivened Harlem cocktail parties—less and less integrated—with humorous definitions equating "liberal" with "phony." Elijah Muhammed, frail autocrat who blended hope with hate, used his Black Muslims to give an anti-Semitic twist to the rising ambitions of less literate people. This taint was explained away, to the satisfaction of many, by sly remarks on the sins of Jewish slumlords and storekeepers. Nice-minded thinkers thus killed two birds with one stone: they blamed Negro anger on the evils of the business system and defended their stereotypes of all Negroes as sweet and gentle like Ole Black Joe.

But the thunder, and later the fire, announced a demand for something other than kind treatment. "Black people are claiming the right *not* to act poor and pure," said Newark's Dr. Nathan Wright, Black Power's most substantial philosopher. Stokely Carmichael, inventor of the power motto, persuaded several young militants in Detroit that welfare workers were a force with a vested interest in keeping Negroes poor and powerless. With his single-track mind on racism, Carmichael even argued that the social workers were consciously conspiring to keep their clients down. Other militants began to talk of the Job Corps as a chain of concentration camps designed to keep troublemakers out of town. Some looked upon proposals for a guaranteed annual income as a down payment on genocide. "Once they prove that black people aren't good for anything in the present economy," an angry dropout mutters, "it's just one step more to wiping us out."

The wild talk set the mood. On a calmer level, public housing began to look like the latest style in slave quarters. Distant school boards seemed unable to understand a parent demand for community-run schools. The case-number method of welfare, under which the recipient is dependent upon the whim of his keeper, seemed to be only part of a general system by which outsiders, in government as in business, could prey upon isolated individuals and prevent the rise of community powers strong enough to help one another. Cops in most cities had long since wiped out the street gangs through which teen-agers defended themselves in the jungle. Defeated gang-types retreated into the final isolation of narcotics, and for the first time turned ghetto streets from Harlem to Buttermilk Bottom into places of random violence. Night life had to move to downtown (white) establishments. The Negro community, never strong, seemed to have been shattered as if by plan into several million helpless individuals.

For contrast, it is useful to compare the urban programs with the New Deal action for farmers and factory workers in the thirties. The difference is total. The older laws gave ragged men and women the power to fight their way into the middle class. The newer laws seem to assume that the remaining poor will be poor always, and the provisions are rigged, innocently, to insure that outcome.

The New Deal gave labor little more than temporary WPA jobs, Social Security—and the all-important right to organize and bargain collectively across the table. The workers took it from there. On the farm half of the New Deal coalition, the programs were more elaborate but the operating principle was much the same. Through the Grange and the Farm Bureau, then militant farmer groups, the programs were designed and run by the participants. As the son of a depression farmer, I saw my father get federal loan insurance to buy a farm, then to lime it, fertilize it and plant it in hybrid corn. The federal agents and university experts who came to see us did so as technical servants, not like case workers sent to spy or sociologists come to study our sex life. It was just as well that nobody tried to gather data for a document like the 1965 Moynihan report on *The Negro Family*. One county farm agent who seemed a bit nosy about a family's living arrangements was escorted down to the creek and allowed to depart by sliding across a foot log, a scaly-bark sycamore, without the comfort of his pants. Farmers were never considered "target populations," to use the welfare-state parlance. Nor did anybody invent a "subculture of the poor" sociology to justify keeping country kids out of the middle-class rat race.

It is argumentative, but necessary, to point out that the New Deal succeeded on farms and in factories because of institutions that no longer exist, or rather which have no proper place in the public-private rhetoric. In order to talk about these institutions coherently, it is convenient to describe a third, or independent, sector made up of organizations that neither make a profit nor serve as branches of government. They include the labor unions, farmer organizations, joint-marketing groups, credit unions, mutual insurance schemes, homemaker clubs, churches, co-ops— and the Democratic Party. The party, then broad-based rather than top-heavy, was not just an election machine that kept New Dealers in office so that they could draft programs. It was one of several community forces, based on belief and interest, through which people could mobilize themselves and, not incidentally, tell government what they did and did not want.

The Black Power movement, ethnic and Populist, is beginning to build independent community strength through which to transform the ghetto from within and to squeeze real, not self-defeating, resources out of both government and business. In many cities, for example, militants are fighting to break out of rental housing, be it public or private. Whites live rent-free in the suburbs; in most years, the increase in sale value of their homes is greater than the interest costs on their mortgages. They also get tax breaks. But public housing, unless turned into co-ops, will continue to put "U.S.A. approved" on the slum's worst economic evil, absentee ownership, and drain a pint of rent a month out of black people. Even Secretary Robert Weaver, head of Housing and Urban Development, has been under pressure enough from militants and from Republicans (mainly Senator Charles Percy of Illinois) to shift toward more FHA insurance for Negro home-buyers.

There is a hidden gold mine in the slums. Where residents grab ownership and thus seize control of their neighborhoods, even in Watts, they quickly improve the environment—and reap substantial profits from the rising price of real estate that is potentially very valuable. These profits can finance much of the cost, otherwise unlimited, of putting poor families on a sound financial footing. In Rochester, Saul Alinsky's FIGHT organization is not only after housing but is bargaining for worker owner-

323

ship of a factory to be built in the ghetto. In Crawfordsville, Georgia, Walter Reuther's Citizens Crusade Against Poverty is testing community ownership of a run-down textile plant that now employs 110 people.

The industrial system now in the making puts extraordinary demands upon the individual and dwarfs him under public and private bureaucracy. Rigidities in the power structures are not, it is obvious, limited to the ghetto. However, this hyperbolized version of similar difficulties in the rest of the society—for example, between college students and their administrators—offers a few hints to the future forms of social tension.

The more obvious lines of current thought clearly heighten a sense of helpless-individualism, and inhibit corrective action. To the surprise of both races, a new breed of black Populists have brought existing programs under bitter attack. It is too early to predict the outcome. But in their ethnic anger, the new Populists are building new instruments of community power that may, in the light of New Deal experience, turn out to be effective. If so, their success may suggest that the modern crisis of the individual arises more from failure of the intellect than of the nerve. Meanwhile, an increasing number of people will feel, as the hillbilly saying goes, "like I been sent for and cain't get there."

BENJAMIN DeMOTT

America the Unimagining

"Has the nation from the start been
the captive of theories about the formation of individual selfhood that are
wrongheaded—theories that are in
themselves obstacles to self-realization?"

*The tendency to see the problem of the relationship between the
individual and society solely in terms of the dissidence of minorities or of individual alienation may be misleading. The apparently happy conformist may represent another aspect of the
problem. If the most basic professed aim of our entire social,
political and economic system is to maximize the opportunity
for individual self-realization, we ought presumably to have a
reasonably clear idea of what self-realization means. Benjamin
DeMott suggests that what we most need is a better understanding of our inner selves.*

A man in his early fifties, vigorous, strong-faced, well-liked
in his town. Family man, business success (small-city merchandising operation). No reader but a great keeper-up—business papers, hard news, world events, facts that matter. Pleasures?
He "gets a kick out of" gadgets and machines—wild stereo lay-
out in the cathedral living room, complicated ship-to-shore gear
on his boat, a genuine systems approach for stock control in the
stores. Further pleasures: he's outdoorsy, handy at home, a Dartmouth man, skier, active in business and community clubs, non-
churchgoer, non-political argufier . . .

At parties he doesn't talk much to women. Also he stands back a little from his kids. Pleasant-tentative with his bright daughter, straight-arrowish "Dad" with his teen-aged boys. Stands back too from the "creative" phases of the business—buying, advertising, display and so on—leaving this to a younger brother. (Let something "real sticky" turn up anywhere, though, and nobody but himself can cope. Who else for instance would be up to a face-off with the old family friend, one of his store managers, when the detective service reports the man is robbing them blind?) As for a personality profile:

"I am more interested in a man's behavior than in his inner life." Check. "In shaping character, externals are more important than inner tendencies." Check. "I sometimes have trouble figuring out the behavior of people who are emotionally unstable." Check. "Math is one of my best subjects." Check. "I think I'm practical and efficient when there's something that has to be done." Check. "I don't have the temperament for the 'romantic' point of view." Check. "I have few emotional problems." Check. "A first principle with me is that it's a man's duty to adjust himself to his environment." Check. "I am a fairly conventional person." Check. "My relations with other people are usually uncomplicated." Check. "My ideas are more often sound and sensible than unusual or imaginative." Check. "I say what I have to say in a few simple words so that I'm easily understood." Check. "There's a lot in the economic interpretation of history." Check. "I find it easier to deal with concrete facts in one special field than with general ideas about man or nature." Check. "I think science offers as good a guide as any to the future." Check. "When I'm working out a problem I try to stick as close as possible to the facts." Check. "I enjoy an intimate conversation with one person more than general conversation with several." No. "When I hear a person talk, I think more about his personality than I do about what he's saying." No. "I think I have a good understanding of women." No. "I love to talk about my innermost feelings to a sympathetic friend." Nah. "I often think I can feel my way into the innermost being of another person." No.

326

"It takes a good deal to make me angry." Check. "Unselfishness and sympathy are more desirable than high ideals and ambitions." False. "I'm apt to make up stories by myself about the private thoughts and experiences of the people I meet." No. "I believe the world may be well lost for love." No. "I live in my imagination as much as I do in the external world." No. "I dislike everything that has to do with money—buying, selling, bargaining." Oh sure. "I like being in the thick of the action." Yes, emphatically. "I like to have people about me most of the time." Yes, emphatically. . . .

Other items (not on the Harvard clinic test) worth noting about this man? One: inclined to treat characters as functions, he regularly "explains" people by telling you what they do (a parenthetical phrase—Harry's a doctor, Hank's a cop, Lucille's had a pair of twins). Another point: the fellow is good to tie up by on a sloppy night at Southwest Harbor and makes, in general, a fine summer neighbor—fun outings to the island, family picnics, softball on the sand, sun's over the yardarm and so on. Further point: when you step away from him, sit in judgment, dwell on his limits, you feel like a heel. You discover again that one of the several reasons for not judging is that the minute it's done, the judge is judged, stands fully visible in his own fatuity and self-congratulation, beyond sympathy, ripe for sentence himself. Yet another item: the man "beheld" is representative. Tens of millions are excluded from his place, just at this moment; going up from the middle in society is where you're likely to find him, not from the middle down. But the excluded millions can't forever escape; even now they are being graded "up" on his curve. Every year the movement of economic life shoots tens of thousands toward him—into his set of mind, his style, his inward truth. He is no "middle-class stereotype," in short; he is an American destination or finish line, the possible end of the race.

Finally, last point about the man: he is in trouble. There's a withering in him, a metaphorical arm gone, some limb, some key part missing, something stunted or ungrown. The present judge speaks quickly, on the run, hoping to hide himself from the next judge: the man just described is, in one flat word, *unfulfilled.*

To say as much is, by instant extension, to discount the seriousness of the famous American commitment to the ideal of individual self-fulfillment. And while such discounting is standard practice among the knowing, it isn't at first glance easy to defend. Granted, the language in which national commitments and values are usually spelled out—the language of civics classes and Scouting Award nights—does beg to be mocked. "The social organization of America is compatible with its free political institutions. . . ." "America is a society in which equality of opportunity is supported by specific social mechanisms, including classlessness, a wide spectrum of inviolable and equal individual rights guaranteed to all individuals, guarantees of minimum welfare for all and special assistance to any that are at unusual economic disadvantage. . . ." "Enhancing the dignity of the individual citizen, developing his capabilities for self-fulfillment, is a prime concern of the American government. . . ." "The environments which help to shape the character of the individual—his home life, education, religious training, occupation, etc.—are in varying degrees matters of public concern. The object of this concern is to develop typical traits of character—independence of spirit, respect for the rights of others, cooperativeness, sense of civic responsibility—and others which will make the individual a better, more constructive citizen." Formulations like these cry out for qualification, amendment, hints of stylish self-restraint. Some humility, please.

But the cry for humility can itself become cant. Spells of living abroad in middle-class communities—leafy Edgbaston in England, say, or a Costa village in Portugal—offer only ambiguous testimony on the matter of the American versus European sense of civic responsibility. But in the area of attitudes and policies concerning education, those ambiguities disappear. The cause of "trained excellence" is Everyman's cause in America; my right to as much education as I can bear goes relatively unchallenged. No events, no crisis, seemingly, can interrupt the national dream of self-realization through mental strife. And no taxpayer protest ever badly smutches this piety. A day or so after the fearful October 1967 peace demonstration at the Pentagon, the President, meeting with a group of teachers at the White House, turned eloquent—some might have said moving—on the subject of self-realization and the school. Appointments this morning, he explained, with the National Security Council and with the President of Mexico—but you, you teachers, you're more important. Whatever else they said about him, the President went on, they would have to say that because of programs he instituted, a million people were in college this year who would not otherwise have had a chance to go. And how much more remained to be done! Four men out of ten on earth could not read or write! He himself hoped to return to teaching when his political career was over.

The books on the Cabinet Room shelf suggested an absence of a passion for the higher literary culture—O. Henry, a high-school physics text, a high-school chemistry text and the like. The few educational institutions in the country where the idea of standards is well-rooted are meritocratic in assumption—which means not only anti-aristocratic but anti-democratic as well. By far the larger part of the huge federal expenditures in the field of education supports phases of the defense program. And, more important than any of this, profound inequities still exist in the American system of public education. But from none of this does it follow that the cause or dream in question was a sham. The old programs and the new—Headstart, the regional educational laboratories, the proposed tuition loan bank—have flaws, cannot meet every need. But the motive behind them is, in essence, no more suspect than the motive behind the foundation of the first free public education system on earth. That motive is the nurture of a citizen useful to the community at large but also decently developed for himself—gifts realized, mind awake, wholeness intact. An unmockable aim, in sum: dignity for man.

*   *   *

And yet, and yet: the Product of It All looks out from the mirror and reveals himself to be—stunted. Somewhere—not simply in the stereotype of himself but in his actuality—he is locked in himself; somewhere he is fixed in an inhuman rigidity; somewhere there is a "malfunction." How to account for this? Has the nation from the start been the captive of theories about the formation and nurture of individual selfhood that are wrong-headed—theories that are obstacles in themselves to self-realization? Is there a uniquely American muddle about fulfillment? If so, what is its nature? How is it to be solved?

Stupidity alone answers confidently—but several relevant observations come to mind. Chief among them is that, for complex social, historical and cultural reasons, the nature of human growth—in particular, the central role of the imagination in determining its rate and quality—has not often been placed clearly before the national view.

Commentators by the hundreds score the country off for garishness, gross materialism, unspirituality; few focus on the poverty of its conception of personal growth. Yet that is the fairer target. The nation prates of self-realization, and rests in near obliviousness that my humanness depends upon my capacity and my desire to make real to myself the inward life, the subjective reality, of the lives that are lived beyond me. The nation feeds itself on rhetoric about "individual rates of progress"—and yet possesses little knowledge, if any, of the steps by which the human being becomes itself, the separate, private acts of the imagination on which the achievement of personhood depends.

And, to repeat, this ignorance or obliviousness is no mystery. Human growth stems from the exercise of our power to grasp another being's difference from within. How can that truism maintain itself among a people convinced of the fundamental sameness of men? As Tocqueville long ago pointed out, the myth of sameness is a keystone in the deep structure of American belief. (Tocqueville's specific point was that the American protest on behalf of "the individual" was rooted in the assumption that all individuals, once free "to be themselves," would desire the same things and feel in the same ways.) And it is a fact that the moral imperative of the imaginative act is rarely proclaimed in American public or cultural life. A Negro singer invited to a White House conference bursts out in condemnation of the guests for the unreality of their proposals, their abstractness when seen in the light of her experience. The First Lady's eyes moisten. Shaken but proud, she responds that she "cannot understand" the outburst, she has not had the same experience. And in the morning the country's best newspaper, *The New York Times*, editorially salutes the First Lady for her "candor," agrees that the feelings and sense of life of the black community are beyond our imagining, and consigns all whites to blank, useless, uncomprehending pity.

And the story is not different on the contemporary intellectual scene. It is a French voice—Jean Paul Sartre's—not an American voice that is heard urging men to more intelligent conceptions of human growth, demanding that they break free of the notion that others have no life except that which they "exhibit when serving as the material out of which we fashion our experience." (". . . there are men who die without—save for brief and terrifying flashes of illumination—ever having suspected what the *Other* is. The horizons of my life are infinitely shrunk.") And among recent philosophers it is a German voice—Max Scheler's —not that of an American, which dares to formulate an equation setting out relations of identity between individual growth, the perfection of love, and a grasp of the full distinctness and separateness of another human being. ("Love calls explicitly for an understanding entry into the individuality of *another* person *distinct in character* from the entering self . . . a warm and wholehearted endorsement of 'his' reality as an individual, and 'his' being what he is. . . . In love . . . there is built up, within the phenomenon itself, a clear-cut consciousness of two *distinct* persons. This consciousness is not merely a starting point; it reaches full maturity only as love pursues its course.")

What is more, a backward glance at the American cultural heritage confirms that the most powerful voices of American literary

331

culture have been precisely those which, in one manner or another, have been most committedly hostile to the enterprise of
attentive imaginative concentration on the fathoming of individual differences. D. H. Lawrence, in his *Studies,* broods hard on
the stunted quality of the selves created in the writing of Poe and
Whitman, and attributes it in the end to their incapacity to imagine and value a *separate* otherness. Love was a theme for both,
but for neither was it a possibility; each man was drawn by fantasies of merging, total engrossment, loss of awareness of the other
as separate—fantasies that teased him into confusing "understanding" with the act of sinking one's soul in another. And
wherever the engrosser or merger disappears from American letters, an even more frightening figure—the self-bound man (Captain Ahab is the Prince)—stands forth in his place. In Emerson,
for example, self-fulfillment appears to require an absolute denial
of others, a massive, unrelenting independence, a readiness for
isolation. Responding to a culture of conformity, this sage declared that a man bent on realizing himself must learn to carry
himself in separation from otherness—"as if everything were tit-
ular and ephemeral but he." Widen the gulf, Emerson cries:

> We must go alone. I like the silent church before the
> service begins, better than any preaching. How far off,
> how cool, how chaste the persons look, begirt each with
> a precinct or sanctuary! So let us always sit.

Or again:

> At times the whole world seems to be in conspiracy to
> importune you with emphatic trifles. Friend, client,
> child, sickness, fear, want, charity, all knock at once at
> thy closet door, and say, 'Come out unto us.' But keep
> thy state; come not into their confusion.

Or yet again:

> Live no longer to the expectation of these deceived and
> deceiving people with whom we converse. Say to them,

O father, O mother, O wife, O brother, O friend, I have
lived with you after appearances hitherto. Hencefor-
ward I am the truth's . . . If you are noble, I will love
you; if you are not, I will not hurt you and myself by
hypocritical attentions.

Emerson does allow that he could love another, if the person
were noble, but it is separateness, not love, that rouses him to
lyricism. In his view, to say it once more, becoming a fulfilled
man means drawing oneself more tightly, consciously, firmly
back within the limits of the primal, existent self.

And the Emersonian stance turns up repeatedly in American
literature, in popular culture (the art Western), everywhere in
American society. (It may even whisper to us in the writings of
David Riesman and Nathan Glazer; the utopian archetype of self-
realized man described by them as "autonomous" has a definite
taste for Emersonian gestures against otherness.) Over and over
we are enjoined to find "our own thing," "our own bag," in the
hippie phrase. And again and again the success of our search is
presumed to depend upon our power to cut ourselves off, to
harden the wall around us, not only to march to the beat of our
own drum, but seemingly to hear no other sound.

There are, of course, counter voices here and there. Though
his message did not cut through, smothered in clichés of life adjustment, John Dewey frequently dwelt on connections between
human growth and sound education of the imagination—that
instrument by which people gain in "flexibility, in scope, and in
sympathy, till the life which the individual lives is informed with
the life of nature and society." More than one American research
psychologist has convinced himself of the centrality of imagination in the course of human development and has attempted in-
quiries into the nurture of the imaginative man—witness the
labors of Henry Murray and his associates at Harvard in the late
1930's. "Self-Other" theories of growth, which stress self-
dramatization and imaginative role-playing, have a place in the

333

history of American philosophy, owing chiefly to the writings of George Herbert Mead. ("The self by its reflexive form announces itself as a conscious organism which is what it is only so far as it can pass from its own system into those of others, and can thus, in passing, occupy both its own system and that into which it is passing . . . Shut up within his own world . . . he would have no entrance into possibilities other than those which his own organized act involved. . . . It is here that mental life arises.")

And there is one great, almost forgotten American who put the case for fulfillment as dependent upon imaginative growth in utterly unambiguous terms—I speak of Charles Horton Cooley, a founder of American sociology. In *Human Nature and the Social Order* (1929), Cooley laid it down that:

> . . . the imaginations which people have of one another are the *solid facts* of society . . . I do not mean merely that society must be studied *by* the imagination —that is true of all investigations in their higher reaches —but that the *object* of study is primarily an imaginative idea or group of ideas in the mind, that we have to imagine imaginations. The intimate grasp of any social fact will be found to require that we divine what men think of one another. Charity, for instance, is not understood without imagining what ideas the giver and recipient have of each other; to grasp homicide we must, for one thing, conceive how the offender thinks of his victim and of the administrators of the law; the relation between the employing and hand-laboring classes is first of all a matter of personal attitude which we must apprehend by sympathy with both, and so on . . .

Nor did Cooley stop here—with a mere definition of an appropriate area of inquiry for his field. He went on to assert that the

334

quality of imaginative sympathies is the surest measure of the degree of human growth and fulfillment:

> One's range of sympathy is a measure of his personality, indicating how much or how little of a man he is.

And he was certain beyond doubt that those who deprecated this sympathy, shrugged it off with prattle about *sensitivity*, missed its richly complicated nature and meaning:

> [Sympathy] is in no way a special faculty but a function of the whole mind to which every special faculty contributes, so that what a person is and what he can understand or enter into through the life of others are very much the same thing. We often hear people described as sympathetic who have little mental power, but are of a sensitive, impressionable, quickly responsive type of mind. The sympathy of such a mind always has some defect corresponding to its lack of character and of constructive force. A strong, deep understanding of other people implies mental energy and stability; it is a work of persistent, cumulative imagination . . .

But if there is a native tradition which understands the nurture of the imagination to be a key to general human growth, it is, by all odds, a minority tradition, far away from the center of popular belief. The weight of the general culture presses continually toward feats of objectification—objectification of labor (the assembly line, time study), of love (sex research), of desire (image-making, consumer research). At the center stands the conviction that fulfillment is deliverance into a function—a job, a title, a carpet, an income, a pool, somebody else's respect. I, the free American, am free to "find my own place," my "social niche," my "professional slot." I go forth from myself, I *go places*, ranch house to White House, dropout to Ph.D., twelve dollars weekly to a hundred dollars a day. And up the line, where I have it made, I "am more interested in a man's behavior than in his inner life," I believe man's first duty is to "adjust himself to his environment," I doubt that anyone can "feel his way into the innermost being of another person," I don't seek inward truths . . .

Is mockery in order? The objectifying American culture can be damned for having only once in its history concerned itself intensely with the matter of precisely what this or that individual man felt in this or that instant of time (the occasion was the period of witch trials in the seventeenth century, when it was found useful to know the inward workings of the devil). It can be damned as well for having consistently refused to introduce into its elementary educational system those "studies"—improvisation, mime, dance, dramatics—that elsewhere in the West are accepted as the basic human efforts at developing an imagination of otherness. It can be damned, more fiercely, for its incalculable failures of imagination—for example, its incapacity to make real to itself the inward life, man by man, woman by woman, child by child, of its black people.

But there are, here as always in life, qualifications to be entered: if there is no imagination of deprivation among us, there is at least guilt at good fortune, and this has sufficed to rebuild a world and feed a dozen famines. And in any event, it is not seemly for a professing humanist to lay down accusations here, for the American humanist—the teacher and scholar whose texts and knowledge should have been the greatest resources of those in pursuit of the truth of "the other subject"—has himself been a cop-out, an objectifier, a character madly eager to turn art itself into a "body of objective knowledge" to be "mastered" for "career examinations."

The point of substance, in fine, lies beyond accusations or "cultural critiques." It is a matter simply of a general, culture-wide dimming of the lights of inward life, a matter of failed encounters, missed meetings, hands that do not reach out, minds that hear the lock turn in their prison doors.

It is nighttime, the Maine harbor again. A lantern in the rain,

336

motion of shore waters, a welcome, a beginning . . . But we don't go on, neither he nor she nor I. "My ideas are more often sound and sensible . . ." "I say what I have to say in a few simple words . . ." No hardrock, an occasional pot putterer, we would nevertheless prefer that people "not get ideas about us." And as for the famous still sad music of humanity, "we" don't hear it much. We don't flow, we hold on tight inside, we do the generous thing over and over and invariably do it ungenerously, we see and feel and imagine ourselves to be highly responsible, competent, the solid people of the earth, the independents, the resilients, the unwhiners.

And for that idea or vision of self some among us pay a lot—gouge their innerness—become less than men.

NOTES ON CONTRIBUTORS

KENNETH E. BOULDING is currently director of the Institute of Behavioral Science at Colorado University. Between 1949 and 1967 he was a professor of Economics at the University of Michigan and previously had taught at Iowa State College, McGill University, Fisk University, Colgate University and the University of Edinburgh. At present he is president of the American Economic Association and a Fellow of the American Academy of Arts and Sciences and of the American Philosophical Society. He was vice-president of the American Association for the Advancement of Science in 1966–67 and has held many similar positions of honor in the past two decades. He is the author of twelve books—*The Meaning of the Twentieth Century* being the most recent.

JAMES W. CAREY is an associate professor of journalism and a research associate professor in the Institute of Communications Research at the University of Illinois. His principal interests are in propaganda and popular culture, and he has written a score of essays on the subject, the best-known of which is "Harold Adams Innis and Marshall McLuhan."

HENRY STEELE COMMAGER, one of America's best-known historians, is currently professor of history and American studies at Amherst College and adjunct professor at Columbia University. He has taught widely, both in this country and abroad, and has edited many studies, including a forty-volume work, *The Rise of the American Nation*. Among the best-known of his many books are *The American Mind; Europe and America Since 1492;* and *The Spirit of Seventy-Six.*

BENJAMIN DEMOTT is chairman of the English Department at Amherst College and visiting professor of humanities at the Massachusetts Institute of Technology. Among his publications are *The Body's Cage* and *Hells and Benefits.* He also conducts a regular column in *The American Scholar* and reviews books for *Harper's* magazine.

GEORGE GALLUP was educated at the University of Iowa. In 1935 Dr. Gallup founded the American Institute of Public Opinion, of which he is a director. He is chairman of the board of Gallup & Robinson, Inc., and chairman of the board of The Gallup Organization, Inc., as well as president of the International Association of Public Opinion Institutes. He has written the following books: *The Pulse of Democracy; A Guidebook to Public Opinion Polls; The Gallup Political Almanac; Secrets of Long Life;* and *The Miracle Ahead.*

OTIS L. GUERNSEY, JR., is the editor of the *Dramatists Guild Quarterly* and the annual theater yearbook *The Best Plays.* He was educated at Yale University, where he was the author of three college-produced plays. In 1941 he joined the staff of the New York *Herald Tribune,* where he remained for nineteen years as—successively—theater reporter, movie critic, theater critic and performing-arts editor. He was drama critic and a senior editor at *Show* magazine and associate editor for the arts at *Diplomat* magazine.

T GEORGE HARRIS is a senior editor of *Look* magazine. Before joining *Look* he worked for Time Inc. and was successively assistant to the publisher, chief of the Chicago Bureau, economics correspondent attached to the Washington Bureau, national-affairs writer and *Time-Life-Fortune* bureau chief in San Francisco. He has received the Economic Writing Award for an article in *Look* titled "Automation—We Can Handle It." Mr. Harris was educated at Yale and Oxford universities.

WILLIAM JOVANOVICH is president of the publishing company Harcourt, Brace & World, where he has been since 1947. He was educated at the University of Colorado, from which he received the Norlin Award for distinguished achievement, and at Harvard University. He is a member of Phi Beta Kappa and the author of *Now, Barabbas.*

RUSSELL KIRK is a writer, editor, columnist and lecturer. He has been an associate professor at Michigan State College, a member of the faculty of the New School for Social Research and a lecturer at the University of Detroit. He is the author of a syndicated column for the General Features Corporation and is a regular contributor to the *National Review.* He was the founder of the quarterly *Modern Age* and is editor of the *University Bookman.* In addition to many magazine articles, Mr. Kirk is the author of fifteen books, the best-known of which is *The Conservative Mind.*

ROBERT M. MACIVER recently retired from his post as chancellor of the New School for Social Research in New York. For twenty-three years, 1927–1950, Professor MacIver had been associated with Columbia University, first at Barnard College and later as Lieber Professor of Political Philosophy at Columbia. He had previously taught at the University of Toronto and the University of Aberdeen, in his native Scotland. Professor MacIver has received honorary degrees from eight colleges and universities as well as many additional honors. He is the author of twenty-two books, among the best-known of which are *The Modern State; Leviathan and the People; The Web of Government*; and his recent autobiography, *As a Tale That is Told.*

GEORGE MCGOVERN, Senator from South Dakota, was educated at Dakota Wesleyan University and Northwestern University. He was a professor of history and government at Dakota Wesleyan University. He was elected to the House of Representatives in 1956 and reelected in 1958, serving as a member of the Committee on Education and Labor and the Committee on Agriculture. Senator McGovern was elected to the United States Senate in 1962. He is the author of two books, *War Against Want* and *Agricultural Thought in the Twentieth Century*, as well as of numerous articles.

FLOYD B. MCKISSICK, executive secretary of the Congress of Racial Equality (CORE), was educated at Morehouse College in Atlanta and at the Law School of North Carolina College. He was admitted to the North Carolina Bar in 1952 and the United States Supreme Court in 1955. Mr. McKissick was elected national chairman of CORE in 1963 in Dayton, Ohio. He has spoken at many colleges, universities and conventions—including the convention of the American Society of Newspaper Editors in 1967. He has been called to give expert testimony to the Senate Committee on Urban Problems (Ribicoff Committee) in 1966 and has written many articles and essays.

ERIC M. MANN was graduated from Cornell University in 1964. He spent a year, 1964–1965, as a field secretary in the northeast region for CORE. He worked for two and a half years as an organizer for the Newark Community Union Project, a community organization in a Negro ghetto. He is a national officer of Students for a Democratic Society (SDS).

JAY MARTIN is associate professor of English and American studies at Yale University, where he teaches courses in American literature and culture. He is the author of *Conrad Aiken: A Life of His Art;*

Harvests of Change: American Literature 1865–1914; and *The Waste Land: A Collection of Critical Essays,* as well as of numerous articles and reviews in the *Nation, Kenyon Review* and other journals. He has recently completed a biography of Nathanael West.

ROGER D. MASTERS was educated at Harvard University and at the University of Chicago. As a Guggenheim Fellow for the academic year 1967–68, he conducted research on the political implications of recent research on organic and human evolution as well as animal behavior. Among the books he has written are *The Nation is Burdened: American Foreign Policy in a Changing World* and *The Political Philosophy of Rousseau.* He has written essays and book reviews for the *Yale Review,* the *Reporter* and the *New Republic,* among other journals. He is an associate professor in the Department of Government at Dartmouth College.

WILLIAM PFAFF is co-author (with Edmund Stillman) of *Power and Impotence; The Politics of Hysteria;* and *The New Politics.* He is foreign affairs commentator for *Commonweal* and has contributed articles to *Foreign Affairs, Dissent, Interplay* and *Harper's,* among others. He is currently at the Hudson Institute.

BERNARD ROSENBERG is a professor of sociology at City College in New York and has been associated with Hunter College, Harpur College and Brandeis University. His books include *The Vanguard Artist* and *Mass, Class and Bureaucracy.* He is an editor of *Dissent* magazine and a contributor to *Commentary,* the *New Leader, Social Research, Social Problems* and other professional journals.

ELSPETH DAVIES ROSTOW (Mrs. Walt W. Rostow) was educated at Barnard College, Radcliffe College and Cambridge University. She has held many teaching positions both in the United States and abroad; she was a research associate with the Office of Strategic Services, 1943–45; and was the Geneva correspondent for the London *Economist* from 1947 to 1949. She has been a board member of the League of Women Voters World Affairs Council, Overseas Educational Fund, World Affairs Forum and Barnard College. She is the author of the book *Economy After the War* and of many articles, reviews and poems.

RICHARD H. ROVERE is an editor and a writer. He has served, in various editorial capacities, with *New Masses,* the *Nation* and *Common Sense.* He has been a staff writer for the *New Yorker* since 1944. Among the many books he has written are *The General and the Presi-*

dent (with Arthur Schlesinger, Jr.); *Affairs of State: The Eisenhower Years; Senator Joe McCarthy; The American Establishment;* and *The Goldwater Caper.* Mr. Rovere has been on the board of editors of the *American Scholar* since 1958.

EDMUND STILLMAN is a graduate of Yale University and the Columbia Law School, and is a member of the New York Bar. He was an American diplomatic officer in Bulgaria, Yugoslavia and the Netherlands from 1947 until 1962. Subsequently he directed research and analysis for the Free Europe Committee, and was later associated with the Hudson Institute. He is presently senior associate and lecturer in international politics at the School of Advanced International Studies of Johns Hopkins University. Mr. Stillman is author of *The Balkans* and co-author, with William Pfaff, of *The New Politics; The Politics of Hysteria;* and *Power and Impotence.*

FRANK N. TRAGER is a professor of international affairs, Graduate School of Public Administration, New York University. He was United States Economic Aid Director ("Point Four" Program) in Burma from 1951 to 1953, and is presently a member of the Department of State's Advisory Panel on East Asian and Pacific Affairs and AID's Southeast Asia Development Advisory Group. Currently, he is a member of the editorial boards of *Orbis* and *Vietnam Perspectives,* and has authored, edited or co-authored many books on politics, foreign policy and economics.

HOWARD ZINN is a professor of government at Boston University. He was educated at New York University and Columbia University, and in 1961 he was a Fellow at Harvard University's Center for East Asian Studies. He has received awards from the Ford Foundation, the American Historical Association and the American Philosophical Association. His books include *SNCC: The New Abolitionists; New Deal Thought;* and *Vietnam: The Logic of Withdrawal.* He has contributed articles to some thirty magazines.

INDEX

Abolitionists, 42

Acheson, Dean, 99

Adams, Henry, 187, 204

Adams, John, 64

Adorno, Theodor W., 194, 197

African emerging nations, American ritualistic liberalism in action, 114–24

African revolutions, 119

Africa's Challenge to America (Bowles), 117, 118, 119

Agricultural Adjustment Act (1938), 172

Aguinaldo, Emilio, 76

Aid programs, *see* Economic aid; Foreign aid; Military aid; Social aid

Alaska, purchase of, 75

Algeria, 122

Alienation, future of democracy and, 279–92; movements of, 32–35; radicalism and, 257–75

Alinsky, Saul, 323

Alliance for Progress, 137

Alliances, foreign, 89, 100

Amana Colony, 72

Ambassador, The (James), 80

America Hurrah (Van Itallie), 236–38

American, The (James), 81

American Commonwealth, The (Bryce), 50

American Democrat, The (Cooper), 279

American Dream, The, 308

American experiment, the, 3–23

American History at a Glance (Smelser), 38

American Politics in a Revolutionary World (Bowles), 117, 118, 121

American Tobacco Company, 178

Americanism, 115, 117–18, 120, 124

Americanization, 26, 71

Anti-Americanism, 27

Anti-colonialism, 124

Anti-communism, 127–28, 129

Anti-Semitism, 80

Antioch Review, 293

Arendt, Hannah, 272

Arnold, Thurman, 177

Arrogance of power, 31

Arts, the, culture and, 206–10, 214, 226–29; people versus, 230–44

Asia, American foreign policy objectives in, 99–102

Asian and Pacific Council (ASPAC), 105, 106

Asian Development Bank, 105, 106, 138–39, 166

Assassination, political, 38

Association of Asian Nations (ASEAN), 105, 106

Association of Asian States (ASA), 105, 106

Atomic bomb, the first, 192

Auden, W. H., 110

Australia, multilateral treaty with (1951), 100

Australia–New Zealand–United States Treaty Organization (ANZUS), 100

Authoritarian Personality, The (Adorno), 194

345

Authoritarianism, 196–97, 202, 207

Bacon, Francis, 29, 205
Bacon's Rebellion (1676), 43
Balanchine, George, 240
Baldwin, Faith, 221
Ball, George, 108
Barbé-Marbois, François de, 187
Barzini, Luigi, 264
Batista, Fulgencio, 127
Bay of Pigs disaster, 125
Beard, Charles A., 69, 97
Beauvoir, Simone de, 27
Belief-complexes, 4–5
Belief-systems, 4–7
Bell, Daniel, 200–01, 273, 274
Bellamy, Edward, 198
Bellow, Saul, 268
Benét, Stephen Vincent, 62
Bensman, Joseph, 224 n.
Bentham, Jeremy, 222
Benton, Thomas, 240
Berdyaev, Nikolai, 205
Beveridge, William, 199
Big Picture, The (Cort), 195 n.
Bilateral security treaties, 100
Bill of Rights, 74, 197, 280
Birch Society, John, 320
Birth rate, world, 135
Black Hawk War, 39
Black Muslims, 320
Bodard, Lucien, 105
Bohemian versus Bourgeoisie
(Grana), 294 n.
Bonus Expeditionary Force (1931),
43
Boorstin, Daniel, 124, 318
Boulding, Kenneth E., 143–61, 170
Bowles, Chester, 117, 118–21, 122,
124, 197
Brown, H. Rap, 281–82
Brown, John, 43
Bryce, James, 50
Buchan, Earl of, 66
Buckley, William F., Jr., 318
Burke, Edmund, 124

Calder, Alexander, 240
California, rebellion against Mexico, 40–41
Calvert, George (Lord Baltimore),
41
Cambodia, 100, 104
Campaign expenditures, political,
scandal of, 54
Camus, Albert, 199, 200, 304, 318
Canadian-Alaskan frontier, contest
of, 40
Canning, George, 75
Capital stock, 144–45
Capitalism, 84, 143, 144–45; cybernetic, 155; tenet of political
creed, 4
Carey, James W., 293–305
Caribbean, intervention in, 40, 68
Carmichael, Stokely, 265, 281–82,
289
Carnegie, Andrew, 73
Carnegie Steel Company, 44
Castro, Fidel, 130, 133
Caulfield, Holden, 266
Caulfield, Max, 297, 298
Census Bureau, U.S., 151
Central Intelligence Agency (CIA),
68, 82, 84
Charles I of England, 45 n.
Chase, Stuart, 174, 175
Chayefsky, Paddy, 243
Checks and balances, system of,
14–16, 64
Chiang Kai-shek, 127, 225
China, Communist, U.S. policy toward, 127, 129; Soviet Union
and, 92, 130, 131
China, Republic of, security treaty
with (1954), 100
Chinese immigrants, violence toward, 38–39, 42
Church, the, role in society, 312–
314
Citizenship, 69
Civil Disobedience (Thoreau), 279
Civil War, American, 6, 26, 29 n.,
37, 46
Cleveland, Grover, 40, 68

Cold War, 87, 92, 125, 127, 129, 130, 295
College Board examinations, 248–249
College education, 271–75; students and, 245–56
Columbia Broadcasting System, 200–01
Coming of Age in America (Friedenberg), 213
Commager, Henry Steele, 39, 40, 43, 59–86, 87, 107, 114
Commercial exploitation of generational differences, 303–04
Commission on the Humanities, 196
Commission on the Year 2000, 201
Committee on the Next Thirty Years, British, 200
Communications, mass, 223–25; revolution in, 133
Communism and Communists, 7, 68, 82, 84, 89, 91–93, 127–30; economy of, compared with American, 167–69
Community, role of, in democracy, 20
Comte, Auguste, 220
Concentration camps, 85
Congo, intervention in, 123
Congress of Industrial Organizations (CIO), 44
Congressmen, professional, inadequacy of, 49–56
Conrad, Joseph, 223
Conservatism, political, 114
Constitution of the United States, 7, 15, 16, 29, 31, 38, 44, 64, 114, 124; *see also* Bill of Rights
Constitutional Convention, 64
Consumption, 145, 146
Containment policy, 92
Cooley, Charles Horton, 334–35
Cooper, James Fenimore, 279, 280, 285
Cort, David, 190, 195 n.
Council of Economic Advisers, 177
Cox, Harvey, 320

Coxey's Army (1894), 43
"Credibility gap," 11
Credo, American, 28–29
Crèvecoeur, Jean de, 62–63, 69–70, 187; *quoted*, 24
Cuba, annexation attempt, 76; intervention in, 68, 89, 92; missile crisis in, 85
Culture, American, 183–275; arts and, 206–10, 214, 230–44; education and, 211–14; future, the, interest in, 200–01, 214; machine and, 190–95, 198, 205; nature of, 201; past and future, intersection of, 185–215; public taste, the, 217–29; radicalism and alienation, 257–75; science and, 205–06; students and their universities, 245–56; technology and, 189–95, 198, 206, 207; utopian revival and, 199–200, 202, 214
Culture and Behavior (Kluckhohn), 186 n.
Culture and the Evolution of Man (Montagu), 187 n.
Culture of poverty, 151–53, 159
Culture of wealth, 159
Custer's Last Stand (1876), 39
Cybernation, 189, 193
Cybernetic Capitalism, 155

Daedalus magazine, 198, 225
Daisy Miller (James), 81
Davidson, Robert, 71
Declaration of Independence, 3, 25, 37, 71, 74
Decree-laws, 15
Defense Department, U.S., 153, 155
De Gaulle, Charles, 88, 105, 130
Democracy, American, bases of, 1; beliefs about, 4–7; character, role, and function of, 7–15; checks and balances in, 14–16, 64; community in, role of, 20; future of, alienation and, 279–292; genius of, 3–23; individual

347

Democracy, American (*continued*)
liberty in, 20–21; minority dissent in, right of, 21–22, 23; misconceptions concerning, 10–15; personality in, value of, 20; popular rule in, extent of, 14–21; pragmatic and experimental nature of, 22; principles of, 36; reform within, movements for, 9–10; responsibility of, 13; separation of powers in, 15, 16–19; short-comings of, types of, 8–9; tenet of political creed, 4; war as enemy of, 14

Democracy and the American Party System (Ranney and Kendall), 19

DeMott, Benjamin, 325–37

Depression of the 1930's, 154–55, 158, 161, 171, 173, 262, 264

Devillers, Philippe, 105

Dewey, Admiral George, 76

Dewey, John, 174, 175, 179, 181, 212, 333

Dickens, Charles, 27

Dictators, 122, 123

Dien Bien Phu, battle of (1954), 128

Diseases, human, cure of, 204

Disposable income, per capita, 146–147

Dissent, minority, right of, in democracy, 21–22, 23

Distribution of income, 150–53

Dolci, Danilo, 265

Dominican Republic, intervention in, 40, 41, 89

Dostoevski, Fëdor, 198

Douglas, Paul, 173, 181

Duffus, R. L., 200

Dulles, John Foster, 128

Dystopias, 199

Economic aid, 30, 114, 122, 135–136

Economic ethics, 160

Economic growth, 46, 147–48, 149, 159

Economic planning, 177–78, 179, 180

Economy, American, 141–81; characteristics of, 164–65; Communist economy and, differences between, 167–69; competitive system in, 162–63; future of, conditions affecting, 159–61, 169; government in, role of, 155–56; growth of, 46, 147–48, 149, 159; internal structure of, 149–56; organizational structure of, 153–155; partnership, political economy of, 162–69; planning, 177–178, 179, 180; politics of, 170–81; position of, relative to other nations, 149; problems of, 156–59, 171–72; success of, qualified, 143–61

Education, American, culture and, 211–14; expenditure on, expansion of, 165; mass, 211–14; public, 152, 183, 211–14, 247–49; radicalism and alienation, 257–275; responsibility of, 11–12; students and their universities, 245–56; universal, 286

Egalitarianism, 301

Egypt, 122, 123

Eisenhower, Dwight D., 18, 55, 68, 158, 225; foreign policy objectives expressed by, 93–94, 100, 101, 102

Eisenhower Doctrine, 83

Eliot, T. S., 239, 265

Elliott, Sumner Locke, 243

Ellison, Ralph, 198

Ellul, Jacques, 272

Emerson, Ralph Waldo, 332–33

Emigration, 69, 70

Employment, level of, 156–57

Equality, social, 189

Esslin, Martin, 227

Ethiopia, 122

Experimentalism, 172

Extralegal coercion, 42–43

Fair Deal, the, 170, 172

Federal Bureau of Investigation, 7
Fitzgerald, F. Scott, 262
Food production per capita in India, 131–32; in Latin America, 137
Forbes magazine, 208
Ford, Henry, 118
Foreign aid, 100, 166, 178
Foreign Assistance Act (1967), 135
Foreign challenge to America, 34
Foreign policy, American, 8, 17, 57–139; assumptions concerning, 87–89; characteristics of, main, 89; goals of, Rusk on, 26; liberalism in action, ritualistic, 114–24; motives, problem of, 107–13; myths and realities of, 59–86; objectives of, 87–106; today and tomorrow, 125–39
Fortune magazine, 208
Founding Fathers, 3, 14, 15, 64, 65
Free enterprise, system of, 141, 162
Free World, the, 57, 82, 84, 88, 130
Freedom, 88, 112–13, 115, 283–84, 287
Frémont, John Charles, 40–41
French revolutions, 43, 44, 79
Freneau, Philip, 65
Freud, Sigmund, 196, 317
Friedenberg, Edgar Z., 213
Fuchs, Victor, 272
Full Employment Act (1946), 155
Future, the, interest in, culture and, 200–01, 214
Future of an Illusion, The (Freud), 196
Future of Mankind, The (Jaspers), 198
Futuribles project, 200

Galbraith, John Kenneth, 162, 207, 272, 286, 316–17, 318
Gallup, George, 49–56, 209
Gallup Poll, 53
Gandhi, Mohandas K., 275

Gans, Herbert J., 219
Gardner, John, 271
Garfield, James A., 38
General Motors Corporation, 153, 178
Generations, American society and, 293–305
Geneva Conference (1954) and agreements, 82, 104
Ginsberg, Allen, 197; *quoted*, 24
Glazer, Nathan, 333
Goethe, Johann Wolfgang von, 27, 72
Goodman, Benny, 239
Goodman, Paul, 213, 260
Gordon, Theodore J., 200, 201
Government, American, 1–56; control by, fear of, 179; democracy, genius of, 3–23; disillusionment with, 49; economy and, role of, 155–56; intervention in world affairs, political, 30–31; leadership, failure of, 49–56; messianism of, 25–27; misinformation and secrecy of, 11; opposition to policies of, freedom to express, 13–14; politics, violence in, 36–48; premises of, intellectual questioning of, 31–32; reason, limits of, 24–35; reform in, need for, 53–56
Grana, Cesar, 294 n., 295
Granger cases (1877), 178
Great Aberration, the, 75
Great Depression, *see* Depression of the 1930's
Great Society, the, 170, 171, 172, 280
Greece, intervention in, 31
Griswold, A. Whitney, 206
Gross national product (GNP), 146, 154, 157, 159, 164, 175, 178; percentage of, by various sectors, 154
Guatemala, intervention in, 68, 85
Guernsey, Otis L., Jr., 230–44
Gulf of Tonkin Resolution (1964), 101

Haiti, intervention in (1915), 40
Hamilton, Alexander, 162
Harris, T George, 315–24
"Have" and "have-not" nations, gap between, 131–39
Hawaii, annexation of, 76; intervention in, 40
Hayes, Miles Van Valzah, 230–31, 244
Heckscher, August, 208
Heller, Joseph, 198
Helmer, Olaf, 201
Helpless-individualism, from rugged-individualism to, 315–24
Hemingway, Ernest, 239
Henry, Jules, 191–92, 213
High-culture, 217, 220–29
Hiss, Alger, 266
Hitchcock, Alfred, 236
Hitler, Adolf, 158
Ho Chi Minh, 103, 112, 128
Hocking, William Ernest, 174
Hoffer, Eric, 286
Homestead Massacre (1892), 44
Hook, Sidney, 93, 116
Hoover, Herbert C., 176
House, Colonel Edward, 116
Housing, public, 171, 176
Howe, Irving, 269
Human Nature and the Social Order (Cooley), 334
Humanitarianism, 173
Humphrey, Hubert H., 108
Humphreys, David, 65
Hutchinson, Anne, 41
Huxley, Aldous, 194, 198
Huxley, Sir Julian, 200, 205

Illiteracy and ignorance, world, 132
Immigration, 6, 28, 38–39, 46, 69–71, 79
Imperialism, Western, 127, 129
Income, distribution of, 150–53; taxation of, 164
Income per capita, disposable, 146–147; real, 147–48; world, 132
Independence, political, 63–64

India, living standard in, 131–32; war with Pakistan, 130
Indian tribes, lands of, expropriation of, 39
Individual, the, American society and, 277–337; alienation and the future of democracy, 279–92; generations and, 293–305; Negroes and, 306–14; rugged-individualism to helpless-individualism, from, 315–24; self-realization, 325–37
Individual liberty, desirability of, in democracy, 20–21
Individualism, from rugged- to helpless-, 315–24
Indochina, 128
Industrialization, 46, 122, 164, 296
Inflation, wage and price, 156–57
Innis, Harold Adams, 293
Innocence, American, 79, 80
Intellectualism, 272–73, 274–75
Inter-American Development Bank, 138
International Development Organization, 136, 138
International Workers of the World (IWW), 44
Intervention in world affairs, political, 30–31
Intolerance, 80, 196–97
Invention, rate of, 190
Investment, 146; foreign, American, 135
Isolationism, American, 26, 28, 29, 60, 64, 65, 66, 67–68, 69, 77–78, 80, 82, 83, 86, 97

James, Henry, 63, 80–81, 187
James, William, 204
Japan, security treaty with (1951), 100
Jaspers, Karl, 195, 198
Jefferson, Thomas, 25, 37, 56, 65–67, 69, 71, 82, 117, 118, 119, 162, 280, 313
Job Corps, 321
Johnson, Alvin, 12

Johnson, Lyndon B., 17, 18, 38, 68, 86 n., 122–23, 175, 180, 284, 286, 329; foreign policy objectives expressed by, 95–96, 100, 101, 102, 105
Johnson, Nunnally, 236
Jovanovich, William, 257–75, 293
Judicial review, 64
Jung, Karl, 205

Kafka, Franz, 192
Kahler, Erich, 200
Kashmir, 130
Katanga, 122, 124
Katz, Elihu, 224 n.
Kauffmann, Stanley, 260, 266
Kazin, Alfred, 298
Kendall, Wilmore, 19
Keniston, Kenneth, 267
Kennan, George, 287–88
Kennedy, John F., 26–27, 38, 68, 81, 180, 312; foreign policy objectives expressed by, 94–95, 98, 100, 101, 102
Kennedy, Robert F., 38
Kenyatta, Jomo, 119
Kerr, Clark, 271
Khrushchev, Nikita, 130, 233
Kierkegaard, Sören, 302
Killens, John, 320
King, Grace, 186
King, Martin Luther, Jr., 38
Kirk, Russell, 114–24
Kluckhohn, Clyde, 186 n., 191
Knights of Labor, 44
Korea, intervention of, 89, 92, 128
Krock, Arthur, 124
Krutch, Joseph Wood, 302
Ku Klux Klan activities, 42
Kuwait, 150

Labor unions, violence in suppression of, 44
Lacouture, Jean, 105
Lactantius, 205
Laos, 100, 104
Latin America, 130; intervention

Latin America (*continued*) in, 68; revolutions in, 74–75; trade relations of, 137
Laurence, William L., 192
Lawrence, D. H., 332
Lazarus, Emma, 69
Lazersfeld, Paul, 224 n.
Leadership, failure of, 49–56
League of Nations, 17, 68, 78
Leary, Timothy, 218, 219
Leavis, F. R., 191
Lebanon, intervention in, 83, 89
Legal process, American willingness to ignore, 44
Legitimacy, dynamics of, 161
Lenin, Nikolai, 27, 111
Levin, Murray, 320
Lewis, C. S., 258
Lewis and Clark expedition, 67
Lewisohn, Margaret, 12
Liberalism, 174; ritualistic, in action, 114–24
Liberty, individual, desirability of, 20–21
Life expectancy, increase in, 204
Liliuokalani, Queen, 40
Lincoln, Abraham, 25, 38, 118, 134
Lippmann, Walter, 52, 53
Lippold, Richard, 240
Literature, American, creation of, 71
Living standards, world, 131–32
Locke, John, 6, 118
Lodge, Henry Cabot, 17, 68
London *Sunday Times*, 281
Louis XVI of France, 45 n.
Louisiana Purchase, 67, 75
Lovejoy, Elijah P., 42
LSD, 218
Lukacs, George, 301

Macdonald, Dwight, 220, 221, 284, 289
Machine, the, culture and, 190–95, 198, 205
Machlup, Fritz, 212
MacIver, Robert M., 3–23, 24
Mafia activities, 42

Mahan, Admiral Alfred Thayer, 76
Mailer, Norman, 197
Maintenance, 146
Majority coercion, 42–43
Malik, Michael Abdul, 281
Malnutrition, world, 132
Maltz, Maxwell, 296 n.
Manifest Destiny, 39, 59–60, 73, 74, 75, 76, 77
Manila Pact, 100, 103
Mann, Eric M., 245–56, 257
Mann, Horace, 211
Mann, Thomas, 200
Mao Tse-tung, 111, 112, 128, 133
Marquand, John, 262
Marshall, George C., 92, 99
Marshall Plan, 138
Martin, Jay, 185–215
Marx, Karl, 232
Mass communication, 223–25
Mass culture, 217–29, 270
Mass education, 211–14
Massachusetts Bay Colony, 72
Masters, Roger D., 36–48, 306
Mayflower Compact, 41
McCarthy, Eugene, 280
McCarthy, Joseph R., 42, 179, 289
McCarthy, Mary, 283–84, 285, 286
McClure, Michael, 197
McGill, Donald, 261
McGovern, George, 125–39
McKinley, William, 38, 40, 76
McKissick, Floyd B., 36, 306–14
McLuhan, Marshall, 218, 272, 293, 296 n.
Mead, George Herbert, 334
Means, Gardiner, 157
Meany, George, 181
Medicare legislation, 165
Mekong River Valley Development Project, 105, 106
"Melting pot," the, 46, 70
Melville, Herman, 268
Mergers, business, 196
Messianism, American, 25–27, 109
Mexican War (1846–48), 39
Mexico, annexation of territory of, 75; intervention in, 40, 68;

Mexico (*continued*)
Texas and California rebellions against, 40–41
Michael, Donald N., 193
Michaux, André, 67
Mid-culture, 221
Migration, 70
Militarism, threat of, 158
Military aid, 114, 128
Military coups and insurrections, 15
Mill, James, 120
Mill, John Stuart, 302
Miller, Arthur, 221
Miller, Henry, 193, 197
Millikan, Robert, 53
Milton, John, 305
Minority dissent, right of, in democracy, 21–22, 23
Minority groups, ethnic and racial, treatment of, 23
Misconceptions concerning democracy, 10–15
Miss Lonelyhearts (West), 192
"Missouri Legion," expedition of (1823), 39
Mitchell, Arnold, 207–08
Mobutu, General, 123
Monroe, James, 68
Monroe Doctrine, 67, 68, 75, 78
Montagu, M. F. Ashley, 187 n.
Montaigne, 302
Montesquieu, 15, 16
Moral code, 19
Moral law, 59
Moral superiority of America, 59–60, 78, 80, 83–86
Morgan, Lewis, 35
Mormons, intoleration of, 42, 72
Morocco, 122
Morse, Jedidiah, 71
Mosel, Tad, 243
Motion pictures, 243–44
Moynihan, Daniel, 322
Muhammed, Elijah, 320
Multilateral security treaties, 100
Mumford, Lewis, 191
Murdock, George P., 210

Murray, Henry, 333
Myth-complexes, 4–6

Napoleon I, 79
Nasser, Gamal Abdel, 122
Nat Turner's Rebellion (1831), 43
National Art Materials Trade Association, 208
National Association of Manufacturers, 175
National defense, rise in, 153, 157–158
National Planning Association, 201
National Recovery Act, 172
Nationalism, African, 124; Asian, 127
Naturalization, 69, 70–71
Negroes, economic gap between whites and, 133; militancy of, 32, 33–34, 35, 47–48, 177, 181, 320–24; second-class citizens, 81; segregation and confinement of, 9; social revolution of, 4; society and, 306–14; violence in the ghettos, 36–38, 47–48
Neutrality, 66, 68, 79, 128
Neutrality Act, 53
Nevins, Allan, 39, 40, 43
New Deal, the, 170, 171, 172–75, 176, 180, 181, 316, 322
New Economics, 319
New Freedom, the, 25
New Frontier, the, 172
New Harmony, Indiana, 72
New Left, the, 32–33, 294, 296, 302, 303, 304
New Principles for a New Age (Bowles), 197
New Republic, The, 260
New World, the, 60–62, 64–65, 70, 72–74, 81
New York Times, The, 331
New Zealand, multilateral treaty with (1951), 100
Newes from Virginia, 62
Newspapers, news distorted and falsified by, 10–11
Nicaragua, intervention in, 40, 68

Nicholas II of Russia, 45 n.
Niebuhr, Reinhold, 25, 175
Nietzsche, Friedrich Wilhelm, 301
Nigeria, 121, 123
Nihilism, 35
Nissen, Henry, 205
Nixon, Richard M., 233
Nkrumah, Kwame, 119, 122
"Non-economic" personality, the, 160–61
North Atlantic Treaty Organization (NATO), 82
North Korea, communism in, 92, 99
North Vietnam, 84, 85, 92, 102, 128–29
Northrop, F. S. C., 200
Nuclear weapons, 84, 188–89, 203

Olson, Floyd, 180
O'Meara, Francis E., 200
Opinion polls, 10, 52–53
Opposition to governmental policies, freedom to express, 13–14
Organizational structure of the economy, 153–55
Orwell, George, 198, 261, 266
Ostend Manifesto, 75–76

Paine, Thomas, 71
Pakistan, war with India, 130
Pan-Americanism, 68
Panama, intervention in, 40
Panama Canal territory, acquisition of, 75
Paris, Treaty of (1783), 79
Partnership, political economy of, 162–69
Party system, political, 7
Pax Americana, 60
Peace Corps, 254, 303
Peale, Norman Vincent, 316
Péguy, Charles Pierre, 26
Penal Colony, The (Kafka), 192
Pequot War (1637), 39
Percy, Charles, 323
Personality, 20, 193–95, 197, 202, 207, 212

Pfaff, William, 107–13, 114
Philippine Islands, annexation of, 75, 76–77; independence of, 127; security treaty with (1951), 100, 103
Picasso, Pablo, 234
Pike, Nicholas, 71
Pilgrims, 41
Planning, economic, 177–78, 179, 180; social, 175
Platt, John Rader, 200, 203
Plymouth Colony, 72
Pocket History of the United States (Nevins and Commager), 39
Polak, F. L., 200
Police brutality, 9
Political assassinations, 38
Political candidates, votes and, 10
Political creed, 4
Political economy of partnership, 162–69
Politics, American, of economy, 170–81; violence in, 36–48
Polk, James K., 67–68
Pollock, Jackson, 240
Poor-nation and wealthy-nation, gap between, 131–39
Popular rule, problems of, 14–21
Populist movement, 26, 45
Post-Historic Man (Seidenberg), 194
Pound, Ezra, 187, 287
Poverty, culture of, 151–53, 159; income distribution and, 151–53; "war" on, 175–81; world, 131–34
Poverty programs, 175–81, 196–97, 255
Pragmatism, 172
Presidential assassinations, 38
Press, the, freedom of, 282, 311–12
Primitivism, 197
Privacy, right to, 282
Production, 145, 146
Production and Distribution of Knowledge in the United States (Machlup), 212
Providence Plantations, 72
Psycho-Cybernetics (Maltz), 296 n.

Public Philosophy, The (Lippmann), 52
Public school system, *see* Education
Public taste, the, 217–29
Puerto Ricans, segregation and confinement of, 9; social revolution of, 4
Puerto Rico, annexation of, 76
Puppet states, 84–85
Puritans, 72
Pynchon, Thomas, 198

Quakers, 42
Quemoy-Matsu, intervention in, 89, 92
Quirk, John, 304

Race Relations Act (1965), British, 281
Racism, 309, 311, 312, 321
Radhakrishman, Sir Sarvepalli, 200
Radicalism, alienation and, 257–275
Railroad strikes of 1877 and 1894, 44
Rand Corporation, 201
Ranney, Austin, 19
Rationalism, 300
Read, Herbert, 229
Real capital, 144
Real income, per capita, 147–48
Reason, limits of, 24–35
Reconstruction period, post-Civil War, 6
Reform movements, 9–10; governmental, need for, 53–56; social and economic, 26–27
Reforming of General Education, The (Bell), 273
Religious communities, 72
Religious intolerance, 41–42
Resources, squandering of, 176–77
Resources in America's Future (Landsman *et al.*), 201
Reuther, Walter, 324
"Revolution of rising expectations," 127

Revolutionary War, American, 37, 42
Rhee, Syngman, 127
Rhodesia, 122
Riesman, David, 333
Right-to-die crisis, 319
Robertson, Nan, 283, 289
Rodgers, John, 72
Roosevelt, Franklin D., 26, 38, 78, 116, 117, 128, 172–73, 174, 175, 176, 180, 224
Roosevelt, Theodore, 26, 38, 40, 68, 76, 286
Root, Erastus, 71
Rosenberg, Bernard, 217–29, 230
Rosenberg, Harold, 219
Rosten, Leo, 221
Rostow, Elspeth Davies, 162–69
Rousseau, Jean Jacques, 45, 118–119, 320
Rovere, Richard H., 279–92
Rugged-individualism, from, to helpless-individualism, 315–24
Rush, Benjamin, 65
Rusk, Dean, 26, 108, 122

Santo Domingo, annexation attempt, 76; intervention in, 68, 84, 125
Sartre, Jean-Paul, 27, 258, 331
Scheler, Max, 331
Schlesinger, Arthur, Jr., 226
Science, culture and, 205–06, 214
Secular City, The (Cox), 320
Security, national, 125, 126
Security treaties, 100
Seidenberg, Roderick, 194, 198
Seldes, Gilbert, 220, 221
Self-determination, 120, 121–22
Self-expression, 285
Self-image, America's, 25
Self-proletarianization, process of, 35
Self-realization, individual, 325–37
Seminole Wars, 39
Separation of powers, 15, 16–19, 64
Separatism, 64, 65, 72
Shays's Rebellion (1786), 43

Shils, Edward W., 226
Short, William, 66
Shulman, Arnold, 243
Simmons, Amelia, 71
Simpson, G. G., 205
Sinclair, Upton, 174, 175, 262
Singularity of America, 26–28
Sino-Soviet relations, 92, 130, 131
Smelser, Marshall, 38
Smith, Joseph, 42
Social equality, 189
Social ostracism, 42
Social planning, 175
Social Problems (Gans), 219
Social security legislation, 164, 171
Social standardization, 193
Socialism, 155; threat to legitimacy, 161
Society, American, alienation and the future of democracy, 279–92; generations and, 293–305; individual and, 277–337; Negroes and, 306–14; premises of, intellectual questioning of, 31–32; rugged-individualism to helpless-individualism, from, 315–324; self-realization, individual, 325–337; traditional, corruption of, 35; violence in, 36–48
Sorokin, Pitirim, 200
South Africa, Republic of, 122, 123
South America, intervention in, 68; *see also* Latin America
South Korea, 84; defense of, 100; security treaty with (1953), 100
South Vietnam, 128–29
Southeast Asia Treaty Organization (SEATO), 17, 83, 100, 103, 106
Southwest Africa, 122
Soviet Union, adversary of American foreign policy, 92–93; China and, 92, 130, 131; economy of, American and, differences between, 167–69
Spanish-American War (1898), 39, 40, 75
Speed, acceleration of, 203
Spender, Stephen, 258

Spillane, Mickey, 221
Spirit of Laws, The (Montesquieu), 15
Stalin, Joseph, 88, 91–92, 94
Standard Oil Company, 44
Standardization, social, 193
Stanton, Frank, 221
State Department, U.S., 123
Status, importance of, 281
Steady Work (Howe), 269
Stein, Gertrude, 239
Stillman, Edmund, 24–35, 36, 114
Students, university education and, 245–56
Students for a Democratic Society, 245, 246
Styron, William, 305
Sudan, 122
Superiority of America, 59–60, 71–86
Supreme Court, U.S., 7, 15, 16, 178

Taft, William Howard, 40
Taiwan, 85
Tashkent Conference, 130
Taste, public, 217–19; arts versus the people, 230–44
Tax receipts, government, 176
Technics and Civilization (Mumford), 191
Techniques, development of, 5
Technological multiplication, deceleration of, 203–04
Technology, culture and, 189–95, 198, 206, 207
Teilhard de Chardin, Pierre, 200
Television, 218, 242–43, 298–99
Tennessee Valley Authority, 171
Term of political office, limiting, 54–55
Texas, annexation of, 75; rebellion against Mexico, 40–41
Thailand, 85, 99
Theater of the Absurd, The (Esslin), 227
Theobald, Robert, 190
Third World, 108, 109
Thirty Years' War, 30 n.

Thoreau, Henry David, 191, 279, 280, 282, 283, 284, 285, 286
Time magazine, 35, 89 n., 201, 260
Tocqueville, Alexis de, 27, 50, 221, 280, 301, 330
Tokenism, 176
Tolstoy, Leo, 191
Total war, likelihood of, 191–92
Totalitarianism, 225, 229, 295
Townsend, Charles, 262
Townsend Movement, 174
Toynbee, Arnold, 200
Trade relations of poor countries, 136–37
Traditional society, corruption of, 35
Trager, Frank N., 87–106
Triumphant Democracy (Carnegie), 73
Trollope, Mrs. Anthony, 27
Trujillo, Rafael Leonidas, 127
Truman, Harry S., 38, 55, 88, 94; foreign policy objectives expressed by, 90–91, 92, 99, 100, 101
Truman Doctrine, 83
Tshombe, Moise, 123
Tufts, James H., 188
Tugwell, Rexford Guy, 175, 177, 181
Turgot, Anne Robert Jacques, 27, 74
Turner, Nat, 43

Un-American Activities Committee, House, 7
Uncommitted, The (Keniston), 267
Underground Railroad, 42
Unequal law enforcement, 42
United Nations, 82, 83, 84, 89, 95, 99, 105, 106, 122, 128, 136
Universal Declaration of Human Rights, UN, 3
University education, 271–75; students and, 245–56
Utopian communities, 72
Utopian revival, 199–200, 202, 214

Valéry, Paul, 189
Van den Haag, Ernest, 220
Van Itallie, Jean-Claude, 236–38
Venezuela, intervention in, 68
Versailles Treaty (1919), 17
Vidal, Gore, 243
Viet Cong, 103
Vietnam, American policy objectives in, 102–06, 125, 126, 127; intervention in, 30, 31, 41, 82, 89, 92, 102–06; puppet state, 85; *see also* North Vietnam; South Vietnam; Vietnam War
Vietnam War, 246, 252, 280, 284, 291, 295; escalation of, 17–18; expenditures on, 176; learning experience, 34; opposition to, 13, 18–19, 26; rejection of American efforts in, 32
Violence in American politics, 36–48

Wagar, Warren, 200
Wagner Act, 172
Wall Street Journal, 11, 201
War industry, rise of, 158–59
War of 1821, 39, 66, 79
War of the Copper Kings (1882), 44
Warhol, Andy, 233
Warren, Robert Penn, 262
Washington, George, 66, 97, 313
Waugh, Evelyn, 258
Wealth, culture of, 159
Weaver, Richard M., 212
Weaver, Robert, 323
Web of Government, The (MacIver), 4
Weber, Alfred, 194
Weber, Max, 160
Webster, Noah, 71, 306
Wedemeyer, General Albert C., 99
Welfare programs, 175–81
Welfare state, 120

West, Nathanael, 192, 210 n.
West Florida, acquisition of, 67, 75
West Germany, domination of, 83
Western Alliance, 130; *see also* North Atlantic Treaty Organization
Western settlement, violence in, 44
Whiskey Rebellion (1794), 43
White, David Manning, 220–21
White alienation movements, 32–33, 34–35
Whitehead, Alfred North, 304
Whitman, Walt, 185
Wildavsky, Aaron, 209
Wiley, Basil, 29
Williams, G. Mennen, 124
Williams, Roger, 41
Wilson, Woodrow, 17, 18, 25, 26, 40, 68, 77–78, 87, 116, 120
Wirtz, Willard, 209
Wolman, Benjamin, 295
Words (Sartre), 258
Work satisfaction, lack of, 196
World Bank, 136
World Design Science Decade 1965–1795 (Fuller and McHale), 201
World War I, 30 n., 69, 77–78, 108
World War II, 30 n., 179
Wright, Frank Lloyd, 233
Wright, Nathan, 321
Wyeth, Andrew, 240
Wythe, George, 66

Xenophobia, 69

Youth movements, 296, 297, 301, 303
Yugoslavia, 168

Zinn, Howard, 170–81
Zoll, Donald, 194

357

John G. Kirk

John G. Kirk was educated at Harvard and Columbia universities. He has been director of Free Europe Press; vice-president and chief editor of Walker and Co., book publishers; and editor of *Diplomat* magazine. He is presently on the corporate staff of Metromedia, Inc.